The Other Freud

Sigmund Freud's major texts on religion and culture have largely been ignored by contemporary postmodern theorists. In *The Other Freud*, James J. DiCenso argues for a rigorous rereading based on the conceptual methodology of contemporary postmodern thought.

Using the works of Jacques Lacan and Julia Kristeva, DiCenso analyses Freud's religious writings, such as *Totem and Taboo* and *Moses and Monotheism*, with the intention of exposing an "other" Freud. The author discovers a Freud who is neither mechanistic nor inflexibly reductive, but rather an insightful investigator of the transformative effect of religion upon the human psyche and culture. The book focuses on the discrepancies of Freudian thought at the intersections between culture and psychology, and demonstrates, with scholarly rigor and impressive freshness, that these are rich, multileveled texts which have the power to foster serious interdisciplinary debate.

James J. DiCenso has produced an insightful, accessible and highly stimulating work which is a major addition to the existing literature on psychoanalysis and religion.

James J. DiCenso is Associate Professor at the Department for the Study of Religions at the University of Toronto. He is the author of *Hermeneutics and the Disclosure of Truth*.

The Other Freud

Religion, culture and
psychoanalysis

James J. DiCenso

London and New York

First published 1999
by Routledge
11 New Fetter Lane, London EC4P 4EE

Simultaneously published in the USA and Canada
by Routledge
29 West 35th Street, New York, NY 10001

Typeset in Times by Routledge
Printed and bound in Great Britain by Clays Ltd, St. Ives PLC

British Library Cataloguing in Publication Data
A catalogue record for this book is available from the British
Library

Library of Congress Cataloguing in Publication Data
DiCenso, James
The Other Freud: religion, culture, and psychoanalysis/James J.
DiCenso.
Includes bibliographical references and index.
1. Psychoanalysis and religion. 2. Freud, Sigmund,
1856–1939–Religion. I. Title.
BF175.4.R44D53   1999
150.19'52'092–dc21
                              98–23772
                                 CIP

ISBN 0–415–19658–2 (hbk)
ISBN 0–415–19659–0 (pbk)

Contents

Acknowledgments

I would like to take the opportunity to thank those who contributed to the improvement of this book through their careful reading and criticism. My colleagues at the University of Toronto, Ann Baranowski, Keith Haartman, Marsha Hewitt, and Eleanor Pontoriero, each, in different ways, helped me see things I was missing, and provided encouragement and support. The readers for Routledge, Frederick Ruf of Georgetown University, Diane Jonte-Pace of Santa Clara University, and Charles Winquist of Syracuse University, provided well-informed, constructive commentaries that helped me to expand on the strengths and, I hope, ameliorate some of the weaknesses of the original manuscript. Without such a community of scholars, the resulting work would have been far inferior.

Introduction

Tensions in Freud, extensions in Lacan and Kristeva

After a century of ongoing influence, Sigmund Freud's work continues to exhibit a remarkable regenerative power. This is related to the interdisciplinary and hybrid quality of his writings, which elude appropriation by any single interpretive approach. Unquestionably, there are also conceptual problems and contradictions ensuing from this play of opposing tendencies. However, such tensions contribute to the production of multiple levels of meaning and lines of argument that expand the horizons of psychoanalytic inquiry. An inherent conflictual quality fosters plurivocity in a way that keeps the Freudian corpus open to fresh encounters. It may be that if Freud's work was more consistent and systematized it would also be more one-dimensional.

A pivotal development in contemporary postmodern thought, occurring in several forms, is the recognition that conflicting tendencies within texts can be *intentionally* emphasized and explored as a resource for expressing new insights. Readings of Freud along such lines have been undertaken by Jacques Lacan, Paul Ricoeur, Jacques Derrida, Luce Irigaray, Julia Kristeva, and many others. These theorists have applied themselves to a wide range of Freud's writings, and have contributed to an ongoing rethinking of psychoanalytic theory. The present inquiry appropriates aspects of the conceptual and methodological contributions of these predecessors, while integrating them into my own line of thought. In this, I am seeking to illustrate how postmodernist strategies of reading elicit new perspectives on the subject that evoked Freud's most reductive and inflexible tendencies: *the psychological function of religious forms within cultural existence.*

Freud's major writings on religion include some of his most important inquiries into the intersections of psychology and culture. There are, of course, rather glaring manifest problems and limitations in these writings, particularly *Totem and Taboo* and *Moses and Monotheism*, but also *The Future of an Illusion* and *Civilization and Its Discontents*. These works have served to establish the dominant psychoanalytic views of the psychology of religion within the closed, essentially dismissive parameters assumed by most theorists. However, assuming a fairly clear, obvious level of surface meaning discourages sustained analyses of these texts. My intention in this study is to rectify this neglect, which seems glaring for several reasons. Freud's writings on religion have shaped so much thinking about the relations among psychology, religion, and culture that their influence alone, their history of effects, warrants re-examination to sort out what may or may not be occurring in them. It is well established that portions of *Totem and Taboo* and *Moses and Monotheism*, in particular, are inaccurate and outdated in many of their manifest claims. Yet the massive influence of Freud, the ongoing impact and appropriation of his texts, calls for delimiting which aspects of his thought on religion and culture might be salvaged, and which merit rejection.

Beyond this, however, close reading reveals Freud's inquiries to be quite complex, multileveled, and fruitful for ongoing interdisciplinary reflection. My argument is that these writings reflect on the meaning of cultural forms related to religion in significant ways, exceeding the scope of Freud's explicit postulates and arguments. Additionally, they open broader questions concerning subjective formation and development. These questions are related to religion in its traditional forms, but extend beyond those confines into other, related cultural and symbolic spheres. They concern the meta-issue of the formation and transformation of human subjectivity within culture, necessarily involving language, values, and ideals. That is, while Freud's analyses purportedly address the question of how religion *originates*, they serve better to illuminate aspects of how it *functions*, psycho-culturally.

Divergent approaches to these intricate problems appear in relation to polarities within Freud's overall views of the human situation. At times, his discourse is entrenched in mechanistic, biologistic, and positivistic tendencies. In this it aspires toward cause-and-effect explanation within closed-system thinking. This quest for closure is related to Freud's pursuit of an ultimate, underlying point of origin for higher-order psychological and cultural developments in a definite force, event, or deed. Thus, on the overt or intentional level, his analyses of religion seek to establish the fundamental determinants of (mainly Western) religious belief and practice. Significantly, however, even on this reductive level the resulting formulations of underlying truth are *multiple*. The latent content discerned behind religion appears variously under the categories of illusion, delusion, and symptomatic displacement of repressed affect traceable to traumatic historical experience. This multiplication of the underlying referent serves to contribute to a destabilizing and de-literalizing of reductive levels of analysis.

Beyond the fissurings created by the failure of literal explanation, alternative counterbalancing orientations are evident throughout Freud's work. These derive from an understanding of human beings as *open systems*, formed by interpersonal relations occurring within cultural frameworks. In Anthony Wilden's terms, "living systems, at the organic level, and social systems, at the person level, are open systems. They depend for their structure and survival on the exchange of matter, energy, and information with their environments."[1] To characterize this dynamic, open-system orientation as it appears in Freud's work, I will frequently employ the term *psychocultural*.[2] This expresses psychological dynamics as inextricably connected with relations to otherness, covering a range of domains. These include the interpersonal realm of specific others, but also what Jacques Lacan calls the symbolic order, or *grand Autre*: language, symbolic systems, judiciary and ethical codes, and other cultural forms. I also follow Wilden in defining culture as "the means of representation" within a given society.[3] Myth, religion, literature, art, and indeed all forms of communicative media play a major role in subjective formation within culture – that is, in *acculturation*. I will argue that Freud's texts on religion illustrate subjective formation as interconnected with *others* and *otherness* in multiple ways. Given a careful reading, they conspire to reveal an *other Freud*, concerned with issues of psycho-cultural formation and transformation.

* * *

Freud's constructions concerning the origin and development of religion intertwine with inquiries into major issues such as the nature of ethical capacity, the interdependency of individual psychology and cultural existence, and possible guidelines for psycho-cultural modification. For our purposes, Freud's narrative constructs are engaged and interpreted only insofar as they explicate the psycho-cultural status and function of religion. Generally, religion is understood as sets of cultural forms conjoining symbolization and idealization with ethical transformations of subjectivity. On the more obvious level, then, religion has to do with specific cultural resources that function in this formative manner (and this in itself extends the domain of religiously significant media beyond the historical religions *per se*). In addition, religious concerns may be further extended to include the psychological and developmental issues intertwined with these cultural forms. In other words, personal development – as psycho-cultural and as involving symbolically and ethically informed modes of subjectivity – is *itself* a focus of the psychology of religion. Freud's writings on religion and culture address all of these issues, under several guises. For example, I will argue that the paradigm of adaptation to reality, formulated in the critical analyses of religion in *The Future of an Illusion*, is intertwined with an inquiry into ethical development. This latter issue, and its interconnection with cultural constructs, becomes more explicit in the subsequent *Civilization and Its Discontents*. Here, the limited, quasi-positivist definition of reality offered in the earlier text gives way to a more elaborate articulation of the cultural construction of reality. This allows for an exploration of multiple faculties and media in the meaningful formation of psycho-cultural existence.

After preparing the conceptual ground through an interpretive engagement with Freud's more straightforward cultural writings, I turn to the more problematic, overdetermined narrative constructions of *Totem and Taboo* and *Moses and Monotheism*. Each of these will be shown to contain a wealth of insights into psycho-cultural developmental issues. These insights have been marginalized and neglected, mainly because of the obscuring influence of the pseudo-historical speculations at the surface of the texts. In the earlier writing, for example, one finds valuable insights into the way symbol systems constructively affect and transform intra-psychic orientations, as well as relations to others and to reality. An issue that arises in a variety of ways is symbolically mediated *distanciation from immediacy*. This sense of immediacy is understood in multiple, but interrelated forms: as drive satisfaction, as narcissistic gratification, and as fixating objectification of the other.

The later text, *Moses and Monotheism*, builds on the latent insights of its precursor. It includes more refined analyses of personal transformations occurring in relation to cultural ideals (with monotheistic religion essentially acting as a paradigm for these). To describe these transformations, Freud often has recourse to language that stands in an uneasy relation to more prominent, well-defined psychoanalytic concepts and agencies. Thus *Moses and Monotheism* is laden with references to "drive renunciation" (*Triebverzicht*), "soul" (*Seele*, consistently mistranslated as "mind"), and *Geistigkeit* (translated as "intellectuality," but also having the sense of "spirituality"). While Freud seems to be attempting to employ a completed psychoanalytic model to explain the origins and nature of religion, there is in fact *a reciprocal impingement of religiously derived concepts and issues upon psychoanalytic theory*. A series of intersecting themes emerge that pressure and alter the boundaries of the original explanatory model. Their pluralized and interstitial status meaningfully reflects qualities of subjectivity that cannot be collapsed into rigid, self-contained categories.

Freud's writings on religion are vital for understanding and rethinking his metapsychological analyses of cultural forms. Particularly significant is the relation of these forms to intra-psychic transformations, partially embodied in the agency of the super-ego but actually straddling the three agencies. There are indications in these writings of a differentiated model of subjectivity, necessarily formed within the symbolic media of cultures. Thus the surface questions of the literal truth or falsity of religion give way to deeper and more complex analyses of subjective acculturation in qualitative terms. By extracting and extrapolating on such themes, I hope to show that these Freudian writings can continue to make a significant contribution to the contemporary discourse concerning issues of psychological development as intertwined with linguistic and cultural media.

I will argue that, in the margins of these writings, Freud is rethinking *questions of subjectivity* beyond the confines of dominant psychoanalytic models. There is at present a long list of thinkers who critique notions of subjectivity in which the term "designates the relation *of a substance* to itself."[4] This phrase, taken from a recent work by Jean-Luc Nancy, summarizes conceptual tendencies toward establishing the subject as the self-certain foundation for truth and reality. From the start, Freud's work has contributed to undermining such totalized models of subjectivity. For example, the portrayal of subjectivity as differentiated into conscious and unconscious – and later into ego, id, and super-ego – works against assumptions of a punctual, self-transparent individuality. The Freudian subject is also *located* in several ways. It is an embodied and gendered subject, structured by relations to others and by specific cultural influences. The contingency and variability of subjectivity, which are the concomitants of locatedness and embodiment, work against tendencies to elevate specific experiences and perspectives to the status of universality.

One of the paradoxes of Freud's work is that, while it provides important resources for overcoming abstracted, decontextualized models of the subject, it nevertheless sometimes perpetuates an imposition of certain fixed norms. Specifically, Freud repeatedly raises the perspective of the male subject to that of a universal. This occurs most glaringly, but certainly not exclusively, in the formulation of the Oedipus complex as the core of a developmental model. Luce Irigaray has rightly argued, with specific reference to Freud, that "any theory of the subject has always been appropriated by the 'masculine.'"[5] There is little doubt that Irigaray is correct in this assessment, and she undertakes important work in formulating a discourse more reflective of gendered experience. Nevertheless, I do not believe that all analyses of subjectivity are necessarily compartmentalized within gender-specific categories, just as they are not necessarily and entirely culture-bound. To my mind, the key differentiation is between elevating specific finite perspectives to an exclusive universality and attempting to speak, from within finite categories, to shared issues of the human condition. The great artistic, literary, philosophical, and religious creations throughout history display something of this latter quality. Freud's work prioritizes male experience, and builds its symbolic and conceptual world around primarily male terms. Certainly, in *Totem and Taboo* and *Moses and Monotheism* this androcentrism is glaring. Nevertheless, when de-literalized, Freud's analyses can continue to reflect meaningfully on shared issues. These include the fact of locatedness within cultural forms, tensions between freedom and determinism that ensue therefrom, and resources and strategies for increasing awareness and autonomy. I will discuss these matters further in Chapter 1, with specific reference to the Oedipus complex, and they will reappear throughout my analyses of the writings on religion.

The interdependency of subjectivity and culture, increasingly recognized by Freud, indicates the necessary, constitutive infiltration of external realities into the core of personhood. These Freudian insights are the basis for many of Jacques Lacan's formulations. As one commentator summarizes, "the theory of the subject is at the same time a theory of culture for Lacan, since both arise through the process of symbolization."[6] Thus the present use of terms such as "the subject" and "subjectivity" derives from Lacanian usage. However, in prioritizing the de-reification of subjectivity, Lacan's work is certainly not free from the excesses characterizing much postmodern thought. In other words, like Derrida, Foucault, and others, Lacan often seems to take pleasure in simply undermining traditional, totalized notions of subjectivity (particularly as entrenched in notions of the autonomous ego). Overall, however, I believe that Lacan's work transcends the playful, if sometimes irresponsible, *dissolution* of the subject. He extends Freudian inquiry into subjectivity as differentiated and culturally located, so that issues of language and communication related to modes of relationality become paramount.

As I will argue and illustrate at some length in the chapters which follow, Freud's concerns extend beyond a more simplistic placement of the individual within culture. They examine the symbolic vehicles necessary to both psychological and cultural formation in a manner that is truly dynamic, and that offers conceptual resources for critique and transformation. In other words, while the psychoanalytic model developed here indicates a dependency of subjectivity upon cultural symbol systems, it also shows symbolic tools, mediated by significant others, to be necessary resources for human agency.

Freud's inquiries point to developmental exigencies related both to interpersonal relations and to the cultural ideals and values informing these relations. In this regard, questions concerning the *ethical* possibilities of subjective development within culture will be raised. In his great work on Freud, Paul Ricoeur describes the "ethical significance" of psychoanalytic speculation as related to its transforming effects on the alienated individual.[7] Hence Ricoeur distinguishes ethics from morality in the narrower, prescriptive sense. Because they can contribute to transformations of subjectivity fostering self-awareness and reflective capacity, Ricoeur makes a case for psychoanalytic theory and practice as having ethical dimensions. I will expand on these arguments by showing that Freud's writings on religion, in exploring the problem of subjective development structured by cultural ideals, make major contributions to this type of ethical inquiry.

* * *

I have noted that strategies for approaching Freud's work as manifesting conflicting trajectories with multiple registers of meaning have been formulated by several theorists. The French psychoanalyst Jean Laplanche provides a model for the present inquiry in discerning an "unspoken dimension," and "unconscious lines of force" in the Freudian corpus.[8] In this he appropriates the differentiation between *manifest* and *latent* levels of meaning formulated in the *Interpretation of Dreams*. This concern with an interplay of incongruous meanings can become the springboard for hermeneutical encounters with Freud's own texts, whereby insights contrary to the surface (manifest) lines of argument are elucidated rather than repressed. Of course, the language of manifest and latent, or surface and depth, should not be taken too literally. In textual interpretation, as in dream interpretation, the surface itself contains the depth. It thus becomes a matter of discerning the ruptures in a manifest viewpoint or line of argument; these provoke a troping of the text so that it is seen in a different way. Therefore in reading Freud I am not concerned with positing an underlying, hidden level of meaning. Rather, my procedure is to follow lines of tension in the text that disclose alternative perspectives.

In a similar vein, Jane Flax has summarized the issue by stating that "ambivalence, ambiguity, antinomies, and paradoxes pervade Freud's theories."[9] She further emphasizes that these numerous forms of tension and, indeed, contradiction, should not be glossed over. The *inconsistencies* in psychoanalytic theory need to be addressed; at the same time, a fuller appreciation of the richness of Freud's work requires careful attention to its fluctuating perspectives, levels, and registers. Flax notes that the majority of commentators on Freud, in following an interpretive paradigm governed by principles of consistency and homogeneity, "tend arbitrarily to reconcile the antinomies in his theories or merely to cancel out one pole in favor of the other."[10] Such responses, both within and without psychoanalysis, assume knowledge of what Freud *really* meant. These assumptions characterize critical, anti-Freudian responses as much as doctrinaire psychoanalytic theory. For example, a common feature of object-relations, ego-psychology, Jungian, and existentialist theories is the rejection of biologism, taken as a more or less self-evident dominant explanatory principle in Freud's work. Authors from these schools then introduce what they take to be innovative emphases on freedom, creativity, and spirituality. Unfortunately, the assumption that Freud's work is consistently and coherently biologistic and mechanistic blocks access to other possible readings and ensuing insights. Failure to recognize plurivocity feeds into the practice of surpassing a closed set of texts rather than exploring more fully the resources inherent in those texts. In this way, fixed assumptions about Freud's work are perpetuated and conceptual possibilities inherent in the work remain dormant.

In psychoanalytic theory the tension between manifest and latent content is supplemented by a series of dynamic concepts. Thus Freud offers several explicitly formulated ideas that speak to a contemporary interpretive sensibility. For example, in *The Interpretation of Dreams* notions of *overdetermination* and *overinterpretation* anticipate the rejection of paradigms of univocity by contemporary theories. Overdetermination applies to formative influences in the genesis of dreams, symptoms, and texts. Overinterpretation indicates the consequent multiplicity of modes and levels of meaning that emerge in analyzing these phenomena.[11] Meaning is, in principle, uncontrollable and open-ended. This open-endedness is the product both of an inherent pluralization within language and symbols (as expressed in Paul Ricoeur's emphasis on *polysemy*), and of the proliferation of meaning in relation to contexts and viewpoints (as in Jacques Derrida's *dissemination*). Derrida summarizes the latter thus: "dissemination...can be led back neither to a present of simple origin nor to an eschatological presence....It marks an irreducible and *generative* multiplicity."[12] Derrida certainly accepts Ricoeur's notion of polysemy, but insists further on the creative force of dissemination. This expands the dynamic of meaning production beyond an *inherent* plurivocity of discourse. It expresses an ongoing process that can never be reduced to the text or phenomenon *in itself*. An ever-shifting other or outside is necessarily operative in establishing the sense of a text. This outside might be understood in terms of context, as long as we bear in mind Derrida's caveat that "no context can determine meaning to the point of exhaustiveness."[13] That is, no context is final or closed. Again, it is particularly fruitful to direct these interpretive procedures toward Freud's densely imbricated discourse (as Derrida has himself done to some degree).[14]

* * *

The following interrogations illustrate that in Freud's writings on religion and culture an apparent surface consistency and homogeneity is continuously disrupted. In these writings, the most reductive assumptions are often conjoined with insights and ideas that resist and subvert the more limited surface or manifest content. My strategy of reading highlights such contradictions, and then offers means whereby potential insights contained in the contradictory moments are developed and articulated. If one delves into Freud's writings and works out their sometimes inchoate latent insights their unparalleled range and penetration of conceptualization becomes enhanced as a resource for ongoing reflection. This does not mean that a systematic alternative view to the manifest theories is cleverly hidden in Freud's work. Appearing in tension with some of the dominant arguments and, often, in a literary, symbolized form, the counter-insights to the manifest arguments remain fragmentary and incipient. The task of the present work will be to bring these latent insights to a more coherent and well-articulated state of development. This is accomplished both in the interpretive engagement with the writings on religion and culture, and through extrapolations on key ideas.

A meaningful analysis of the tensions within texts such as *Totem and Taboo* and *Moses and Monotheism* requires a strategy of *reading against the grain* that does not assume a uniform flow, a homogeneous current of meaning. This potentially allows counter-moments or seemingly marginal aspects of the work to enter into the interpretive process, altering the status of the dominant arguments. This strategy for reading Freud is enriched by his use of polysemous narrative constructs, including figurative and myth-like images and symbols, in the presentation of his ideas. This is in line with Freud's numerous references to the intuitive discernment of psychological truths in the works of poets and artists. However, the more poetic moments in Freud's work also conflict with his predominant resistance to embracing literary and figurative forms of discourse as scientifically valid. This is one of several sources of tension in these writings. It is engendered partly by Freud's inability or unwillingness to develop his more poetic insights systematically and partly by his somewhat restricted, quasi-positivistic understanding of scientific inquiry.

I will not argue that Freud's empirically based critiques of religion are unfounded or entirely incorrect. Indeed, empirical and experiential bases are essential to critical reflection on cultural and subjective modes. However, there is a line where an empirical attitude hardens into doctrinaire forms of radical empiricism, scientism, or positivism. A standard definition of positivism's standpoint is that "science is the only valid knowledge and facts the only possible objects of knowledge."[15] In Freud's work, such positivistic views appear in many guises. The early trauma theory, the postulation of libidinous drives and infantile wishes as the bases of psychical and cultural phenomena, and the reduction of the origin and meaning of religion to determinate primal events are all manifestations of positivistic tendencies.

In regard to the mixed elements of scientism, positivism, and radical empiricism in Freud's work, I will illustrate that these surface orientations can be subjected to a deconstructionist type of analysis. That is, the positivistic elements in Freud's thinking are qualified and overturned by elements *within* his own inquiries. My approach is again influenced by Derrida in this respect. He argues that empiricism predicates truth on a form of experience designating a "relationship with presence."[16] In this form of inquiry the postulation of truth becomes embedded in a privileging of a single interpretive modality of the phenomenally given. Therefore more comprehensive and differentiated forms of understanding require resistance to the closure sustained by fixation on presence. What is present, or empirically manifest under specific conditions to a particular observer, needs to be held in relation to other possible experiential and conceptual configurations. The interplay or complementarity between perspectives and interpretations yields deeper insight into any given phenomenon. Elsewhere, in commenting on the nature of logocentrism and metaphysics as representative of closed or totalized systems of explanation, Derrida again discusses empiricism. As he states, "realism or sensualism – 'empiricism' – are modifications of logocentrism."[17] Any orientation that privileges a determinable reference point as the final ground and arbiter of truth is, in this sense, logocentric or *metaphysical*. The latter terms become pejorative by indicating closed and controlled systems of reference, whether materialist or idealist, resisting intrusions of new, alternative perspectives.

In "Freud and the scene of writing," Derrida undertakes a deconstruction of the focus on "presence" in Freud's topographical model of conscious and unconscious, as developed in relation to dream interpretation. He overturns the paradigm of an underlying unconscious content or referent, determinable in itself apart from the modalities of representation by which it comes to be known.[18] Yet, for all his fascination with psychoanalysis, Derrida never applies the deconstruction of empiricism to the Freudian writings on religion and culture, in which positivist and empiricist paradigms figure most prominently. The present work makes a new contribution by undertaking a deconstructive analysis that overturns a metaphysics of radical empiricism and its correlative reductionisms. Freud's discourse on religion, combining a "scientific" mode of explanation with a high degree of literary depth and complexity, provides a unique test case for this strategy. Subverting and splitting open the positivist shell of these writings discloses elements of an alternative orientation to psycho-cultural realities, unassimilable with the dichotomized categories of empirical and ideal.

Roland Barthes has noted that overturning fixed readings and attending to the *playing* of the text "coincides with a liberation of symbolic energy."[19] Barthes's formulation traces disclosures of new meaning and insight to the unraveling procedures of deconstruction and other postmodernist styles of reading. However, this argument goes beyond a fascination with mere dissection and dissolution. It indicates what may be termed a *reconstructive* component that can ensue from postmodernist analyses. A twofold inquiry, moving from fissuring surface meaning to assembling symbolic resonances and fragments of alternative lines of thought, reflects the strategy of the present undertaking. The analysis proceeds from moments of tension in the Freudian texts to the discernment and elucidation of latent insights concerning the psycho-cultural function of religion. Such alternative levels of meaning can be understood in terms of narrative or disclosive, rather than historical or correspondence, models of truth.

A useful definition of narrative truth, within a specifically psychoanalytic context, is provided by Donald Spence:

> Narrative truth can be defined as the criterion we use to decide when a certain experience has been captured to our satisfaction; it depends on continuity and closure and the extent to which the fit of the pieces takes on aesthetic finality.[20]

Spence is particularly concerned with narrative criteria for truth in the psychoanalyst's understanding and interpretation of the analysand's recollections. The significance of narrative truth, however, extends beyond these parameters. It exhibits important points of contact with Freud's notion of the truth value of *psychical reality*. In each, self-accounts, like dreams, may reveal profound psychological realities of an individual's life. That is, what is at issue are symbolized expressions of subjective experience and self-understanding. These can be psychologically "true" – that is, disclosive of personal meaning – even if they do not literally correspond to external events. As Spence emphasizes, "narrative truth has a special significance in its own right...making contact with the actual past may be of far less significance than creating a coherent and consistent account of a particular set of events."[21] Spence contrasts the narrative approach to truth with the criterion of correspondence with definite facts that characterizes historical truth. The latter, he argues, "is time-bound and is dedicated to the strict observance of correspondence rules; our aim is to come as close as possible to what 'really' happened."[22] Spence tends to see Freud as firmly rooted in a historical approach to truth. This view certainly captures the dominant intentional and surface orientation of both *Totem and Taboo* and *Moses and Monotheism*. It is in line with Freud's arguments concerning the historical, as opposed to the material, truth of religion (discussed in Chapter 4). Yet this historical approach represents only one dimension of these texts, and perhaps not the most significant one. Without assuming an unproblematic fit of Spence's categories to Freud's writings, a narrative approach helps reveal much that remains obscured by Freud's predominant focus on historical validity. However, emphasis on narrative levels of meaning must be supplemented by *deconstructionist* procedures. These are required to disclose and interrogate textual conflicts and tensions in a way that moves beyond surface levels of meaning. If there are narrative and symbolically portrayed insights in these texts, they emerge sporadically, covertly, and in points of negation at the literal and manifest levels.

On a manifest level (that is, as a set of pseudo-historical constructs) the narrative account first formulated in *Totem and Taboo* shapes the analysis in *Moses and Monotheism*. It is transposed onto the biblical setting, with Moses partially re-enacting the role of primal father. Freud also uses the earlier narrative as the explanatory backdrop to the subsequent one. Thus he invokes phylogenetic memories of the primal parricide to explain patterns of affective behavior and irrational eruptions of guilt. This attempt at a causal link, however, serves to divert the focus from narrative repetitions that are indicative of deeper psychical and symbolic levels of meaning traversing the two texts. The etiological accounts of Freud's pseudo-historical constructs act as *myths* informing us about the *status and impact* of ideal cultural forms. The significance of these mythical constructs parallels Mircea Eliade's interpretation of cosmogonic myths as establishing *paradigms* for cultural worlds or the order of things. The symbolic order, representing the establishment of reality *in the time of origins*, is not historical but paradigmatic.[23] Similarly, Freud's narratives – seemingly describing the origins of religion, culture, and morality – better serve to symbolize dynamic psychocultural processes. Freud's narratives use particular historical materials, and constructive extrapolations thereon, to make points reflecting more broadly on religious dimensions of psycho-cultural existence. In remarkable contrast to the materialist views habitually associated with psychoanalysis, these texts especially highlight *language*, *symbolization*, and *ideals* as forming and transforming humanly experienced reality. The precise nature and function of ideals, values, and worldviews, of course, varies enormously in different cultural and historical contexts. Nevertheless, it is their *necessary* intervention in personality formation that is the core latent insight of Freud's religious writings.

* * *

In examining Freud's cultural and metapsychological writings, the initial construction of psychoanalytic method and theory within a therapeutic context cannot be ignored. Generally speaking, there are two sides to the matter: the normalization of pathology and the pathologizing of normality. With regard to the first point, even in Freud's earlier writings the boundary between normal and pathological begins to be blurred. Similar "mechanisms" are evident in pathological, neurotic manifestations such as hysterical symptoms, compulsions, and phobias, and in everyday occurrences such as dreams, faulty acts (parapraxes), and jokes. It can be argued that this blurring works against the segregation and disenfranchisement of the mentally ill by locating their experience and behavior within general human terms.[24] Reciprocally, however, there is an extension of the therapeutic model to cultural levels, which are seen to require critical amelioration. Freud's tendency to pathologize is quite evident in most of his cultural writings. Pathologizing provides the basis for a critique of specific cultural formations and practices, among which religion figures prominently. Here the following question becomes crucial to my inquiry: Does the prominence of a pathologizing attitude toward culture obscure lines of critique informed by *constructive* goals? The concerns of this question are sustained by many underlying arguments in Freud's writings on religion and culture. These do not merely *undermine* existing structures and orientations, but point beyond them in a manner governed, quite explicitly, by ethical ideals and concerns with meaningful human development.

The overtly pathologizing, reductionistic, and atheistic stance of the texts on religion has too often been taken as predetermining their possible meaning. Of course, it seems clear that Freud's intentional stance toward traditional religions *is* both atheistic and predominantly critical. In *Moses and Monotheism*, for example, Freud is quite explicit about his views on literally understood religious postulates. Speaking of the satisfaction found in the belief in a higher being, he concludes: "We can only regret that certain experiences in life and observations in the world make it impossible for us to accept the premise of the existence of such a Supreme Being."[25] One must respect Freud's avowed position. Moreover, Freud's arguments outlining the pathological and regressive dimensions of specific forms of religious belief and practice demand serious engagement. Yet this atheistic and generally critical orientation does not mean that his analyses do not yield constructive insights. This argument does not involve positing that Freud was secretly religious. Rather, the point is that Freud's writings inquiring into the psycho-cultural dimensions of religion are not fully governable by his manifest intentional stance. These writings are, on some levels, critical and patholo-gizing, but they disclose much more about religion and culture than symptomological and positivistic models allow.

One might further argue that Freud's atheism, combined as it is with a spirit of critical scientific inquiry, acts like a creative catalyst as much as it forms a restrictive prejudgement. A critical, questioning orientation impelled Freud's detailed psychodynamic inquiries into religion, morality, and culture. Beginning with a rejection of literal, metaphysical self-under-standings of religion and morality, Freud sought the sources and meaning of religion *within* culture and psychology. The care with which Freud elaborates an explanatory model yields numerous valuable insights into the human significance of religious forms. These incorporate symbolic, representa-tional, and aesthetic activity concerning meaningful worldviews related to ethically informed subjective maturation. As overdetermined, religious forms speak to issues of meaningful interpersonal subjectivity in a manner that cannot be reduced to their constitutive components. Thus my analysis of Freud is not directed toward a final definition of religion, but rather toward further unfolding modes of subjectivity informed by symbolic frame-works of meaning, values, and ideals. The emerging insights may, I hope, be reapplied to transform our understanding of traditional religious forms, but this task is not undertaken here.

* * *

From among the various *postmodern* theorists to have engaged Freud, the work of Jacques Lacan and Julia Kristeva most expressly informs my anal-yses. They provide strategic conceptual tools for the project of rereading Freud and offer structural concepts that extend the insights emerging from this reading. However, my intention is to address and appropriate the work of either theorist not *in toto*, but only insofar as it contributes to my line of inquiry.

I approach Lacan as one who continually stimulates fresh reading and understanding. He opens our interpretive eyes, both generally and with particular respect to Freud, and also provides new concepts and categories that extend aspects of Freud's thought. Attempts to classify Lacan's work either as a coherent system or as a failed attempt at systematization seem misplaced. Lacan understood his work mainly as an exegesis of and extrapolation on Freud, and it is in this spirit that it is employed here. Lacan contributes to a mode of interpretation and model of subjectivity that develop the dynamic conceptions *within* Freud's work while resisting its reifying tendencies. Ultimately, using Lacan to enhance a reading of Freud on religion and Freud's texts on religion as a context for reading Lacan illustrates previously unseen points of convergence between the thinkers. My analyses will illustrate the point that Freud's inquiries into religion seem to call for Lacanian categories of interpretation, such as the *imaginary* and the *symbolic*. In this I am less concerned with legitimating Lacan than with clarifying and strengthening certain insights and lines of inquiry he develops out of Freud.

Like Freud, Lacan was an avowed atheist.[26] He should therefore be understood as contributing to a psychology of religion in functional terms. Again, for my purposes this has to do with issues of meaningful and ethical subjective development within cultural forms. Even on this level Lacan does not offer a comprehensive theory of religion, and it may well be that formulating such theories is predicated on systematizing and totalizing premises which are no longer tenable. Lacan's work, however, provides an insight into the psychological significance of religion, or into what may more accurately be termed the religious dimensions of subjectivity. He illuminates broadly religious issues by addressing interconnections among language, symbolism, ideals, and the formation of ethical and reflective capacities through his open-system model of the subject.

One of Lacan's few direct statements concerning religion supports the view that problems of meaningful psycho-cultural development are in themselves religious ones. He describes religion as being at once a mode of posing "the question of existence in the world" and of the subject's self-interrogation.[27] There is an evident interconnection between these two points of focus. That is, religion is related to the question of the subject's mode of being, and to sets of symbol systems and practices that express and inform those subjective modalities. The Lacanian orientation offers a means of conceptualizing self-transformation and maturation as relational, and as involving linguistic and symbolic resources. The Lacanian model, variable and open-ended as it is, encompasses both the ethical dimensions of human relations and the cultural symbol systems that structure them. I believe that these aspects of Lacanian thinking are brought into much sharper focus by juxtaposition with Freud's inquiries into religion and culture.

Julia Kristeva's writings, more directly than Lacan's, delve significantly into the Freudian texts on religion. *Powers of Horror*, for example, includes a great deal of reflection on issues and themes related to *Totem and Taboo*. Although the present work undertakes a new, sustained analysis of Freud's writings on religion and opens original lines of inquiry, Kristeva's analyses will be incorporated into my interpretations at several important points. In addition, Kristeva develops conceptual tools that extend Lacanian models of the subject-in-process, especially as it is related to meaningful development within symbolic forms. Overall, Kristeva does not always agree with Lacan, but much of her work refines his analyses of the intersections between individual psychology and culture. Kristeva furthers these analyses, particularly with her model of semiotic forms of expression connected with religious and artistic production. The category of the semiotic enriches the Lacanian understanding of the nature and role of linguistic media in the interplay of cultural and individual development. It also contributes to an understanding of psychical trauma, conflict, and the breakdown of symbolizing capacities, while providing strategies for addressing these issues. In these inquiries Kristeva opens issues concerning critical and transformative responses to existing symbolic social structures. In other words, while Freud and Lacan tend to illuminate issues of symbolic *structuring*, Kristeva moves to issues of *restructuring*. In this way, her work speaks to many issues emerging from my reading of Freud.

By extracting some latent themes in Freud's work, and extending them through insights and ideas derived from Lacan and Kristeva, I hope to develop further the dynamic model of subjectivity they share. Following the thread provided by issues concerning the subject-within-culture establishes more intimate connections between these key figures in French psychoanalysis and Freud's foundational texts on religion and culture. This shared project reveals Freud's analyses of religion to be more intrinsic and essential to psychoanalytic theory, and much more complicated and innovative, than has generally been considered. If the present work is successful in its endeavors it will be difficult (if not impossible) henceforth to read Freud on religion and culture according to previously standard assumptions.

Chapter 1

Trauma, Oedipus complex, and the exigencies of subjective formation

Traumatic experience and psychical reality

I have argued that tensions between positivistic tendencies and counter-tendencies toward open-system thinking appear throughout Freud's work. One important manifestation of these tensions appears in the early attempts to establish a definitive explanatory model for neurotic disturbances. As he pursues these concerns, Freud reflects on the *representational* dimensions of human experience, as well as on *disruptions* in subjective experience and development. These interconnected issues provide more than a test case for delineating key points of creative tension in Freud's metapsychology. Permutations of these themes (representational forms, trauma, subjective formation) appear repeatedly in his writings on religion and culture. The problem of trauma, in addition to indicating how Freud's inquiries exceed the scope of a positivistic paradigm, also provides a thematic point of departure for larger psycho-cultural issues.

The initial psychoanalytic approach to neuroses evinces a basically causal-mechanistic view of the problem. As Freud summarizes, "traumatic neuroses" were understood in terms of fixation on a disrupting event occurring in early life. "Neuroses could then be equated with a traumatic illness and would come about owing to inability to deal with an experience whose affective coloring was excessively powerful."[1] The experiences related by Freud's analysands were predominantly of a sexual nature, and his initial explanation of neurosis came to be known as the "seduction theory." It is evident that this theory, as Ian Hacking has pointed out, reveals a tendency on Freud's part to "anthropomorphize" trauma. Hacking states that "Freud's traumas almost always involved somebody doing something, an intentional action."[2] This model often obscures the relation of traumatic experience to events that are not strictly the result of human agency (for example the death of a loved one by natural causes). Another limitation of Freud's initial line of explanation is its reliance on specific contingent causal events, a reliance that serves to segregate neurotic from normal psychology. William McGrath summarizes the issue as follows:

By focusing on sexual traumas, this theory had the effect of sharply separating the personal history and psychical characteristics of the mentally ill from the world of normal mental development, thereby blocking the way to a more general and unified conception of mental activity.[3]

However, Freud did not modify his model only for theoretical purposes, but also because of its inadequate representation of clinical experience. In recounting the transformation in his thinking, Freud goes on to state, in relation to an example of father fixation in a female patient, that the trauma formula "is not sufficiently comprehensive."[4] In some instances, memory was found to be conjoined with fantasy and narrative reconfiguration. The modification of Freud's views is evident in his stating that "phantasies of being seduced are of particular interest, because so often they are not phantasies but real memories. Fortunately, however, they are nevertheless not real as often as seemed at first to be shown by the findings of analysis."[5] Here, it is clear that Freud does not *rule out* the existence of actual experientially based traumas alongside of and enmeshed with instances of fantasized remembrances. However, the experientially based traumatic events posited by the original seduction theory are not *necessary* factors in the etiology of the neuroses. Freud's position accommodates a plurality of factors affecting individual development and remains open to numerous possible experiential paths. In a significant passage, Freud concludes that "there is no need to abandon the traumatic line of approach as being erroneous: it must be possible to fit it in and subsume it somewhere else."[6] The nature of this "somewhere else" is of key import for the present inquiry, particularly because one version of the displaced trauma locates it prehistorically, within the psychodynamics involved in establishing culture and religion.

Often, however, Freud seems to dismiss the veracity of accounts of actual seduction. Relating how virtually all his female patients told of an early seduction by the father, Freud states: "I was driven to recognize in the end that these reports were untrue and so came to understand that hysterical symptoms were derived from phantasies and not from real occurrences."[7] While this transition to a model in which fantasy is an essential factor in memory and illness is constitutive of psychoanalysis, it has positive and negative consequences. These issues have informed a great deal of ongoing controversy in psychotherapeutic circles. Essentially, the prestige of psychoanalytic theory served to create a psychotherapeutic bias against actual accounts of seduction and traumas based on abuse. More recently, there has been a backlash against the predominant psychoanalytic tendency to treat memories of real events as fantasies.[8]

For my purposes, the key issues concern Freud's recognition of the representational features of psychical reality. This is constituted by an interweaving of memory and experience with narrative and symbolization. Summarizing the transformation in Freud's thinking, McGrath notes:

> his insight involved the realization that in the unconscious a screen memory phantasy worked both backward and forward in time, recasting old memories in the service of the fantasy's forward-driving force, a process in which language played a central role.[9]

Freud shifts from a model predicated upon events operating in a causal manner, to an overdetermined etiological formulation involving symbolic, developmental, and interpersonal factors. As this occurs, Freud's thinking also transcends a narrow positivist paradigm of human experience and psychical functioning.

Freud undertakes a partial transition to a modified theory where psycho-dynamic processes are as significant as external events. A precedent for this development occurs in *The Interpretation of Dreams*, where Freud introduces the notion of "psychical reality" (*psychische Realität*) as "a particular form of existence not to be confused with material reality."[10] The category of psychical reality, key to the nature of dream experience, is also applied to fantasy life and symbolic constructs. This broader application serves to increase the significance of the category. Freud summarizes his modified views by stating that "the phantasies possess *psychical* as contrasted with *material* reality, and we gradually learn to understand that *in the world of the neuroses it is psychical reality which is the decisive kind*."[11] Similarly, in *Totem and Taboo* Freud emphasizes the effective force of psychical reality in neurotic and compulsive activity: "We find no deeds but only impulses and emotions, set upon evil ends but held back from their achievement. What lie behind the sense of guilt of neurotics are always *psychical* realities and never *factual* ones."[12] One begins to see that, within Freud's thinking, the issue of subjective experience of and relation to reality is far more complex than can be accommodated by a positivist model. The expanded psychoanalytic understanding of reality, as including active and creative psychical components, is crucial to interrogating Freud's treatment of religio-cultural constructs.

These themes resurface, following the First World War, in the analyses of traumatic experience in *Beyond the Pleasure Principle*. In that work Freud takes his point of departure from the repetition compulsion ensuing from severe trauma. He points out that "dreams occurring in the traumatic neuroses have the characteristic of repeatedly bringing the patient back into the situation of his accident"[13] Freud proceeds to argue that it is not at all self-evident that dreams related to traumatic experience should recur in this manner and that this repetition is in stark contrast with conscious attempts to forget the event. Many lines of thought emerge from these reflections. These include the postulation of the "death drive," which tends to internalize and biologize the sources of psychical conflict. Other lines of thought emerge from the often discussed account of the *fort–da* (gone–here) game of Freud's grandson. The latter has provided an example of the function of *symbolizing* in attempting to integrate and master negative experience such as absence and loss.[14] In discussing these matters, Cathy Caruth has noted that the compulsive repetition of painful experience indicates "the absolute inability of the mind to avoid an unpleasurable event that has not been given psychic meaning in any way."[15] This perspective shifts the focus from the intensity of an event to the manner in which the event is symbolically grasped and integrated. In other words, the ability *meaningfully to represent* a painful experience distinguishes between a "deathly" compulsiveness and the possibility of therapeutic working-through.

Two intersecting insights emerge from Freud's modifications of his initial cause-and-effect model. The first, as we have seen, involves the complexification of the nature of psychical experience related to traumatizing events. The second concerns traumatic aspects of human existence, with specific reference to the maturation process. This view represents a transition from specific traumatic events to universal formative processes that shifts Freud's theoretical focus "from neurotic abnormality to the general human condition."[16] Human maturation, with its unformed nature, its needs, open-endedness, dependencies, breaks and contingencies, is almost necessarily infused by some degree of *traumatization*. Maud Mannoni further clarifies this point by stating that "the child must pass through necessary conflicts, which are identification conflicts, not conflicts with the *Real*."[17] As the ensuing chapters will illustrate, this broader sense of traumatization is associated with the formative processes of acculturation involving *symbolic remove*, that is, distanciation from immediacy and givenness. With these formulations, the Freudian model accommodates and responds to a spectrum of varying degrees of psychical health. This is related to personal experience and suffering, the ability or inability to function in everyday social life, and other individually variable phenomena. However, psychoanalysis partially breaks down the barrier between normal and pathological, insofar as all human beings experience *some* degree of traumatization related to developmental exigencies. This is one aspect of Freud's progression from a psychopathologist to an inquirer into broader psycho-cultural issues.

Concerns with fissures and conflicts in human development become most clearly evident in Freud's formulations of a maturational dynamic within the framework of Oedipal imagery. Thus one of the major ways in which Freud reinterprets accounts of seduction is as representing the developmental travails associated with the "typical Oedipus complex."[18] An etiological model emphasizing specific traumatic experiences of a sexual nature is overshadowed by a model in which libidinal and relational vicissitudes are clustered about the Oedipus complex. These developmental exigencies account for repressions, fixations, regressions, and so forth. Rather than invoking disruptive events that *may* happen, the Oedipal model seeks to articulate *structures of interrelational development*. These, to be sure, necessarily include contingent and variable individual relations, vicissitudes, and conflicts. Again, abusive traumatic events occur all too frequently and are highly pertinent to analysis – Freud never denied this. Yet, as a theorist of the human condition, Freud turns from an emphasis on the possible, particular traumatizations to the necessary, universal exigencies of libidinal and relational development. Freud has supplemented a simpler causal model with a more intricate and overdetermined set of developmental interactions that accentuate individual variability and psychical creativity.

Oedipal dynamics and entry into the symbolic

Earlier I argued that Freud's explicitly atheistic and reductionistic stance need not predetermine an inquiry into his writings. Additionally, it could be said that Freud's avowal of a scientific attitude, frequently bordering on positivism, actually plays a constructive role in the creative yield of these texts. Freud's disavowal of religious worldviews is linked to a broader anti-idealism. This attidude appears in numerous assertions concerning the primary and originary status of sexuality, libido, id, and unconscious wishes and desires. I will not address the issue of the extent to which this anti-idealism holds up in its strictest form. However, it does compel Freud – scrupulous inquirer that he was – to find non-idealist explanations for the coming into being of ideal and symbolic structures in culture. These ideal forms represent standards of quality and value that counteract, to some varying degree, the motivational force of more immediate inclinations and needs. They include ethical, intellectual, and creative capacities for representation and symbolization, and they involve functions associated with each of the psychical agencies: id, ego, and super-ego.

In both *Totem and Taboo* and *Moses and Monotheism* Freud formulates explicit theories that account for the coming into being of religion, culture, and morality in specific contexts. The impetus behind Freud's inquiries into culture and religion can be analyzed on several levels. For example, these inquiries may be understood as instances of psychoanalysis "colonizing" the unconquered territory of cultural theory. On this level, Freud's analyses of cultural formation posit mechanisms, forces, dynamics, and pathologies parallel to those manifested in individual psychology. Specifically, these forces and dynamic structures are seen as analogous to those discerned in the Oedipus complex. Freud appears to undertake a reductive conquest, replacing the mystery and complexity of ideal cultural structures with a closed-system explanation governed by instinctual conflicts.

However, closer inspection reveals that Freud's psychodynamic model remains open-ended. It is necessarily incomplete, in that it postulates a dependency of individual development on interpersonal relations and, ultimately, on extant cultural forms. This is one way in which the closed-system thinking characteristic of many of Freud's positivistic and mechanistic formulations is subverted by an awareness of individual psychology being located within the variable systems of culture. This open-endedness sustains conceptual flexibility, stimulates the ongoing modification of psychoanalytic theory, and offers insight into creative relational processes. Yet it tended to be seen by Freud as posing the danger of infinite explanatory regress, and hence as a problem to be resolved. On the level of synthesizing conceptual loose ends, one issue in particular made cultural inquiry significant for psychoanalytic theory. This was the question of the *origins of conscience and morality*.

At the time he was writing *Totem and Taboo* the problem of culture was becoming increasingly important to Freud. Cultural concerns were not just tangential to a theory rooted in individual psychology, but were beginning to be seen as intrinsic to the dynamics of subjective maturation. Individual psychological development was increasingly understood as inseparable from interpersonal and cultural existence, including abstract forms such as language and ethics. These issues were of particular significance to the problem of the ego-ideal and would take on increased importance as its successor, the super-ego, became more fully formulated. Issues related to the super-ego – such as the nature of conscience and sublimation, as well as problems of intra-psychic tension, guilt, and anxiety – inform much of Freud's later metapsychological work and are given important treatment in his analyses of religion. Even prior to the postulation of the super-ego, however, the internalization of symbolic cultural resources it represents was becoming an increasingly significant aspect of psychoanalytic theory.

In a psychoanalytic approach to individual development the crucial points of contact between subjectivity, interpersonal relations, and acculturation are condensed into the framework of Oedipal dynamics. This configuration contains various levels, and functions accordingly in a thoroughly overdetermined manner. My eventual concern will be to analyze *Totem and Taboo* and *Moses and Monotheism* as key texts reflecting on the intersections of desire and culture. In these inquiries the Oedipus complex is a dominant paradigm (conjoined with "historicized" versions of the trauma theory). The Oedipus complex symbolically condenses a model in which individual psycho-sexual development is inherently dependent on interactions with cultural representatives. On an etiological level which remains shaped by a causal-deterministic orientation, the core complex impels Freud's inquiries into the origin of religion. However, this transposition to the cultural sphere is not without difficulties; and this is a point that can be used to emphasize the non-literal dimensions of the Oedipus complex. Its figurative and symbolic qualities become more prominent as the persuasiveness of its literal, explanatory logic diminishes.

The Oedipus complex is clearly subject to multiple levels of interpretation.[19] In Freud's writings on the Oedipus complex as signifying structural relations in the formation of subjectivity there is a discernable spectrum of understanding and application. Moreover, the Oedipus complex is overextended and overdetermined apart from its application to cultural forms. The spectrum of meaning compacted into Oedipal dynamics ranges from the highly particular and concrete to the more general and abstract. That is, at one end of the spectrum the analyses focus on specific relations to individual parental figures, shaped variously by factors such as the gender of the developing subject, the attitudes of the parental figures or guardians, and the degree and nature of their presence or absence. This forms the more particularized, interpersonal level of analysis. The other end of the spectrum is partially predicated upon the first level, but examines issues on a less individually variable and particularized scale. Here the analyses still relate to the developing individual but focus on a more generalized dynamic of desire and conflict. This dynamic is related to the internalization of cultural structures and authority in the formation of the super-ego. These processes are founded on the interpersonal level but concern broader cultural and social dimensions of subjective development. This more abstract end of the spectrum is the point of departure for Lacanian extrapolations relating the negotiation of the Oedipus complex with accession to the symbolic order of one's culture. At this level what is *universal* is the necessity of some form of acculturation, including immersion in a linguistically shaped world governed by codes of conduct. The specific constructs of language, moral codes, as well as the nature and degree of individual internalization, are open to innumerable variations.

My concern, then, is not with Freud's theories of psycho-sexual development on the more particularized and concretized individual level, nor with the Oedipus complex as the key moment in specifically determined familial interrelations. Rather, my focus is the other end of the spectrum, where a dialectics of desire interfaces with problems of acculturation. Still, the two levels, which I have characterized as ends of a spectrum, are not fully separable, and certainly are not clearly differentiated in Freud's work. Furthermore, Freud often tends to transfer the Oedipal configuration from the individual to the cultural realm, as if it were complete on the individual level and as if the cultural level were a separate but parallel domain. In this form the Oedipus complex serves a crucial explanatory function in the analogical thinking of *Totem and Taboo*, *Moses and Monotheism*, and, to a lesser extent, *The Future of an Illusion*. What also emerges in these analyses, however, is a disruption of the closed-system view and the analogical method that accompanies it. That is, in the cultural writings the end of the Oedipal spectrum revealing the individual–cultural *interdependency* occurring within symbolic systems becomes increasingly prominent.

Of course, a literal reading of the Oedipus complex on the level of individual psycho-sexual development remains prominent throughout Freud's work, although it is subject to modification.[20] Indeed, Freud's suspicion of innovative and symbolic treatments of his ideas is often evident. For example, in one place he warns against "twisted re-interpretations" of the Oedipus complex.[21] In this comment Freud is concerned with the ideas of Alfred Adler and, most particularly, C. G. Jung; and it must be said that his resistance is not entirely unwarranted. Jung, for example, turns from the interpersonal dynamics of the Freudian model almost entirely, interpreting mythic and literary images as expressions of an innate archetypal order. Jung conceived of his approach as the antithesis of Freud's anti-idealist stance. It expressly posits a *sui generis* spiritual dimension, as against manifest Freudian reductions of religion and culture to sexuality. With this type of approach Jung begins to navigate the territory of symbolically mediated inner transformation. However, in relinquishing the constitutive, interpersonal paradigm of Oedipal dynamics Jung's formulation of a spiritual realm tends toward reification. Because of its emphasis on unchanging psychical structures (the archetype *an sich*), the Jungian model retreats from issues related to the interplay of psychology and culture.

There are, of course, numerous difficulties in Freud's renditions of the Oedipus complex. One of the most significant is the neglect of pre-Oedipal relations (a problem that partially carries over into Lacan's work in spite of the latter's introduction of the mirror stage).[22] This could be seen as a gap in an otherwise acceptable model, filled in by numerous subsequent psychoanalytic theorists and practitioners such as Melanie Klein, D. W. Winnicott, and, in a different way, Julia Kristeva. More egregious are Freud's tortuous attempts to construct a normative female version of the Oedipus complex.[23] Yet even these problems are damning only when the literal, more particularized, and variable levels of Oedipal dynamics are given generalized status. That is, when contingently variable features are raised to the status of universality we are confronted with an apparent *necessity* of the misogynistic reading of female anatomy in terms of essential lack and castration, the postulation of penis envy, a literal threat of castration directed at male subjects, and other dubious hypotheses.

However, Freud himself continually indicates *symbolic* dimensions of the Oedipus complex that counteract the literalism, biologism, and determinism of many of his formulations. For example, on one occasion in *Totem and Taboo* Freud modifies his use of "father complex" to "parental complex" (*Elternkomplex*).[24] This indicates a widening of interpersonal dynamics in a way that subverts gender stereotypes. Another crucial instance of this opening is the portrayal of Oedipal dynamics in what Freud calls a "bisexual" reading. This takes us beyond the literal, gender-specific level of analysis and mitigates some of the problems in the accounts of female sexuality. Thus in *The Ego and the Id*, while discussing "identification with the father" in the formation of the ego-ideal, Freud appends the following footnote:

Perhaps it would be safer to say 'with the parents'; for before a child has arrived at a definite knowledge of the difference between the sexes, the lack of a penis, it does not distinguish in value between its father and mother.[25]

We may bracket the implication that the parents will and should later be distinguished in value, and that the distinguishing feature is the possession of a penis. For the present argument the important point emerging from Freud's modification is that relations to the persons representing the *authoritative other*, regardless of sexual specificity, are crucial in self-formation. This matter is developed shortly after the above footnote. Freud breaks up the stereotypical male and female version of the Oedipus complex by introducing the issue of psychical bisexuality as connected with the possibility of identifying, to varying degrees, with both parents. "Closer study usually discloses the more complete Oedipus complex, which is twofold, positive and negative, and is due to the bisexuality usually present in children."[26] Here, with the "complete Oedipus complex," the identifications work both ways: boys and girls with mothers and fathers. This is important even beyond its disruption of gender stereotypes. It points to the function of the parental figures in a relational dynamic that is not sexual and gender-specific in any limited or obvious sense. This opens the way to de-literalizing parental authority so as to highlight its mediation of cultural structures. This line of interpretation is ultimately extended by Lacan and Kristeva, as we shall see.

The formulation of Oedipal bisexuality has symbolic significance in pointing to the cultural dimensions of interpersonal development overarching gender-specificity. This view does not neglect the facts that we are gendered beings and that this will have a considerable impact on the individual nature of subjective formation. However, it highlights the irreducibility of psycho-sexual development to *fixed* male and female stereotypes. As one Lacanian analyst notes, "a female could play the part of the intervening father, just as a male could play the part of the loving and caring mother."[27] To make this point is not to forget that social conditioning can affect male and female psychological development and identity formation in restrictive stereotypical ways. It serves, indeed, to highlight this problem *as a cultural one* mediated through particular others. These are insights and resources offered by Freudian theory to contemporary thought, although they require careful extrication from the dated, culture-bound views that frequently obscure them.

Granting its conditioned and particularized elements, the configuration of the Oedipus complex provides an overdetermined symbolic portrayal of developmental dynamics within culture. This is a point made by Gananath Obeyesekere, who discusses the Oedipus complex as *fictitious*, emphasizing that this is "a way of expressing a truth that cannot be expressed otherwise."[28] A crucial feature of this fictive portrayal is its linking of individual development with both interpersonal relations and cultural forms. Even when it is understood on a restricted and literalized level, the model of Oedipal dynamics necessarily involves more than libidinal relations among family members. Its resolution is inextricably connected with the introjection of the parental imagos and the ideals associated with them. This describes an essential aspect of self-development that connects the individual much more deeply than before with cultural values.

Some of the cultural dimensions of Oedipal dynamics are evident in the following summary statement by Freud:

> The daughter finds in her mother the authority which restricts her will and which is entrusted with the task of imposing on her the renunciation of sexual freedom which society demands....In the son's eyes his father embodies every unwillingly tolerated social restraint.[29]

This statement emphasizes the *symbolic* status of the parents, in the Lacanian sense, as representatives of cultural norms and values. This is a vital point, even if the insight is marred by the normative assumptions that necessarily link mother with daughter, father with son. The "complete" Oedipus complex would seem to qualify this normative view. The overdetermined, multileveled nature of Oedipal dynamics is also indicated by Freud in the following passage from the *Outline of Psychoanalysis*. Freud is discussing the formation of the super-ego ensuing from the "resolution" of the Oedipus complex. He states:

> The parental influence of course includes in its operation not only the personalities of the actual parents but also the family, racial and national traditions handed on through them, as well as the demands of the immediate social *milieu* which they represent.[30]

Here, parental figures are not merely individuals, but bearers of culture, although the personal presence of some parental-type figure is essential to the formative process. In addition, Freud's comments indicate that the Oedipal phase serves as a model for engagements with cultural authorities extending into adult life. When moments such as this occur in Freud's work we may see that the Oedipus complex can never really function reductively as a fixed explanatory reference point, as might originally have been intended. There are simply too many overlapping forces at play here.

The developmental dynamics configured in the Oedipus complex exceed the scope of the ego and its functions of rationality and reality-testing. That is, all aspects of subjectivity – characterized as id, ego, and super-ego – are included in the formative process. In emphasizing the symbolic value of the Oedipus complex one does not, therefore, wish to desexualize it, keeping in mind the broader psychoanalytic understanding of sexuality.[31] The libidinal or desiring component of Oedipal dynamics reveals personality development as necessarily *interpersonal*, and as occurring on many levels of psycho-physical and psycho-cultural existence. Jane Flax summarizes the Freudian account of human existence as one "that is simultaneously embodied, desiring, rational, speaking, historical, social, gendered, subject to laws both 'immutable' and unconscious and temporal, and capable of autonomy from social and biological determinants."[32] Not all of these dimensions are always brought out clearly; nor are they fully reconciled in Freud's numerous accounts. Nevertheless, the Oedipus complex remains valuable as a developmental paradigm incorporating a multiplicity of levels and factors that are, in their variable intertwinings, constitutive of the human condition. This point is crucial to my overall argument concerning the psycho-cultural status of religion-like symbolic forms in the mediation of ideals and values.

Oedipal dynamics offer a condensed representation of an extended transitional phase of individual development. The initial object-relation expresses how libidinal ties bonding human beings are formative of the self. The dynamics of maturation indicates that human psychological development does not occur on a merely cognitive level and is not a self-enclosed process.[33] Yet furthering autonomy and self-formation necessitates that initial attachments be counteracted by cultural prohibitions. This veto establishes a conflictual dialectic between desire and cultural authority, resulting in identifications and introjections fostering the accession to culture. It is along these lines that Freud indicates the status of the Oedipus complex in personality development. He states that its resolution allows the individual "to divert his libido from its infantile attachments into the social ones that are ultimately desired."[34] Psychological maturation occurs within affective and interpersonal processes characterized by love and hate, attraction and repulsion, identification and differentiation. In these interactive processes cultural structures embodied in significant others intrude into and inform the psychological make-up of the individual. As Lacan expresses the matter:

> the value of the Oedipus complex as a closing off of a psychic cycle results from the fact that it represents the family situation, insofar as by its institution this situation marks the intersection, in the cultural sphere, of the biological and the social.[35]

Incorporated into the Oedipal dynamic is what Lacan has called the "*non/nom de père*."[36] This plays on the homophony between the French for *no* and *name*, indicating the relationship between the "Name of the father," representing cultural codes and laws, and the prohibitions and restrictions that are an essential aspect of the Oedipal conflict.[37] The ensuing identification (as a response to the "no") with a parental figure fosters the internalization of cultural codes in the form of the super-ego. The Oedipal construct condenses critical intersections of force, resistance, and transformation in subjective development related to acculturation. Interpersonal and cultural dynamics transform the individual intra-psychically by introducing qualitative structuring which acts as a constraint upon desire. As Wilden states, "constraints are the basis of complexity and the conditions of creativity."[38] Thus the process of internalizing constraint is essential to the formation of an individuality differentiated from the attachments of the pre-Oedipal phase.

For Lacan, the Oedipal stage represents the first definitive constellation of subjectivity within culture, linked to the incipient formation of the super-ego and the capacity for sublimation. Lacan's de-literalization extends the Oedipus complex into interpersonal and cultural dynamics generally applicable to men and women. However, despite the movement beyond Freud's literal, male-oriented Oedipal imagery, there remains a residue of patriarchalism in the very form of the Oedipal symbols and in Lacan's phrase "Name of the father." This residue may also be associated with a tendency on Lacan's part to privilege the symbolic, whereby its dynamic interdependency with the two other registers of the real and the imaginary is often obscured.[39] Nevertheless, the Lacanian formulations illustrate that, irrespective of gender, human beings normally go through a process of confrontation with the laws and structures of culture and a formation within language, and this confrontation will be mediated by particular others. The encounter with and the internalization of cultural authority are impelled by desire; that is, the need for others and for love relationships. The de-literalized Oedipus complex symbolizes this dynamic of desire, restriction, internalization, and subjective transformation. It therefore represents, *mutatis mutandis*, a core constellation in the development of subjects as cultural, speaking beings.

Freud's anti-idealism resists positing in human beings an a priori capacity for cultural accomplishments, particularly ethical ones. Although it is variously defined as drive, libido, or id, what is psychically innate is always lacking higher-order functions. Among the most mechanistic descriptions of innate force is Freud's definition of the id as "a chaos, a cauldron full of seething excitations."[40] By contrast, the agencies representing higher-order functions – both the ego and the super-ego – have a secondary, constructed nature. Their formation is dependent on some form of experiential, culturally located dynamic. Of course, in metapsychological works such as *Civilization and Its Discontents* there is a partial shift in emphasis from cruder id energies to a more creative portrayal of innate force as *Eros*. This is in fact one expression of creative tension in Freud's metapsychology. Freud's invocation of *Eros* functions to accentuate constructive libidinal qualities related to loving and binding. These qualities, obscured by purely mechanistic renderings, should not be neglected. However, although there is a gradual deepening of the meaning of the id and the drives in Freud's later work, more mechanistic and reductionistic views remain alongside these modifications.

The varying descriptions of id and *Eros* do not affect Freud's concern with an empirical and historical grounding for psychodynamic processes. Freud never invokes his more poetic and mythic renderings of innate force to qualify his arguments concerning the *secondary* nature of higher-order processes. It remains important to recognize the biological and energetic models governing Freud's insistence on the primacy of "blind" id drives. Despite the inadequacies of these models, their resistance to idealist orientations yields important insights. An approach to ethics, culture, and even rationality that resists positing heterogeneous ideal sources for the agencies that embody and enable these higher-order activities must provide a *dynamic* account of their genesis. An interactive model will thereby accommodate the cultural and individual variables in the processes of psychical formation.

A concern with dynamic etiology is evident in Freud's accounts of the genesis of the super-ego as the agency related to conscience and ethical capacity. Some important implications of Freud's analyses may be obscured, because the issue usually highlighted is the super-ego's temporally secondary, dependent, non-ideal nature. As Freud summarizes:

> Even if conscience is something 'within us', yet it is not so from the first. In this it is a real contrast to sexual life, which is in fact there from the beginning of life and not only a later addition....The part which is later taken on by the super-ego is played to begin with by an external power, by parental authority.[41]

However, the self-evidence of the parental authority breaks down with the locatedness of the family within culture. The function of parental authority already presupposes the existence of language and moral codes. The original source of ethical capacity becomes a question for psychoanalysis, as has also been noted by Hans Loewald, who refers to the "circularity" evident here.[42] The need to escape such circularity is one factor that leads Freud to the problematic historical constructions of the texts on religion, positing both traumatic and Oedipal events at the origins of cultural forms.

On more than one level, Freud's concern with the *literal* – that is, historical – validity of both *Totem and Taboo* and *Moses and Monotheism* is related to the cultural components of the Oedipus complex. On both the more restricted familial level and the broader symbolic level, Oedipal dynamics reveal that individual development is predicated on the prior existence of cultural forms, including language, ideals, and values. Without such higher-order cultural resources, personality formation could not occur. This problem seemed to lead Freud to inquire into the origin of these cultural forms in a way that might trace them back to original, constitutive libidinal dynamics. It is in this initially highly curtailed way that religion, morality, and culture become major areas of concern for psychoanalytic theory.

Chapter 2

Religion, ethics, and acculturation

Freud's critique of religion and the latent issue of ethical transformation

As with the trauma and Oedipal theories, positivistic and counter-positivistic tendencies are co-present in Freud's writings on religion. When Ricoeur, in discussing Freud's views on reality and the concomitant critical analyses of religion, concludes that "Freud's view is positivist," he is conveying only one side or one dimension.[1] In fact, Freud's treatment of subjective and objective realities, and their connection with religion and other cultural forms, is in a state of unresolved tension, mirroring the wider tensions in his work. My task will be to *amplify* these points of tension, showing that alongside the manifest arguments there are seminal latent dimensions to these writings. Finally, after elucidating such counter-positivistic trends, I will develop the implications of this other Freud.

Of course, it is important to acknowledge the predominance of the positivistic paradigm at the surface of Freud's analyses. It structures the manifest level of the arguments and acts as a force displacing and suppressing other insights. It tends to function as a set of interpretive brackets, distorting and delimiting the texts' projection of possible meanings. Therefore my inquiry into Freud's analyses of religion is framed by his most explicit positivistic arguments, as they appear in a variety of theoretical or metapsychological texts. The limits, contradictions, and aporias that emerge within Freud's explicit positivistic critique provide points of departure for deconstructing the parallel manifest levels in each of the texts on religion and culture.

Some of Freud's most forthright positivistic arguments concerning truth and reality with specific reference to the question of religion appear in *The Future of an Illusion*. The psychological method of this text is an application of the *hermeneutics of suspicion*, which yields such illuminating results when applied to phenomena such as dreams, parapraxes, and obsessive actions. Freud's interpretive approach is generated by a distrust of the surface, manifest form and content of the phenomena at hand. Truth is seen to have a latent, concealed status, requiring both deciphering and disentangling from the distortions and substitutes concealing it. In *The Future of an Illusion* the latent content discerned behind religious ideas and practices is associated with the "father complex," as it is in both *Totem and Taboo* and *Moses and Monotheism*. Here, however, this complex is not linked to a posited (pre)historical father figure (except in comments marginal to the main argument). Rather, human helplessness is seen to elicit infantile desires for wish-fulfillment, projected on to and realized in religious cultural forms of a primarily patriarchal nature.

Freud predicates his analysis of wish-fulfillment and projection on the vulnerable character of human beings. He emphasizes that, even in adulthood, we ultimately remain defenseless against "the superior forces of nature, of Fate," and "the painful riddle of death." Thus we are compelled to form communities both for physical survival and, most importantly, to assuage the mental pressures arising from human existence.[2] The overt arguments of *The Future of an Illusion* reflect Freud's tendency to assume a positivistic model of knowledge and reality. That is, the meaning and truth of "higher-order" psycho-cultural developments is explained by underlying substantive realities divided into biology and external materiality. This assumption leads him to interpret social-psychological constructs as evasions of the pressures of these primary realities. Here, the *pathological* manifestations of cultural forms, as evasive mediations between biology and external reality, become an issue. As a mediating safety mechanism, communal organizations of human existence exact a high price from the individual for the benefits they grant: "every civilization must be built up on coercion and renunciation of instinct [*Triebverzicht*]."[3] Freud's analysis hinges on the inescapable presence of psycho-physiological impulsions of a sexual, aggressive, and infantile nature within the individual. Civilization suppresses and channels these impulses to allow some degree of peaceful coexistence, entailing the establishment of prohibitions that frustrate drive satisfaction and create a condition of privation. This portrayal of a relentless tension between forces is also one of the surface themes of *Civilization and Its Discontents*. Yet even at this level of argument there are intimations of deeper psychodynamic processes at work. For example, the term *renunciation*, particularly crucial to the analyses of cultural forms in *Moses and Monotheism*, expresses far more than simply the relinquishment or repression of primary drives. It is indicative of complex, qualitative psychological transformations in relation to acculturation. In this, as I shall argue, it exhibits parallels with the mysterious processes of sublimation.

The underlying issue of *qualitative transformation* appears more clearly, as Freud turns from an economic or energistic portrayal of cultural dynamics to the realm of ideas and ideals. In relation to the pressures of socialization and acculturation, religion functions as one of the *mental assets* (*seelischer Besitz*) of civilization.[4] These represent non-coercive means of integrating unruly, instinctually motivated individuals into cultural matrices. Such vehicles of culture include *ideals* with which individuals can identify and "substitute satisfactions" such as art.[5] Generally, these mental assets are seen by Freud not only as fostering culturally necessary psychological transformations, but as related to important scientific and artistic production. In fact, one of the peculiarities of the text is its recurring praise for intellectual activity and accomplishments. (For example, Freud asserts that "civilization has little to fear from educated people and brain workers.")[6] Despite the one-sided hyperbole of these comments, they indicate a profound recognition of and respect for ideas and ideals – that is, for higher-order secondary-process activity. However, *illusion* (i.e. religion), described as "perhaps the most important item in the psychical inventory of a civilization,"[7] has an ambiguous status. Although it stems from deep psychological needs and shares the formative qualities and attributes of other cultural structures, religion is ultimately seen as regressive and harmful.

Classifying religion as illusion, Freud argues, has nothing to do with the truth or falsity of its claims. The differentiation from delusion (involving false assertions about reality) is made explicitly. By contrast, "what is characteristic of illusions is that they are derived from human wishes."[8] In defining illusion as a manifestation of essential psychological forces, Freud is consistent with his earlier formulations concerning the pervasive nature of wish-fulfillment in primary-process activity, as reflected in symptoms, dreams, and faulty acts (parapraxes).[9] Just as wish-fulfillment is a fundamental latent motivation behind the manifest contents of individual psychology, so it is a powerful determinant of cultural forms. While religion is acknowledged as having a socially integrating function and as fostering acculturation, its origins link it to regressive tendencies. Religion inscribes in cultural formations a repressive mechanism that restrains the drives while offering wishful substitute satisfactions. It thereby inhibits human potential for independence by sustaining an infantile psychical organization dependent on authority (i.e. "the father"). Freud summarizes his reductive, pathologizing views as follows: "Religion would thus be the universal obsessional neurosis of humanity; like the obsessional neurosis of children, it arose out of the Oedipus complex, out of the relation to the father."[10] Assuming that the reductive argument is clear, there are nevertheless complexities and overinterpretations that, as we have seen, emerge from a closer inquiry into the nature and meaning of the Oedipus complex.

Even on a straightforward, literal level, the relation between religion and the Oedipus complex is twofold. Religious ideas, as Freud presents them, alleviate anxiety and fear by producing substitute satisfactions of wishes: "In the end all good is rewarded and all evil punished, if not actually in this form of life then in the later existences that begin after death."[11] Here, God fulfills the Oedipal fantasy of the omnipotent loving and protecting parent.

Yet the Oedipus complex has another side that appears in the prohibitive and punitive roles of the deity.

In *Beyond the Pleasure Principle* the drives are polarized into anabolic (life drives) and catabolic (death drives) modes.[12] There are, of course, serious arguments against Freud's postulated death drive in its literal, biologized form.[13] However, the construct nevertheless serves to highlight issues of conflict and negation in psychological dynamics and experience. One aspect of psychical life this revision of drive theory is invoked to clarify is the severity of the super-ego in relation to the ego. Aggression, renounced or reduced in outwardly directed forms in the clash with authority during the Oedipal phase, "is taken over by the super-ego and increases the latter's aggressiveness (against the ego)."[14] In *The Ego and the Id* Freud reveals the religious significance of this tendency: "even ordinary normal morality has a harshly restraining, cruelly prohibiting quality. It is from this, indeed, that the conception arises of a higher being who deals out punishment inexorably."[15] Taken literally, the explanatory hypothesis behind this formulation is that the destructive or deathly side of the id is channeled through the super-ego. However, it might be more accurate to say that the super-ego becomes "deathly" when it functions in a rigid, inflexible manner (for various personal and cultural reasons).

The agency of the super-ego is a product of the Oedipal phase and bears its parental stamp. That is, it internalizes both fear and hatred of, and love and respect for idealized authority figures. These internalizations can be projected and acted out in relation to anthropomorphized god images. Thus, however one understands the postulation of the death drive, relationships to a personified deity are doubly marked by infantile tendencies. God is both the protector who rectifies the injustices and evils of the world and the wrathful overseer whose interdictions restrain drive activity. However, in each case it is most significant that religion is located within the complex interplay of *psychology* and *cultural formations*. Its mode of functioning within this dynamic interplay is actually the key issue in Freud's critique of illusion. In this instance, we might note that manifestations of super-ego harshness can be associated with a more infantile or, in Lacanian terms, *imaginary* orientation. The hypostatization of an idealized source of moral authority provides a relatively stable reference point for codes of conduct; yet as literalized it can induce fixation upon particular, culturally delimited norms.

The psychoanalytic distinction between *illusion* and *delusion* is crucial, yet it is one that Freud does not consistently maintain. This inconsistency also reflects differentiations within Freud's object of inquiry; that is, religion actually falls into both categories. Thus Freud notes that religious forms often lapse into the realm of delusion. Religious statements concerning reality sometimes contradict what has been collectively and empirically established to be the case, especially by the culturally dominant methods and paradigms of science.[16] Insofar as Freud's critique is predicated on religion's delusional opposition to reality as known through scientific inquiry, it differs little from well-known empiricist arguments. However, Freud insists that the essential contribution of psychoanalysis is the disclosure of the *latent psychological contents* behind the manifest contents of monotheistic doctrines. Under this definition, as Freud reiterates, illusion represents the "fulfillment of the oldest, strongest wishes of mankind."[17] The thrust of Freud's psychoanalytic critique of religion is therefore predicated on the pejorative connotations of illusion as regressive and infantile. The *delusional* aspects of religious belief are secondary, occurring when representations of unconscious forces become conflated with external referents.

Yet, having established that his analysis of religion places it firmly in the category of illusion because of its relationship with unconscious needs and forces, Freud increasingly emphasizes the clash between religious worldviews and the scientifically determined experience of reality. As this occurs his critique becomes sharper and more focused, but also more conditioned by positivistic assumptions. Freud argues that the infantile impulses of illusion are dysfunctional because they conflict with the requirements of reason, *Logos*, and necessity, *Ananke*. This pair of "gods" provides the basis for a complete rejection of religion. The final focus of Freud's argument concerns the effect religion has on our capacity to constructively engage reality. Here Freud unequivocally asserts that "scientific work [*wissenschaftliche Arbeit*] is the only road which can lead us to a knowledge of reality outside ourselves."[18] These views of the nature of reality, and of adaptation thereto, are highly constricted. However, Freud's critique also involves a parallel or supplementary *exhortation to personal development*. This remains rather narrowly characterized as a more mature, rational, and fulfilling psychological organization and relation to external reality. Religion becomes antagonistic to this project because its consolations are seen to work in opposition to an empiricist and rationalist agenda. "Religion brings with it obsessional restrictions" and it "comprises a system of wishful illusions together with a disavowal of reality."[19] Hence Freud argues that "the time has probably come, as it does in analytic treatment, for replacing the effects of repression by the results of the rational operation of the intellect [*rationelle Geistesarbeit*]."[20] In this argument more nuanced, underlying issues of subjective transformation are indicated.

It is noteworthy that, far from exhibiting a deterministic stance in these propositions, Freud argues for the *mutability* of the human psyche in dynamic relation with cultural change. He grants that in their current condition human beings are mainly irrational and "governed by instinctual wishes," but asks "whether they *must* be like this, whether their innermost nature necessitates it?"[21] The familial and social influences on early development make it impossible for us to have direct, unmediated knowledge of our own natures. Indeed, in line with *open-system* thinking, the psyche in itself is simply an abstraction; it can never, in actuality, be dirempted from the cultural forces that mold it. Thus Freud advocates an open-ended, non-deterministic view of the human condition, which at the same time emphasizes cultural locatedness. In this view, *human potentiality is constrained and curtailed not by immutable innate predispositions, but rather by outmoded cultural structures and their formative influences.*

Freud proposes a wager; that is, he invites us to take the risk that we might indeed realize human potentialities masked and curtailed by domi-nant cultural and, especially, religious influences. On this basis, Freud offers us the goal of attaining "primacy of the intelligence [*Primat der Intelligenz*]."[22] The main characteristic of this primacy would seem to be a practical, utilitarian relationship to the external world, which Freud describes as an "*education to reality.*"[23] Freud acknowledges that his wager may itself contain a dimension of wish-fulfillment, but argues that "my illu-sions are not, like the religious ones, incapable of correction."[24] It seems that Freud is implicitly acknowledging the importance of *regulative ideals* guiding possible psycho-cultural transformations. As he sees it, however, an essential feature of his ideals, as opposed to religious ones, is their flexibility and adaptability. However, the question arises: *adaptation to what?* As a rational response to the forces of necessity and reality, *Logos* actually seems to be a vehicle for responding to new cultural situations, new knowledge, new psycho-cultural needs and possibilities. It is therefore related to ongoing, open-ended processes of psycho-cultural transformation, including ideals, values, and worldviews.

The nature and scope of the ideals compacted into Freud's notion of *Logos* emerge more clearly in relation to one of the central underlying themes of *The Future of an Illusion*: ethical transformations of the human condition within cultural constructs. The book appears to give precedence to a model of human development structured along the lines of adaptation to material reality and necessity. Yet one of its crucial themes is the transition from irrational to rational morality. This might also be characterized as a shift to *a more reflective mode of ethical consciousness.* Reflective ethical capacity is not necessarily welded to the fixed, reified, culturally imposed norms and values Freud associates with traditional Western monotheism. Freud's well-known critique of the Christian love commandment ("love thy neighbor as thyself"), formulated in *Civilization and Its Discontents*, is rele-vant in this respect. Freud, assuming a rigid reading of this commandment, offers a detailed psycho-cultural critique based on its being impossible to fulfill, its being unfair to those who deserve our love, its neglecting that not everyone is worthy of our love, its fostering a self-righteous attitude leading to aggression against outsiders, and, finally, its creating personal unhappi-ness.[25] A close analysis of these arguments shows that what Freud is attacking are not ethical ideals as such, but overly abstracted, reified ideals disconnected from the realities of human collective existence. Reified ideals repress the reality of the drives, and subsume relations to particular others under closed, generalized categories. Therefore, as Wallwork has argued, Freud attacks one version of an ethical ideal on the basis of an alternative set of ethical ideals.[26]

Similarly, in *The Future of an Illusion* when Freud criticizes religion for its inadequacy as a foundation for morality he utilizes a set of criteria differing from those related to the task of mastering *Ananke*. Since religious precepts are linked to belief in a being or beings who mete out rewards and punishment, Freud argues that their persuasive force will disintegrate as belief is outgrown.[27] In other words, one way in which religion becomes repressive is by curtailing rational reflection by welding ethical ideals to reified belief systems. Thus the *rational* operations with which Freud is concerned also include an *ethical* dimension involving the task of "reconciling men to civilization."[28] Mature ethical capacity requires the participation of a rational, reflective subjectivity, i.e. of *Logos*. Yet it also involves culturally constituted ideals and values that inform relations to others along qualitative lines. The issue emerging here is the nature or status of those ideals and the mode of subjective relation to them.

As the argument comes to a conclusion, Freud continues to mix the discourse of a scientifically informed adaptation to reality with ethical amelioration of the human condition. Commenting on the goal of "primacy of the intellect," he states (to his imaginary interlocutor): "It will presumably set itself the same aims you expect from your God...namely, the love of man and the decrease of suffering [*die Menschenliebe und die Einschränkung des Leidens*]."[29] In this statement there is far more at stake than an ideal of instrumental control of the empirical world by means of scientific procedures. The discourse of empirical science and the model of adaptation to determinable material reality actually conceal proposals for *psycho-cultural transformations in accordance with regulative ethical ideals*. It is quite revealing that the critic of the love commandment here emphasizes the importance of a more psychologically informed and flexible ideal of love.[30] I want to emphasize that, rudimentary as these arguments may be within *The Future of an Illusion*, they nevertheless provide a touchstone for a series of related concerns which appear in Freud's other writings on religion and culture. The question of ethical development – irreducible either to libidinal development or to adaptive, reality-oriented ego development – continually reappears as an underlying theme of these texts.

Freud's inquiry extends beyond a positivist and empiricist critique of religion to address more complicated and differentiated cultural and ethical issues. Likewise, there is an implied extension of meaningful subjectivity beyond the adaptive ego to include ethical capacities classified under the agency of the super-ego. These extensions ultimately pressure the exclusively pejorative reading of illusion. To be sure, the category of illusion also describes regressive strategies, linked to religious representations of a wish-fulfilling deity or cosmic order, for fulfilling infantile needs through literalized projections. Yet religion also intersects significantly with potentially creative components of illusion. These are related to the representational features of cultural ideals that do not merely reflect extant, material realities, but *structure* relations to others and to alterity. Some of the progressive dimensions of illusion appear in Freud's investigations into psycho-cultural reality as requiring both aesthetic forms and ethical ideals. In these reflections Freud further engages some of the concerns that appear in his discussions of "psychical reality," as discussed in the previous chapter. Psychical reality designates representational and narrative forms that give meaningful expression to subjective experience. Similarly, illusion categorizes more than mere infantile wish-fulfillment; it also encapsulates representational abilities and productions, whose validity is not adequately measured by the touchstone of objective facticity. Here, of course, is the precedent for linking the Freudian category of illusion with D. W. Winnicott's "transitional space," crucial to personal and cultural development.[31] It is perhaps this many-sided pressuring of the more purely pejorative use of the category of illusion that leads Freud to drift into a focus on the delusional aspects of religion. The latter category seems to express a more obvious problem, wherein literally construed religious postulates are adamantly maintained in the face of rationally persuasive counter-evidence.

The shift in the definition and critique of religion from the category of illusion to a focus on its links with delusion becomes more firmly established in *Civilization and Its Discontents*. This book appeared shortly after *The Future of an Illusion*, and is in some ways an extension and modification of the earlier inquiry. Here Freud explicitly emphasizes the delusional nature of religion:

> a special importance attaches to the case in which the attempt to procure a certainty of happiness and a protection against suffering through delusional remolding of reality is made by a considerable number of people in common. The religions of mankind must be classed among the mass delusions of this kind. No one, needless to say, who shares a delusion ever recognizes it as such.[32]

It would seem that the tension between the critiques of religion as illusion and as delusion has been resolved in favor of the latter. But the reclassification of religion as delusion cannot annul the previous arguments that link religion to illusion by virtue of the psychological processes it reflects and to which it responds.

There may be an underlying, unspoken factor in the rather sudden emphasis on the delusional nature of religion. It serves to keep religion separate from the more nuanced and constructive analyses of cultural forms related to the broad category of illusion that emerge quite explicitly in *Civilization and Its Discontents*. Thus, having isolated religion safely within the category of delusion, the book contributes significantly to developing an understanding of the creative dimensions of illusion related to psycho-cultural development. A significant portion of the text is devoted to reflections on the interplay between psyche and culture, illustrating that psychical relations to external reality are as complicated as intra-psychic relations. As with so many of Freud's far-ranging inquiries and insights, however, these are partially disguised within a more limited argumentative structure.

The surface inquiry of the book is shaped by an analysis of the program of the pleasure principle, especially the economics of pleasure and unplea-sure within cultural repression. The harshness of life, which was instrumental in engendering the illusions of religion, is analyzed by Freud in a manner indicating that some form of psychologically effective escape, protection, or compensation is required for happiness and health. Three such means are "powerful deflections, which cause us to make light of our misery; substitutive satisfactions, which diminish it; and intoxicating substances, which make us insensitive to it."[33] These comments already indi-cate that human existence and the pursuit of fulfillment are more complex than an education to reality. Indeed, he seems to take an antithetical stance, focusing on inner forces. The meaning of life, a question Freud sees as standing or falling "with the religious system" (whatever that means), is one he here addresses in terms of "the programme of the pleasure principle."[34] The endless search for pleasure and happiness, he argues, supersedes the rational and technological control of our environment. However, more is contained in this argument than a mere acknowledgment of psychological hedonism. Emphasis on the pleasure principle introduces issues concerning human creativity within cultural existence. In essence, Freud argues that we do not simply *accommodate* ourselves to a pre-existent reality, but *modify* our environments in relation to internal requirements. Cultural existence is not informed by reason or necessity alone, but by the wider range of human desires and capacities. Because the pleasure principle "is at loggerheads with the whole world," an *aesthetic* amelioration of our experience of the world is essential to its program. Again, one should stress that this is figurative language, and that Freud's arguments are not teleological. In fact, some-thing of a Lacanian view – in which an inherent lack, open-endedness, or incompleteness pushes us toward ongoing cultural formation – emerges in the course of these reflections.[35]

The drive toward creative modification in our apprehending, repre-senting, and participating in reality is manifest in the relation between culture and beauty. The aesthetic path to fulfillment has a problematic status for the psychoanalytic interpretation of cultural activity. "Beauty has no obvious use; nor is there any clear cultural necessity for it. Yet civilization could not do without it."[36] Later in Freud's analysis, the psychological and cultural worth of aesthetics appears more clearly. Noting that despite the rapid advancements in science and technology during the last few generations human life has not become noticeably happier, Freud remarks that "power over nature is not the *only* precondition of human happiness, just as it is not the *only* goal of cultural endeavor."[37] These arguments are, I believe, all the more compelling today. They not only broaden Freud's criteria for human fulfillment; they indirectly transform the limited definition of reality offered in *The Future of an Illusion*. The task of culture is not simply accommodation to *Ananke*; rather, culture emerges at the intersections of subjectivity and objectivity, bringing new reality into being. In connection with human well-being, a pivotal point is that "happiness is something subjective."[38] It cannot be realized fully in a technical mastery over the external world, but is derived as well from expressing internal, subjective propensities. The aesthetic modification of reality, reflecting an interplay of creativity with experience, emerges as essential to cultural activity and to human fulfillment.

Another component of an intermittent and indirect qualification of the narrower, positivistic model for human development emerges within the course of Freud's response to his friend Romaine Rolland. The latter had proposed that, while the analyses of dogmatic religion in *The Future of an Illusion* are fundamentally sound, Freud misses the essence of religiosity in the form of mystical or "oceanic" experiences of unity with the cosmos.[39] Rising to the challenge, Freud proceeds to an analysis of the nature of the ego, its development, and its relation to the undifferentiated forces of the id. On the surface, what ensues seems to be another instance of Freudian reductionism; mystical experiences are explained away as regressions to more primitive, pre-ego organizations. Yet as Freud draws upon psychoanalytic theory to address issues of ego development, implications emerge for a model of the personality differing from the focus on adaptation.

Freud argues that the certainty we take in the substantiality of the ego is deceptive. Rather, "the ego is continued inward, without any sharp delimitation, into an unconscious mental entity which we designate as the id and for which it serves as a kind of façade."[40] The boundaries delimiting the ego are not impermeable, and this applies to its relation to the external world as much as to the unconscious dimensions of the psyche. Significantly, Freud mentions that the softening of external boundaries can also be seen under normal and, indeed, highly desirable conditions, especially states of love. This example alone serves to qualify the privileging of firm ego boundaries as the major feature of a mature personality. That is, a capacity to *relinquish* boundaries and defenses, to open oneself to otherness, would also seem to be essential to personal maturation and well-being.

The permeability of the ego leads Freud into the area of developmental psychology. He argues that "an infant at the breast does not as yet distinguish his ego from the external world as the source of the sensations flowing in upon him."[41] It is only by a gradual process, in which undifferentiated relations to reality are disrupted by denial and frustration, that "a tendency arises to separate from the ego everything that can become a source of such unpleasure, to throw it outside and to create a pure pleasure-ego which is confronted by a strange and threatening 'outside'."[42] These points recapitulate some of the arguments of *The Ego and the Id*. While this text is highly influential in the subsequent development of ego-psychology branches of psychoanalysis, it also formulates the model of "the ego's dependent relations." The language of alien internal agencies and threatening external forces highlights the deterministic and pessimistic aspects of Freud's portrayal. This has given rise to the predominant psychoanalytic orientation that views the ego as struggling with blind, often pathologized internal forces. Thus the ego is seen as engaged in the heroic task of becoming a rational individual better able to master the forces of nature.

However, another complementary orientation emerges in a re-examination of Freud's analyses. They qualify the model of the fully autonomous rational ego, so that meaningful subjectivity involves relations to otherness, both externally and internally. Freud states that "the ego is that part of the id which has been modified by the direct influence of the external world." The ego becomes a mediator between id and reality "and endeavors to substitute the reality principle for the pleasure principle which reigns unrestrictedly in the id."[43] This developmental model has profound implications for understanding the ego's relations to the id and to externalness. The emphasis on the reality-testing functions of the ego masks the complementary dependency of the ego on the wider psychical dynamics here described in terms of id (but also, in the broader view, involving the super-ego). The rootedness of ego in id implies an internal determination of the nature and perspectives of the ego (as seen, for example, in its initial characterization as a *pleasure ego* dominated by the pleasure principle of the id and manifest in the narcissistic dimensions of the ego). It follows that notions of a complete diremption of rational consciousness from the illusions of the id appear unfounded.

As Paul Ricoeur reminds us, psychoanalysis reveals "the nonautonomy of knowledge, its rootedness in existence, the latter being understood as desire and effort."[44] Ricoeur has further noted that the "very situation explored by psychoanalysis" is that of "the interlacing of desire and culture."[45] Manifestations of desire in cultural existence appear in Freud's analysis of *Eros*. Freud invokes *Eros* as the force that unites individuals into couples, families, and communities. In his words, "Eros and Ananke have become the parents of human civilization too."[46] Thus *Eros* complements external necessity in creating incipient social formations. However, Freud's frequently narrow presentation of *Eros* masks the deeper significance of its association with culture. It is not only the case that internal as well as external forces contribute to cultural life. Moreover, those internal forces exhibit creative potency, and this is irreducible to the "reduction of tension" sometimes seen to characterize the pleasure principle. As Ricoeur states, "Eros is the great exception to the principle of constancy."[47] Hence culture, the vehicle of the human experience of reality, is not merely a tool for mastering the forces of material necessity. It is also a manifestation of *Eros* as a creative factor in the ongoing shaping of reality.

These seemingly divergent discussions within *Civilization and Its Discontents* actually converge in illuminating ways. They establish interconnections between creative representational dimensions of id processes, super-ego functions enabling conscience and ethical capacities, and the constitutive function of cultural forms. One key link between these points is the elusive phenomenon of *sublimation*. This process involves each of the three agencies within an interactive transformative process. Sublimation serves as a concept describing meaningful expression and realization of primary-process (id) activity in connection with secondary-process (ego) articulations. Freud emphasizes that sublimation allows the individual to become more *"independent of the external world* by seeking satisfaction in internal, psychical processes"[48] Here, a different criterion for human development is introduced: not conformity with material reality, but independence or distanciation from it. This distancing is not, of course, the disconnection of delusion, but rather a capacity for mediated and differentiated relations. It is also significant that this liberation occurs through creative fantasy and imagination. Thus, discussing art, Freud states that "satisfaction is obtained from *illusions*, which are recognized as such without the discrepancy between them and reality being allowed to interfere with enjoyment."[49] Illusion here indicates the *creative modification* of the experience of reality consisting of cultural forms. The psychological area that is so problematic when disclosed in religious formations becomes highly significant when channeled into art. Illusion contributes to cultural structures, and so functions as a necessary factor in the existential mediation between psychical and external realities.

Civilization and Its Discontents delineates a series of interconnections between ego and id, *Eros* and culture, fulfillment and art. These combine to offer a view of the relation between illusion and reality differing significantly from that articulated in the context of Freud's inquiry into the nature of religion in *The Future of an Illusion*. The crucial point that follows from these insights, but which is suppressed by Freud's intentional stance, is that for human beings reality is a variable, partially determined by our faculties and modes of apprehension, and shaped within mediating cultural worlds. It may be seen that these lines of force within Freud's analysis parallel the tensions evident in the trauma and Oedipal theories. In each case a positivist model is qualified, if not fully subverted, by awareness of the symbolizing and narrativizing features inherent in the human experience of reality.

In many of his explicit arguments Freud continues to assume that reality is a fixed referent characterized by the force of physical necessity bearing upon human existence. Yet he also shows that our experience of reality occurs as a dynamic interchange between such forces of *Ananke* and human desire, as molded by culture and language. In light of these considerations, aesthetic illusions and creative productions contribute to cultural formations. It follows that scientific inquiry is not the only valid and constructive mediating form in the human experience of reality. In the overview, then, we find both progressive and regressive psycho-cultural formations categorized as illusion, applicable to both religion and art. *Some* of the phenomena associated with religion may indeed be infantile, irrational, and resistant to change. Additionally, however, religion can embody the constructive qualities Freud associates with art: an articulation of meaningful symbolic activity in non-utilitarian cultural production, fostering creative modification of experienced reality. When these constructive dimensions of illusion are conjoined with Freud's concern for *ethical* modifications of the subject-in-culture it appears that, at the very least, a more nuanced analysis of religion is indicated.

Lacan and the problem of modalities of subjectivity

My analyses of Freud's discourse on religion and culture indicate the need for more detailed and precise conceptual categories than are provided by the terms illusion, delusion, necessity, reason, and reality. In this regard, Lacanian ideas can clarify and amplify dimensions of Freud's cultural inquiries. The intersections between symbolic and ethical capacities form a direct link between Freud's work on religion and culture and some of the metapsychological contributions of Jacques Lacan. At this point my concern is to introduce Lacanian concepts that address issues emerging from the preceding discussion. These will, in addition, provide tools for interpreting Freud's more heavily symbolic writings in the next three chapters.

Lacan specifically addresses the interrelations of psychology, language, and culture, and in so doing develops more systematically the underlying, counter-positivistic dimensions of Freud's inquiries. Of particular significance is the Lacanian threefold topography constituted by the "registers" of the *symbolic*, the *imaginary*, and the *real*. This topography extends psychoanalytic approaches to psycho-cultural formation. The Lacanian model applies both to the earlier Freudian topography of conscious, preconscious, and unconscious, and to the later one of ego, super-ego, and id. Indeed, it presupposes and is grafted on to these categories. The term *register* conveys a structure through which specific conditions, in this case psychical and cultural conditions, are regulated or modified. This is indicative of the elusive problem of analyzing *modalities* or qualitative states of the psychical agencies and associated cultural forms.

Lacan's imaginary register should not be confused with the *imagination*. Rather, this category specifically designates rigidly structured patterns of imaging, and hence interpreting, both self and world. The imaginary is generally characterized by mimetic types of identification, and by fixation, narcissism, and closed, non-reflexive modes of relation. Thus the imaginary tends to be defined in more predominantly negative terms. For example, Lacan associates it primarily with the narcissistic ego's orientations of control and closure. Yet, as Julia Kristeva points out, imaginary modes of relation are also connected with the formative identifications necessary for basic personality development.[50] Without these preliminary structurings of the personality, identifications and introjections on the symbolic level, essential to later developments, will lack the requisite foundations in a strong sense of identity.

The symbolic is associated with the manifold resources of language and cultural forms, and is indicative of differentiated and pluralistic relations. (It is thus unconnected with the psychoanalytic sense of symbols as having fixed meanings as presented, for example, in later editions of *The Interpretation of Dreams*.) Overall, the symbolic is defined more positively as the realm of cultural ideals and values, and as the linguistic and representational forms that embody them. In this regard, Lacan also sometimes speaks of *the Law*. As Dylan Evans summarizes, "the Law in Lacan's work refers not to a particular piece of legislation, but to the fundamental principles which underlie all social relations."[51] The symbolic therefore incorporates the major formative, qualitative dimensions of culture, *Logos* and *Nomos*, that shape experience of reality.

Psychologically, the symbolic also represents *transformations of the personality* engendered by introjecting cultural vehicles connected with language and Law. This twofold quality specifically addresses the intersections of inner and outer that are delineated by Freud. However, in its designation of *extant* cultural and social systems, the symbolic also has negative connotations. Many contemporary theorists have analyzed symbolic orders in terms of the problem of privileged social forms, for example repressive patriarchal structures. With respect to these issues, it is important to discern the existence of closed, imaginary orientations within societies. On this level collective imaginary orientations can be linked to the problem of ideology; that is, they designate social forms that reinforce closed modes of identity. Therefore, while the symbolic refers to cultural forms in general as potentially open systems, no existing cultural system is free from the limiting effects of imaginary and ideological tendencies. I will discuss critical concerns ensuing from these points in Chapter 6.

The *real* is that which, at any given time, cannot be integrated into discourse; it "resists symbolization absolutely."[52] For example, the real designates the givenness of the drives, uncharted and unknown dimensions of external reality, and any internally or externally located experience that cannot be fully or directly narrativized within cultural and personal systems of symbolization. As we have seen, traumatic experiences, by virtue of their negatively overpowering nature, exhibit this quality of being unassimilable in everyday discourse. They leave blank spaces in memory, or produce screens, displacements, and fantasies. At the opposite end of the spectrum, mystical experiences might also be understood as overwhelming the individual's symbolic-discursive resources, giving rise to paradoxical and indirect communications at the boundaries of discourse.

For Lacan, human experience of reality is always symbolized in one form or another, whereas the real is known only negatively, indirectly, and inferentially. The real parallels Kant's *noumenal* or *Ding an sich* in having both an internal and external status, and in being apprehended only as a necessary postulate. Lacan also shares the view of neo-Kantian thinkers such as Ernst Cassirer that mediated, phenomenal experience is shaped by variable cultural constructs and symbolic forms. Lacan emphasizes that reality is known only through language and the real is encountered only as it intrudes into language systems. This means that, while there is always a category or register of the real that is inexhaustible, its contents (as it were) are not fixed. Lacan writes:

> one can only think of language as a network, a net over the entirety of things, over the totality of the real. It inscribes over the plane of the real this other plane, which we here call the plane of the symbolic.[53]

More pointedly, Lacan argues that speech "introduces the dimension of truth into the real."[54] These arguments push psychoanalytic cultural inquiry away from a positivist model based on the quest for underlying empirical truth, and towards issues of *the nature and function of symbolic resources*.

It should further be noted that the notion of the real has a critical role in Lacan's thinking. As indicating a dimension of otherness which is always beyond full assimilation into discourse, the real sustains the sense of the symbolic *as symbolic* and hence serves to prevent conceptual closure. This indicates something of an *iconoclastic* quality in Lacanian thought, resisting literalization and reification of symbolic forms. The boundaries of symbolic systems continue to be pressured by intrusions of the real, and the capacity to recognize and respond to this is central to the Lacanian model of subjective development. Inaccessible in itself, the real designates that which resists the solipsistic tendencies of constructions within imaginary and symbolic orders. Thus the concept of the real serves to remind us of the perpetually unfinished and partial nature of psycho-cultural structures and worldviews.

On the subjective level, the real is associated with the id, the imaginary with the ego, and the symbolic with the super-ego. However, Lacan's topography does not map directly on to Freud's. It rather provides a language for interpreting both the spectrum of qualities associated with each psychoanalytic agency, and possible developmental modifications of each agency. The id or drives may be categorized under each of the three registers, while the ego and super-ego are, by definition, outside of the real. The drives appear in the register of the real as need, in the imaginary as demand, and in the symbolic as desire. The variable organization of the drives depends on an individual's psychological development and relational mode of being-in-the-world. Here, the Lacanian topography serves to elucidate conflicting levels of analysis in Freud's formulations of the libido. It is sometimes portrayed mechanistically, in the register of the real, and, at other times, in terms of the symbolic register as *Eros*. The variability in Freud's formulations reflects an understanding that human eroticism is not simply a drive governed by the pleasure principle, as it would be in the register of the real. *Eros*, rather, is transformed within socio-cultural processes, such as language acquisition, into imaginary and symbolic modes.

Both demand and desire involve symbolization and acculturation. Demand, however, seeks immediate gratification and lends itself to the production of stereotypical images and modes of relation. It is also inter-mixed with cultural influences, so that, for example, imaginary orientations of demand are stimulated and sustained by the influences of consumerist culture.[55] By contrast, desire requires full participation of another person; it is fulfilled only with recognition and response. A view consonant with Lacan's is well expressed by Emmanuel Levinas. He states that "desire is an aspiration that the Desirable animates; it originates from its 'object'; it is revelation – whereas need is a void of the Soul; it proceeds from the subject."[56] As we shall see, this intrinsic connection between desire and the Other, shared by Lacan and Levinas, links this category to issues concerning religious and ethical dimensions of subjective development.

The super-ego, as an agency of acculturation, is associated primarily with the symbolic register. In this regard the super-ego represents potentiality for personality development guided by ethics and ideals. However, we may note that harsh and unyielding super-ego formations, often described by Freud, can be associated with personalities dominated by the fixations of the imaginary. Usually because of the influence of parents, guardians, and other bearers of culture, the capacity for ethical reflection can become welded to rigid codes of conduct.[57] When this occurs, ethical aspirations and relations to the symbolic become obsessive and irrational. The Law becomes reified, and one's activities are overlaid with a burdensome weight of anxiety and guilt. Hence, as with other aspects of subjectivity, pathological super-ego formations are often evident.

To summarize, the registers describe modes of psychical organization and orientation that shape the presentation of reality and are reflected in, and reinforced by, cultural constructs. Furthermore, the three registers are defined in relation to each other, and their co-presence contributes to the dynamic nature of the Lacanian psychological model. In his later writings Lacan uses the image of the Borromean knot, with three loops that unravel if one is cut, to illustrate the interdependence of the registers.[58] However, the relation between the registers is also partially *developmental*, exhibiting a general movement from: (1) the predominance of the real in the drives, through (2) an initial (and abiding) structuring related to the imaginary and the ego, to (3) some degree of appropriation of the resources of the symbolic mode in acculturation (represented intra-psychically by the super-ego). Lacan therefore argues for some degree of developmental progression from predominantly imaginary to symbolic orientations. Subjective development within the symbolic has its roots in the resolution of the Oedipus complex, but it is neither automatic nor assimilable to socially adapted maturity. That is, such development is an ongoing process. It has distinctly ethical and transformative dimensions insofar as it indicates a reflective capacity traversing the agencies and oriented toward recognition of the other.

Lacan explicates the limits of imaginary structures in terms of relational and interpretive closure emerging with the establishment of the ego. The notion of the *mirror stage* portrays the manner in which the ego is initially formed as an imaginary gestalt:

> What I have called the *mirror stage*...manifests the affective dynamism by which the subject originally identifies himself with the visual *Gestalt* of his own body...it represents an ideal of unity, a salutary *imago*; it is invested with all the original distress resulting from the child's intra-organic and relational discordance during the first six months, when he bears the signs, neurological and humoral, of a physiological natal prematuration.[59]

In the mirror stage the imaginary is associated with incipient psychic organization. This parallels Freud's view of ego development as occurring through modifications of the id in response to external stimuli. The image of the mirror expresses this formative process as modeled after the image of bodily integrity: either one's own, reflected back, or that of another. Lacan refers to this formation as "orthopaedic;" that is, it *straightens* the personality and thereby necessarily imposes structure and limitation.

Links between the imaginary register and the ego's alienated character appear in Lacan's statement that the ego is founded upon "imaginary, narcissistic, specular identification."[60] The ego thereby comes into being in response to an initial need to structure and consolidate identity. Because of this, it necessarily embodies objectifying and defensive traits that may inhibit further development. In the most pejorative terms, this leads to "the assumption of the armour of an alienating identity."[61] The imaginary ego serves as a defense against, and organization of, the fragmented and incoherent initial condition of infancy. Because of our radically unformed state at birth, we are characterized by an intrinsic openness connected with a lack or a "gap" (*béance*) in our being. This openness, upon which a series of dynamic processes is founded, may be seen as a key to both the creativity and vulnerability of human beings. In response to original chaos, the unity of the ego is gained through what Lacan calls a "fascination" with an image which is also a closed form of identification.[62] The negative consequence of this formation is rejection of what is unassimilable in the delimited identity structure. This establishes the illusion of autonomy and completeness, as well as the self-aggrandizement characteristic of the narcissistic ego. Freud's discussions of "infantile omnipotence," as appear for example in *Totem and Taboo*, are important in this respect.

In covering over or, in Lacanian terms, *suturing* the inherent lack in the human condition, imaginary formation creates a split or alienation within the subject. The irony is that the self-image of the ego is built on identification with external impressions. Yet in becoming formed in its identifications with others the ego closes itself off from dimensions of otherness, both externally and internally (the latter includes aspects of subjectivity such as those characterized as desire). As Samuel Weber summarizes, "a heteroreflective relationship is thus turned into an auto-reflective one marked by the transparency of self-consciousness."[63] Part of the limitations of the ego as a mode of subjectivity, therefore, is its denial of its locatedness within alterity (both intra-psychically and extra-psychically).

The problematic status of the ego is reinforced by the argument that beyond the mirror stage the ego continues to be shaped and conditioned by imaginary forms of identification, compromising its status as objective mediator of reality. Lacan thus argues that "the ego is the sum of the identifications of the subject, with all that that implies as to its radical contingency."[64] Increased awareness of the manner in which ego orientations are contingently shaped allows associated delimitations, biases, and distortions to be worked upon. By contrast, the association of the ego with a "reality principle" feeds into an illusion of objectivity and control that actually serves to entrench internalized perspectives and biases.[65] Fixation in the modality of the ego therefore reinforces cultural as well as personal forms of conceptual and perspectival closure. Although some encounter with and internalization of the symbolic, as indicated in Lacan's reformulation of the Oedipus complex, is essential to personality development, the imaginary retains a stronghold, to a greater or lesser extent, in the organization of the ego.

Imaginary and symbolic modes of being are both products of acculturation, and each therefore mediates experience in certain ways. However, Lacan articulates a qualitative differentiation between modes of symbolization, as linked with modes of psycho-cultural orientation. Similarly to

Freud, Lacan retains a pejorative sense of "illusion," which he associates with imaginary relations. In this respect Lacan delineates two aspects of the imaginary. First, as we have seen, it characterizes a phase of all normal development related to early formative identifications. Second, and most significantly, the imaginary applies "to the relation of the subject to the real *whose characteristic is that of being illusory*."[66] This parallel between illusion and the imaginary is strengthened when we recall that Freud's critique of religious illusion emphasizes imaginary orientations such as demand, fixity, and totalization. For example, Freud condemns the "rigidity and unchange-ableness" of codes of behavior based on religion, and also points to the restricted capacity for critical correction in religious belief.[67] Therefore the Freudian critique of illusion actually highlights tendencies toward *closure* in religious orientations and cultural forms. Freud's critique of illusion as a closed, narcissistic structuring of self and world is augmented in Lacan's analyses of the pejorative aspects of imaginary formations. Illusion is not contrasted with a static, neutral concept of reality as matter and force known through instrumental reason, but rather with a more open-ended, corrigible, and self-transforming symbolic mode of being.

For Lacan, the problem of modes of subjectivity and symbolization becomes the explicit focus of critical psycho-cultural analysis. The essential difference between the imaginary and the symbolic is that the latter repre-sents orientations that do not naively identify themselves with reality in any final sense. In addition, the linguistic media characteristic of the symbolic, such as metaphor and metonymy, offer resources for resisting one-dimen-sional perspectives. This plurivocity allows for perspectival and conceptual reconfigurations in relation to new experience, to manifestations of the real that challenge existing views and assumptions. In this respect Lacan empha-sizes that "reality is defined by contradiction," that is, by difference, otherness, and negativity.[68] The symbolic, as a culturally informed mode of subjectivity, facilitates meaningful responses to contradiction. Thus subjec-tive transformations occur in encounters with others within cultural worlds of communication and in relation to the real in experiences that pressure established forms of social-symbolic understanding.

The pluralized and open-ended resources of language are perhaps the most crucial attributes of the symbolic. This quality applies to the symbolic as both a modality of subjectivity and as a set of cultural structures. Lacan appropriates Ferdinand de Saussure's analyses of the linguistic sign as constituted by differences. That is, linguistic terms have meaning in relation to one another and to the grammatical structures of a given language.[69] As Richard Boothby summarizes, "the imaginary form is essentially a *gestalt* unity. By contrast, the linguistic signifier is structured not by unity, but by difference."[70] This differential structuring has enormous implications for reflections on psycho-cultural existence. Subjective differentiation within language is the correlate of a necessary mediation in experiencing the world.

Lacan emphasizes that signification is "never resolved into a pure indication of the real, but always refers back to another signification."[71] Therefore the task of psychoanalysis is not to pursue the chimera of adjusting subjectivity to a standard of normalized relations to a posited unmediated reality. Rather, psychoanalysis provides a model for and a means of educing the *truth of the subject* as an interactive process occurring within cultural symbolic structures. Here truth is not based on a correspondence model (i.e. the fit between statements and objects). Lacan's truth of the subject is more compatible with the notion of "narrative truth" discussed earlier. Both have to do with modes of being that include self-knowledge and ethical relations with others. The key to this truth is the capacity for mutually meaningful and fulfilling relations, a capacity that is developed through the communicative processes of the symbolic. Intimations of the connections between the truth of the subject and religious and aesthetic symbolism and discourse are evident here, and this is a point where Lacanian contributions clarify and extrapolate on insights occurring in Freud's analyses of religion.

These preliminary explorations prepare us for a fresh engagement with the densely imbricated images and reflections of *Totem and Taboo* and *Moses and Monotheism*. The ensuing chapters will illustrate that valuable insights and resources concerning symbolic transformations of subjectivity appear throughout these inquiries into the intersections of religion, ethics, and culture.

Chapter 3

Displacement, supplementarity, and symbolic meaning in *Totem and Taboo*

There are no grounds for fearing that psycho-analysis, which first discovered that psychical acts and structures are invariably overdetermined, will be tempted to trace the origin of anything so complicated as religion to a single source.[1]

The myth of origins and the problem of origination

The multiple levels of meaning discernible in the Oedipus complex manifest themselves throughout Freud's analyses of religion. It therefore comes as no surprise that *Totem and Taboo* concludes triumphantly by asserting that "the beginnings of religion, morals, society and art converge in the Oedipus complex."[2] Yet rather than coalescing within a sweeping reductionistic point of origin, these links create a series of unfolding interconnections. The relations among society (or, rather, culture), morals (or, rather, ethics), religion, and art enrich our understanding of each component of the explanatory network and subvert simple etiological models. Especially when it is read in light of the Lacanian symbolic order, the Oedipus complex becomes an overdetermined figure for the dynamics of acculturation.

Freud's manifest arguments concerning the origins of totemism take shape mainly through historical and ethnographic hypotheses cobbled together from the work of Frazer, Darwin, and Robertson Smith. These hypotheses are linked by psychodynamic patterns, particularly those emerging from analyses of obsessional neuroses and childhood animal phobias. Together, these components create a causal-explanatory account of the origins of culture. This is the predominant level on which Freud himself saw the text as functioning and on which it has been addressed by most scholars. On this level there has been widespread rejection of the ethnological hypotheses of *Totem and Taboo*; a reliable summary of these critiques is provided by Edwin R. Wallace.[3]

In light of the problematization of the manifest level of argumentation, Wallace and others have indicated alternative insights discernible on more figurative levels. These may be roughly categorized as follows:

1 Biographical factors, especially Freud's status as patriarch of the psychoanalytic movement and his conflicts, primarily with Jung, over the status of religion. Here Freud's concern about being "killed" (supplanted) by Jung has been emphasized.

2 As a more or less direct application of individual psychology, especially the Oedipus complex, in the sphere of culture and history. On this level the pseudo-historical constructions are seen as being of little value in themselves, but as offering a vehicle for narrative expression of psycho-analytic ideas.

3 As offering insight, though mainly indirectly and figuratively, into a series of interrelated psychological and cultural dynamics.[4]

The present work develops issues related to the second and third levels of analysis. It explicates, in a more comprehensive and systematic manner than has been undertaken heretofore, some of the possible symbolic dimensions of the text, primarily those related to psycho-cultural levels of interpretation. My overall argument is that *Totem and Taboo* embodies a variety of ideas and insights relevant to understanding the psychodynamics of acculturation. These involve the formative influence of symbolic orders connected with religion, especially as constituting the ethical orientations of the super-ego. In conjunction with these processes, Freud's analyses specifically address issues related to capacities for renunciation and sublimation as representative of personal maturation along broadly religious lines.

In *Moses and Monotheism* Freud refers to *Totem and Taboo* as "my construction" (*Konstruktion*). He indicates that the text does not describe a single event, but is a figurative condensation of multiple events to which no date can be assigned. In Freud's words, "the story is told in an enormously condensed form, as though it had happened on a single occasion, while in fact it covered thousands of years and was repeated countless times during that long period."[5] Freud is clearly aware of the narrative qualities of his account, although he argues that the construction is not *purely* imaginary, but is indeed (in some broad way) historically based. His method of linking discrete bits of theory and evidence into a "construct" is, however, evocative of the narrative genre suggested by Spence and others. A related point has been made by Paul Ricoeur, who states that the lynchpin of Freud's historical account, the primal parricide, "is merely an event constructed out of ethnological scraps on the pattern of the fantasy deciphered by analysis." Most importantly, Ricoeur continues: "one does psychoanalysis a service not by defending its scientific myth as science, but by interpreting it as myth."[6] Indeed, such possible levels of mythic and symbolic insight, as indicated by Ricoeur, appear in a remarkably consistent manner in the first three essays of *Totem and Taboo* and become condensed into the originary myth of the fourth essay. This should be kept in mind lest we become lost in

Freud's tendency to literalize his constructions and thereby acquiesce in curtailing their range of psycho-cultural insight.

The quest for the etiology of higher psycho-cultural forms provides the catalyst for an inquiry whose yield exceeds its intentionality. In light of Freud's empiricist orientation, the existence of higher processes, such as those related to moral prohibitions, becomes a problem requiring causal explanation. Thus Freud formulates temporal, dynamic models of the development of these forms rather than assuming their existence. The two key prohibitions he isolates are: "not to kill the totem animal and to avoid sexual intercourse with members of the totem clan of the opposite sex."[7] The reason for the development of these prohibitions and the means whereby they came into being, remain unclear. In the earlier portions of the text Freud is content to allow the question to linger unanswered on the periphery of his inquiry. These unresolved dilemmas set the stage for the great explanatory hypotheses of the primal horde and primal parricide introduced in the fourth essay of *Totem and Taboo*.

Freud's discussion of cultural systems of morality, represented by totemism and the incest taboo, contains numerous interrelated insights concerning the psycho-cultural function of symbolic forms. In the first essay Freud argues that cultural structures of exogamy linked to totem clans function to prevent incestuous relations. As he summarizes: "In almost every place where we find totems we also find a law against persons of the same totem having sexual relations with one another and consequently against their marrying."[8] This social structure operates not only to prohibit, but also to distance and differentiate. Thus acculturated human relations are shown to be *symbolically structured along lines of mediated difference*. Freud notes that totemism functioned to "replace real blood relationship by totem kinship," displacing the physical and literal on to the social and symbolic.[9] The symbolic extension of kinship can be located within the multiple dimensions of the Oedipus complex. This appears in an example taken from the Australian aborigines. Freud notes that "the terms used by them to express the various degrees of kinship do not denote a relation between two individuals but between an individual and a group."[10] As examples of this extended usage Freud notes that the terms "father" and "mother" apply to all individuals in the tribe or group who *might* potentially have been one's literal procreator. He summarizes: "Thus the kinship terms which two Australians apply to each other do not necessarily indicate any consanguinity, as ours would do: they represent social rather than physical relationships."[11] This analysis can be read regressively as indicating how social relations are similar to family relations in their embodiment of Oedipal dynamics. However, it can also be read progressively. That is, Freud indicates how systems of *symbolic* relations are superimposed on and supersede literal, familial relations. Indeed, the familial and social levels are equiprimordial, so that one cannot be posited as the basis for the other.

It is easy to overlook the text's insights into the formative effects of symbol systems in psycho-cultural existence. Freud contributes to this difficulty by repeatedly emphasizing the causal-explanatory value of his hypotheses. For example, in summarizing his findings, Freud concludes that the very existence of prohibitions against incest reveals an innate tendency toward incestuous fixation of libido. The pressure of incestuous tendencies is evidenced by cultural developments acting as controlling responses to this pressure.[12] Freud's emphasis is on the lack of anything but id-based desire, and particularly incestuous desire, at the level of innate endowment. This argument seems designed to counter Jungian essentialist views of morality and symbol-forming capacities. The reactive dimension of Freud's thinking leads him to emphasize cause-and-effect arguments antithetical to Jung's teleological views.

Freud now turns to a more detailed discussion of the problem of *displacement*. He notes that in both taboo and obsessional neurosis "the purpose of some of the prohibitions is immediately obvious." These would be cases where an object is avoided because it lends itself to direct association with repressed materials. However, what is most interesting is that "others, on the contrary, strike us as incomprehensible, senseless and silly, and prohibitions of this latter sort are described as 'ceremonial'."[13] A pertinent example of this is the prohibitions of the elaborate sleep ceremony related by Freud in the *Introductory Lectures on Psychoanalysis*.[14] These puzzling, ritualized prohibitions took the form of stopping all clocks in the room, arranging the pillows and blankets in a specific manner, leaving the bedroom door ajar, and other seemingly senseless activities that the individual must *necessarily* undertake before going to sleep. These actions are interpreted by Freud as disguised compromises between acting out and repressing a drive. That is, they are the consequence of displacement, produced by conflict between unconscious impulses and the defenses of the ego. These defenses, by the way, may also occur *unconsciously*, so that the individual is not actually aware of what it is that is being repressed, or why. Because of such repression and conflict, and because of the fluidity of expression along lines of association and contiguity found in unconscious or primary-process activity, "obsessional prohibitions are extremely liable to displacement. They extend from one object to another along whatever paths the context may provide."[15]

Freud summarizes his argument by listing the following parallels between taboo and obsessional neurosis: the prohibitions lack any assignable motive; they are maintained by an internal necessity; they are easily displaceable; and they give rise to injunctions for the performances of ceremonial acts.[16] These processes are also evident in the parallel instance of taboos related to death. Freud notes that the same prohibitions that apply directly to the deceased "apply to those who have been in contact with the dead only in a metaphorical sense: the dead person's mourning relations, widowers and

widows."[17] There is, in effect, a social structuring of relations to others and
to reality occurring along quasi-linguistic lines.

The symbolic and creative dimensions of displacement tend to be overshadowed by Freud's emphasis on the *pathological* features of totemism.
The etiological model Freud constructs operates on a mechanistic principle
of cause and effect coupled with libidinal energetics. Both taboos and other
moral constraints are seen to parallel the prohibitions on expressing libidinal
impulses evident in neurotic behavior. Using the latter as his exemplar,
Freud states that "the prohibition does not succeed in *abolishing* the instinct.
Its only result is to *repress* the instinct (the desire to touch) and banish it into
the unconscious. Both the instinct and the prohibition persist."[18] Here we
have a classic psychoanalytic account of the tension between opposing
forces. The tension is not properly overcome in neuroses, but persists in a
twofold or ambivalent relationship to the prohibited objects: "The principal
characteristic of the psychological constellation which becomes fixed in this
way is what might be described as the subject's *ambivalent* attitude towards a
single object."[19] This ambivalence is linked with the conflicting forces of
psychical life, here portrayed within a mechanistic model of energy seeking
to escape blockage: "The instinctual desire is constantly shifting in order to
escape from the *impasse* and endeavors to find substitutes – substitute
objects and substitute acts – in place of the prohibited ones."[20] The substitutes simultaneously serve the function of providing expiation and
compensation.[21] Later Freud states the dual levels of meaning in other
terms, giving priority to latent causes: "The obsessional act is *ostensibly* a
protection against the prohibited act; but *actually*, in our view, it is a repetition of it. The 'ostensible' applies to the *conscious* part of the mind, and the
'actually' to the *unconscious* part."[22] In other words, obsessional actions
related to prohibitions are displaced manifestations of unconscious
impulses.

Freud notes that "this transmissibility of taboo is a reflection of the
tendency, on which we have already remarked, for the unconscious instinct
in the neurosis to shift constantly along associative paths on to new
objects."[23] Yet this shifting along associative paths occurs in ways that are
hardly mechanistic or quantitative. Freud emphasizes that it acts much as do
the disguises of the "dream work" to allow indirect expression of prohibited,
censored wishes. He states that "the prototype of all such systems is what we
have termed the 'secondary revision' of the content of dreams."[24] This
parallel with the dream work is relevant to the issue of the *formative* nature
of symbolic constructs. Thus it is significant that the operations of the
dream work have been shown by numerous theorists to reflect linguistic or
quasi-linguistic processes. Paul Ricoeur, for example, argues that the two
main processes studied in *The Interpretation of Dreams* – condensation and
displacement – "are meaningful operations comparable to rhetorical procedures."[25] In the same vein, Lacan illustrates parallels between the dream

work and figures of speech. Displacement or transposition occurs along lines of contiguity, much as the operations of metonymy. Condensation acts as a form of substitution, much as metaphorical tropes.[26] Moreover, in dream interpretation the underlying or latent content is disclosed, one might say constructed, only retrospectively through interpretive processes engaging numerous overdetermined variables. This means that the paradigm of a single, underlying meaning or truth existing in itself prior to its displaced and distorted manifestations is forsaken in favor of a more open-ended "overinterpretation."[27] In applying parallel transformative mechanisms to the work of culture, Freud is indirectly subverting a linear, cause-and-effect form of explanation.

The process of displacement, invoked by Freud to explain the psycho-cultural transformations of totemism, cannot be contained within the framework of a mere *evasion* of libidinal force. This would be the case even if the parallel with the formation of dreams in the dream work and in the ritualized activities of obsessional neurosis were an exact one. However, the quantitative model, in which fixed amounts of energy require alternative outlets, is in fact coupled with a *qualitative* transformation. In other words, displacement is not simply a defense mechanism, but intersects with the transformative processes Freud characterizes as *sublimation*. This connection is explicitly made by Freud some years later in *The Ego and the Id*.[28] Thus the processes of displacement are overdetermined and exhibit qualities of symbolic production with distinctly creative (or transformative) attributes. Not only is innate incestuous desire repressed and rerouted, but, more significantly, in these processes symbolic forms come into being that constitute culture and engender far-reaching transformations in psychology. The clan system is a symbolic ordering of cultural reality along lines of *value* constructed in the symbolic language of animal ancestors and totem figures. It is not merely a literal, direct prohibition of particular acts. Rather, *the totemic system fosters a turning away from a condition of self-enclosure and lack of differentiation, as represented by incestuous relations*. This is effected through the vehicle of symbolic displacements and supplements intrinsic to socio-cultural formation.

As we have seen, a key feature of the dynamic of displacement is the presence of *ambivalence*. Freud discusses this attitude in a further attempt to connect neurotic and cultural patterns of behavior by formulating an originary Oedipal mechanism applicable to culture. This explanatory strategy seeks to address a crucial problem, that the formation of "higher-order" faculties and structures in displacement poses a problem for mechanistic and reductionistic paradigms. The key question here, on the psychological level, is: *What is the origin of conscience?* That is, what provides the necessary opposition to actions yielding immediate gratification? To this problem Freud responds:

thus it seems probable that conscience too arose, on a basis of emotional ambivalence, from quite specific human relations to which this ambivalence was attached [the subsequently introduced narrative of the primal father is foreshadowed here]; and that it arose under the conditions which we have shown to apply in the case of taboo and of obsessional neurosis – namely, that one of the opposing feelings involved shall be unconscious and kept under repression by the compulsive domination of the other one.[29]

Ambivalence is the product of simultaneous love and hate, which is reduced by Freud to a tension based on drives or impulses. However, ambivalence also relates to the *qualitative* level of attitudes and feelings. It indicates a twofold relation to the other fostered by an originary *doubling* in the subject's psychological constitution.[30] This doubling may create psychic tension, but it also sustains a capacity for reflection and reflexivity. (Both this reflective capacity and the more pathologized elements of inner splitting become clarified in Freud's subsequent formulations concerning the intrapsychic dynamics of ego and super-ego.) Reflective capacity emerges from ambivalence because an *immediate* response to the other from a single affective orientation is compromised. Indeed, ambivalence indicates breaking with immediacy, both objectively (in terms of the primacy of the real) and subjectively (in terms of imaginary orientations). Each emotional orientation is qualified, held in partial suspension by its opposite, which creates the possibility of a reflective space or moment.

Beyond the implicit insights into creative processes evident in ambivalence, displacement, and symbol formation, another important point emerges from the foregoing analysis. As Freud notes, the parallels between neurosis and totemism break down in one crucial respect. The activities and attitudes associated with the neuroses alienate individuals from society. Their fantasies, rituals, obsessive acts, and displacements are not grasped as interpersonally and collectively meaningful. These phenomena seem senseless and repulsive to others; and their obsessive quality becomes an oppressive burden to those involved. Clearly, neuroses constitute a pathologized relation with social reality both functionally and epistemologically. Totemism, however, is part of the social construction of reality. "After all," Freud notes, "taboo is not a neurosis but a social institution [*eine soziale Bildung*]."[31] The significance of this point emerges as Freud argues that, while the neuroses exhibit "far-reaching points of agreement with those great social institutions, art, religion, and philosophy," they nevertheless "seem like distortions of them." Freud further emphasizes that "the divergence resolves itself ultimately into the fact that the neuroses are asocial structures; they endeavor to achieve by private means what is effected in society by collective effort."[32] There are significant differences between mental constructs that are solipsistic and potentially delusional, that depart from reality as socially established, and symbolic formations that are creatively *constitutive* of an interpersonally meaningful social realm. This point is further elucidated when Freud states:

> the real world, which is avoided in this way by neurotics, is under the sway of human society and of the institutions collectively created by it. To turn away from reality is at the same time to withdraw from the community of man.[33]

In this comment reality has more to do with the *symbolic* than with the *real* (in Lacanian terminology). Similarly, in the relatively early "Obsessive acts and religious practices," mainly devoted to analogies between religion and neurosis, Freud concludes by indicating a key point of divergence between religion and obsessions. The latter are socially dysfunctional, while the former is intertwined with "a progressive renunciation of constitutional instincts, whose activation might afford the ego primary pleasure." This, Freud emphasizes, "appears to be one of the foundations of human civilization."[34] In this seemingly marginal statement Freud indicates significant links between religion, culture, and intra-psychic transformation, wherein the ego relinquishes immediate gratification in the name of some collective principle or ideal. *Moses and Monotheism*, in particular, will develop these themes of psycho-cultural development in terms of Freud's notion of renunciation.

These points indicate Freud's awareness of the limits of an analogical procedure modelling religion and culture on neuroses. Freud's comparative analyses reveal the necessary implication of cultural forms in personality formation and in human experience. Despite Freud's predilection for reductive analogies and his tendency to assume a positivistic definition of reality, a crucial point emerges in the above considerations and, indeed, throughout his analyses of religion and culture: *Human existence is socially constituted and symbolically mediated.* The "supplement" produced by cultural processes is as original as are the (retrospectively constructed) underlying causes. Here Jacques Derrida's remarks concerning the supplementarity inherent in dream interpretation are apposite. As he states: "The supplement, which seems to be added as a plentitude to a plentitude, is equally that which compensates for a lack."[35] In this case the supplement compensates for an intrinsic lack in human subjectivity, an open-endedness requiring culturally mediated structuring. The supplement occurs as a system of cultural forms, including language and values. Other comments made by Derrida in the context of an analysis of Rousseau are also relevant to reading Freud. "Supplementarity," states Derrida, "makes possible all that constitutes the property of man: speech, society, passion, etc."[36]

Intra-psychically, acculturation as a process of supplementarity links up with the Freudian notion of *sublimation*. The term expresses a creative transformation of psychical energy, yielding some form of constructive, socially valued activity. Freud writes: "a certain kind of modification of the aim and change of the object, in which our social valuation is taken into account, is described by us as 'sublimation.'"[37] Sublimation indicates processes of qualitative intra-psychic transformation occurring in relation to acculturation. Religion, in the form of totemism or in any other manifestation, is intrinsic to these processes insofar as it provides sets of symbolically articulated ideals that alter subjective motivations. These modifications are precisely *not* equivalent to repetition along lines of evasive substitution, in which no change or development occurs. In neuroses displacements are not curative because they continually repeat and act out the same thing: there is no working-through (*Durcharbeiten*).[38] One of the tasks of analysis is to *disrupt* the repetition and stimulate understanding and working-through as part of a qualitative transformation in the psychical orientation of the subject.

In the overview, Freud's analyses of religion actually illustrate *both* types of relationship to drive processes, regressive and progressive. Relatedly, Julia Kristeva refers to the "two paths" of sublimation and perversion, and locates religion at their intersection.[39] On the one hand, religious phenomena may be seen to manifest infantile and pathological tendencies toward repetition compulsion. Kristeva refers to the pathologized and regressive components of religion as perversion, by which she specifically means fetishism. Fetishism, in turn, can be understood as imaginary fixation on literalized ideal entities and related symbols and practices. These are invested with an excessive emotional significance that fosters resistance to critical reflection and transformation. On the other hand, religion is also associated with creative, transformative, sublimatory tendencies occurring by means of culturally formed symbols and ideals. These foster transitions from sameness and self-enclosure to differentiated relations to otherness.

Freud's preoccupation with questions of origin and etiology conceived along causal lines, and with an interpretive procedure governed by analogy, diverts him from attending to these pivotal issues distinguishing totemism (his prototype for all religious symbol systems) from neurotic activity. These preoccupations mask deeper insights into cultural dynamics disclosed by his text. Freud turns from the constitutive functions of displacement and symbolic activity to problems of cause and effect, determined to reduce the more complex to the less complex. In this enterprise Freud restricts the use of the model of manifest versus latent content to discerning fixed underlying causes. Freud seems intent on a form of *originary* thinking that postulates a hidden reality behind the displacements. Yet his analyses open another path of inquiry, one that acknowledges that displacements and supplements are constitutive of cultural and psychological realities far more complex and significant than the putative originals from which they deviate.

Omnipotence of thoughts and cultural reality

Before pursuing Freud's explanation of higher-order cultural forms and mental processes, some stocktaking concerning related issues will be helpful. For example, it should be noted that the prominence of Freud's *reductive* orientation is reinforced by numerous aspects of the text. This appears in his seemingly disparaging stance in relation to peoples such as the Australian aborigines and Polynesian Islanders, evident in his use of the term *die Wilden* (savages). Also problematic are Freud's assertions concerning the analogies and parallels between the mental lives of "savages, neurotics, and children."[40] Most significant is the developmental schema ordering "three great pictures of the universe: animistic (or mythological), religious and scientific."[41] This culturally conditioned model is quite consistent with the overt arguments of *The Future of an Illusion*, as discussed in Chapter 3. Both are governed by the sense that adequation to a positivistically defined factual reality is the primary touchstone for psycho-cultural development. This sustains the view that Western natural science provides the model and the conceptual tools for the endeavor of establishing true knowledge of and practical relations to reality. Clearly, there is a consistent line of thought traversing the surface of Freud's texts on religion and culture, rendering it difficult to discern the underlying counter-views.

Nevertheless, in several key respects Freud's work qualifies the hierarchical schema of the modern myth of scientific progress. Even within the context of an evolutionary model based on the normative status of the discursive practices of natural science, Freud discerns the roots of the later in the earlier. Thus, just as Freud often subverts the authoritarian relationship between analyst and analysand, and the boundary between normal and pathological, in a similar way *Totem and Taboo* breaks down the barrier between modern Western ethical and cultural accomplishments and the symbolic forms of other cultures. This blurring is evidenced in the following passage:

> It may begin to dawn on us that the taboos of the savage Polynesians are after all not so remote from us as we were inclined to think at first, that the moral and conventional prohibitions by which we ourselves are governed may have some essential relationship with these primitive taboos and that an explanation of taboo might throw a light upon the obscure origin of our own "categorical imperative."[42]

Of course, one may read this passage as giving evidence of an even more sweeping reductionism. It dispels the Kantian illusion of ethical ideals based on indubitable principles stemming from the innate, God-given endowment of practical reason. It seems, in fact, to indicate a project of reducing all higher-order ethical principles to displacements that evade and repress incestuous impulses.

However, we have seen that the complex mechanisms of displacement subvert the cause-and-effect relationship between origin and supplement. That is, the "supplement" of cultural symbol systems, as the product of displacement, qualitatively exceeds its posited causal origins. Furthermore, an understanding of the reflections on morality in *Totem and Taboo* and other Freudian texts should take shape in relation to the following question: *Does Freud value ethical accomplishments?* We have already seen that *The Future of an Illusion* has as one of its major themes the pressing need for a "rational morality." Thus it seems quite in keeping with the textual evidence to argue, as Yerushalmi has done, that Freud exhibits a consistent positive valuation of "ethical heights."[43] This wider perspective reinforces the claim that the arguments of *Totem and Taboo* are not *merely* reductive. They also illuminate the function of psycho-culturally constituted ideals and values. To be sure, Freud's critiques of conventional morality, and of *idealist, irrational*, and *coercive* ethical orientations, remain prominent and important. Yet the psychoanalytic de-idealization of ethics is coupled with an analysis of the human condition that is essentially dynamic and open-ended, in which the mediations of language and symbols are constitutive, and in which ethical formation is a critical concern. The texts on religion serve to articulate elements of such a view, in however fragmentary and indirect a manner. Freud's critical analyses are not necessarily predicated on a narrow positivist worldview. That is, an anti-idealist, non-essentialist stance need not forgo a constructive analysis of the realm of culturally formulated regulative ideals.

Another significant point of tension between reductive and constructive orientations appears in Freud's presentation and analysis of the belief in the "omnipotence of thoughts" shared by *die Wilden* and neurotics. This is a matter Freud turns to immediately following the discussion of displacement in the second essay of *Totem and Taboo*, and the analysis develops some key explicit and implicit issues. In discussing displacement as a defensive mechanism, i.e. as a means of avoiding painful psychical reality, Freud connects displacement and *projection*. For instance, he uses the example of a hostile impulse toward the deceased:

> the defense against it takes the form of displacing it on to the object of hostility, on to the dead themselves. [That is, the dead are seen as being hostile and potentially dangerous toward the living.] This defensive procedure, which is a common one both in normal and pathological mental life [*Seelenleben*], is known as "*projection*."[44]

On the surface, Freud's argument seems quite simply reductive. Belief in, and fear of, spirits and ghosts has now been "explained" by a psychical mechanism of displacing a hostile impulse on to a realm of imaginary beings. This type of analysis also forms the prototype for the critique of illusion as the projection of wish-fulfillment on to imaginary beings in *The Future of an Illusion*. However, once again Freud's critical analyses include latent insights that lead to deeper and more fruitful territory.

In discussing projection, Freud becomes involved in issues concerning an experiential realm intersecting psychical and cultural realities. He has noted *pathological* instances of projection related to defense. Yet the processes summarized under the heading of projection are both more frequent and more extensive than defensive mechanisms. As Freud states:

> projection was not created for the purpose of defense; it also occurs where there is no conflict. The projection outwards of internal perceptions is a primitive mechanism, to which, for instance, our sense perceptions are subject, and which therefore normally plays a very large part in determining the form taken by our external world.... [Projections] are thus employed for building up the external world [*zur Ausgestaltung der Außenwelt verwendet*], though they should by rights remain part of the *internal* world.[45]

In this statement Freud conjoins two points of view. He maintains a pathologizing orientation based on the presupposition that there are *proper* realms of inner and outer that should remain distinct. Within this argument, however, Freud also emphasizes that the transference of psychical reality on to the experience of the external world contributes to *the formation of cultural symbol systems*. In this respect Freud notes that animism is an instance of such *world-building* projection, "which constituted the *Weltanschauung* of primitive peoples."[46] Cultural worlds cannot simply be derived from internal or mental structures; nor do they mirror an extant physical reality. They are formed within an *interplay of inner and outer* which Freud designates, somewhat inadequately, by the term "projection."

Freud picks up the thread of his analysis of animism in relation to displacement and projection in the third essay of *Totem and Taboo*. The psychical orientation governing the animistic worldview is further developed, again with the help of parallel neurotic phenomena (here taken from the case of the "Rat Man"): "The principle governing magic, the technique of the animistic mode of thinking, is the principle of the 'omnipotence of thoughts.'"[47] This notion designates an inflated sense of mental powers. It involves both an inability to reality-test, i.e. differentiate between inner and outer sources of perception, and the concomitant projection of psychical structures and dynamics on to the external world. In his analysis of the Rat Man case, Stuart Schneiderman points out that in the processes characterized as omnipotence of thoughts "the patient retains his narcissism and adapts it to the exigencies of reality."[48] This indicates the pathologized aspect of projective activity: the world is adapted to subjectivity, rather than vice versa. Schneiderman continues: "It is as though consciousness makes a foray into the world to capture some element and to imprint upon it the stamp of possession, its particular brand; it then retires in satisfaction over its handiwork."[49] The key here is the *narcissistic* aspect of the activity, which links it to the *imaginary* register. Here projection is self-enclosed and self-satisfying; it sustains an order of the same.

Freud argues that a primary instance of omnipotence of thoughts on a cultural level is magic, which "mistakes an ideal connection for a real one."[50] In sympathetic magic the graphic, iconic similarity between the act performed (rituals, making of effigies, etc.) and the desired result provides the operative connecting principle. Other cultural practices are seen to function according to the principles of contagion by similarity, association, and contiguity. One should note that these magical connections parallel those evident in certain figures of speech. Synecdoche takes a part to represent a whole, metonymy takes an attribute or associated item to represent an entity, and metaphor juxtaposes and condenses divergent realms or referents to create new meaning. An example of magical practice involving these symbolic processes, one that returns with greater significance in the fourth essay, is anthropophagy. Here Freud notes that "the higher motives for cannibalism among primitive races have a similar origin. By incorporating parts of a person's body through the act of eating, one at the same time acquires the qualities possessed by him."[51] Thus the animistic worldview exhibits a combination of an illusory, superstitious practice (because it acts out the symbolism literally) with symbolically constituted patterns of behavior. In any event, in addition to their analogies with obsessional neurosis, these examples also show, once again, that human subjectivity and relations to externality are culturally structured along quasi-linguistic lines.

Freud, of course, highlights the magical, wish-oriented, and illusory nature of imitative and projective practices, downplaying the relation to symbolic world-building to which he alludes. These practices suggest that "primitive man had an immense belief in the power of his wishes."[52] The animistic worldview assumes a parallelism between mental processes and external reality. Thus the void in comprehending the physical universe is filled by unconscious projective processes whereby "primitive man transposed the structural conditions of his own mind into the external world."[53] In Freud's analysis, animism represents a distorted and pathologized psycho-cultural orientation. It provides an erroneous pre-scientific explanation of the physical world; that is, it mixes up inner and outer in a way that is *delusory*. It also gives people an *illusory* sense of empowerment in relation to the world, so that it symbolizes a form of collective narcissistic self-aggrandizement. In addition, and perhaps more constructively, animism offers a worldview that meets the need for *meaning* Freud sees as characteristic of religious activity.

The phenomena of projection appearing in animism and religion mix inner and outer reality. These should properly be separated according to the criterion of reality-testing as approximating knowledge of the external, objective world. In this respect Freud speaks of the need to "reverse the process" of projection, and of the need to sort out inner and outer.[54] Clearly, such *deprojection* functions to accommodate symbolic worldviews to material reality as governed by the laws of nature. This accommodation is intrinsic to the rise of science and technology as systematic responses to the material dimensions of reality. Psychologically, deprojection also encapsulates a therapeutic response to illusory formations; that is, it serves as an antidote to unhealthy narcissism. Freud's concerns with delusion and illusion, combined with the positivist model that remains influential throughout his work, orient him toward the developmental schema in which psychocultural progress involves deprojection guided by accommodation to a world of facts.

The overt level of Freud's overall metapsychological stance, later summarized in *The Future of an Illusion*, is also fundamental to *Totem and Taboo*. Both texts present models of development governed by a transition from the predominance of subjective to objective influences. In this schema animism is associated with a subjective, inflated, and infantile sense of human empowerment. In some forms of religion this magical potency is transferred to the gods, who remain partially influenced by human wishes. Full maturity, it would seem, occurs only in the renunciation of illusory omnipotence associated with the scientific capacity for confronting reality. Thus "the scientific view of the universe no longer affords any room for human omnipotence."[55] Here a process of adaptation to reality, conceived in a positivistic manner, is again the overt standard for judging psycho-cultural forms. In the *New Introductory Lectures* Freud summarizes this view most lucidly. The intention of scientific thinking is to arrive at "correspondence with reality – that is to say, with what exists outside us and independently of us and, as experience has taught us, is decisive for the fulfillment or disappointment of our wishes. This correspondence with the real external world we call 'truth'."[56]

We have seen, however, that there are instances throughout his work where Freud expands his perspective to include both psychical and cultural realities. These dimensions of existence require approaches to truth such as are found in the "narrative" model. This expansion offsets the closure of the restricted correspondence definition of truth. Thus, in contrast to concerns with adaptation to a positivistically defined reality of given facts, the second aspect of Freud's argument shows that projection, in the sense of an interpenetration of inner and outer, is also essential to cultural world-building. These constitutive processes are linked with imagination and the creation of ideals that play a formative, constructive role in human psycho-cultural existence. Symbolic ideal constructs, such as the totem system with its animal ancestors and exogamous structures, instill a capacity for understanding self, others, and world in relation to ethical principles. That is, they do not sustain narcissistic gratification, but, on the contrary, act back upon subjectivity in a critical and transformative manner. Cultural symbol systems mirror neither subjectivity nor a fixed and determinate external reality. Instead, these cultural constructs inform subjectivity and *shape* relations to reality, and to others, along qualitative lines.

It is significant that Freud characterizes the mature scientific personality as capable of *renouncing* infantile satisfaction. (Freud does, however, hold out the possibility of deferred, realistic gratifications through applications of scientific knowledge.) Yet this capacity, upon which scientific activity is predicated, requires cultural support. Already in *Totem and Taboo* Freud links religion and renunciation by arguing that "renunciation lies at the basis of taboo."[57] This line of inquiry will be significantly developed in *Moses and Monotheism*. There, as we shall see, Freud illustrates in much greater detail that psychical capacities for renunciation are established in conjunction with the psycho-cultural function of religious and ideational forms. Renunciation requires a means of *distancing* one's sense of self and one's motivations from immediate needs. This means is supplied by culturally structured ideals. In other words, capacities for renunciation involve transformations in the personality effected through symbolic media.

An additional, related point arises here. Far from being an *adaptation* to extant reality, science and technology are in some respects quintessential forms of human *world-building*. They may be partially regulated by the possibilities provided by the real, but they apply concepts, paradigms, and other culturally informed ideational structures that allow for ordered interrogation of experience. A further important issue arises from this cultural locatedness of science. Because of the influence upon them of culture-bound assumptions and agendas, science and technology also require critical coordination in relation to values and ethical ideals.[58] This point further emphasizes the need for a more *differentiated* model of psycho-cultural development than that offered by the adaptive, reality-testing ego, seemingly directed by the force of *Ananke*.

Progression from animism to science is further elaborated in the well-known model which associates these worldviews with stages of *libidinal development*:

> The animistic phase would correspond to narcissism both chronologically and in its content; the religious stage would correspond to the stage of object-choice of which the characteristic is a child's attachment to its parents; while the scientific phase would have an exact counterpart in the stage at which an individual has reached maturity, has renounced the pleasure principle, adjusted himself to reality and turned to the external world for the object of his desires.[59]

Here Freud's linking of animism with *narcissism*, and religion with *Oedipal dependency* is extremely important. These associations indicate that the problems Freud addresses are not exhausted by surface concerns with accommodation to reality. At a deeper level, issues of psycho-cultural development are more precisely understood in relation to the problem of *self-enclosed relations to reality catering to wish-fulfillment*. This psychological problem is also expressed figuratively in terms of the prohibition against incest. Both narcissism and incest represent, among other things, states of psychical self-enclosure.[60] Cultural structures such as exogamy provide vehicles for transcending this closure and lack of differentiation. These forms create a variety of resources for other-directed, symbolically mediated relations. Thus self-development does not occur by paring down subjectivity to a neutral "mirror of nature." Freud's exposition shows that symbolic worlds are intrinsically linked with the formation of ethically oriented modes of existence, including capacities for self-reflection and the renunciation of immediacy.

Freud's discussion of animism contains two distinct yet interconnected levels of analysis. One level concerns projections of psychical contents in the imaginary form of *spirits*; the other concerns key *spiritual* accomplishments of culture. This differentiation between two psycho-cultural modalities, paralleling the Lacanian registers of *imaginary* and *symbolic*, is explicitly indicated: "Thus man's first theoretical achievement – the creation of spirits [*die Schöpfung der Geister*] – seems to have arisen from the same source as the first moral restrictions to which he was subjected – the observances of taboo."[61] The creation of spirits is easily interpreted by Freud as the product of wish-fulfillment empowered by omnipotence of thoughts and projected on to the physical world. This would correspond to the pejorative dimensions of illusion, and to an imaginary orientation in Lacan's sense. From the standpoint of science, which presumably prioritizes accommodation to empirical reality, belief in spirits is forsaken in favor of a more functional relation to *Ananke*. Simultaneously, however, Freud indicates the relation of these illusory projections to *progressive* cultural accomplishments that foster the capacities for intellectualization (*Geistigkeit*), renunciation, and ethical capacity. The belief in spirits merges with the formation of a symbolic "spiritual" (*geistig*) realm that is constitutive of human psycho-cultural existence. Progress in *Geistigkeit*, will be a central theme of *Moses and Monotheism*, but the issues are already anticipated here. Intellectualization may enable adaptation to reality, but it also involves the development of cultural and symbolic resources historically connected with religion and ethics.

Freud's text points, albeit indirectly, to the following conclusion: *Cultural formations displace and modify narcissistic imaginary relations of immediacy to matter and to the drives*. There is an irony to Freud's postulated goal of human development as a closer, "truer" relationship to the real as fact. Contrary to this goal, it is rather the real – facticity unmediated by psychical and cultural symbolic formations – from which human beings *diverge* in becoming acculturated. To be sure, the real remains a touchstone for human activity, a realm of otherness that can intrude on psychical and cultural structures. We may recall that, in Lacan's terms, one of the factors differentiating symbolic from imaginary orientations is the capacity to respond to otherness. This responsiveness, however, occurs through renewals of the symbolic orders of given cultures based on their capacity to transcend themselves. Critical reflection is in some ways a second order of distanciation, allowing cultures to modify their governing paradigms, and to resist closure and stagnation. Thus the real is not a referent for cultural development, but rather the perpetual other. In this sense, however, the real is as inexhaustible as it is unreachable. It acts as a factor incorporated within the dynamic processes of psycho-cultural development, and not as an end at which we arrive. To postulate the real as a given that can be reached is to return to a paradigm of closure in yet another form, obscuring the creative distancing necessary to ongoing acculturation.

Once again, two conflicting paradigms are evident in Freud's arguments. The first posits material reality as a positivistically understood goal of knowledge. The second understands culture, with its mediating resources, to be constitutive of an ever-altering, humanly modified reality. Freud indicates the psycho-culturally formative effects of symbolic distancing from the real in his explication of the displacements, supplements, and doublings occurring in animism and totemism. These symbolic forms counteract the determinism of existence governed by brute force, by the immediacy of drives, and by narcissistic self-aggrandizement. This insight appears in Freud's emphasis on the developmental value of religious institutions: "These cultural products would constitute a first acknowledgment of *Ananke* which opposes human narcissism [*die sich den menschlichen Narzißmus widersetzt*]."[62] What exactly is this necessity that opposes narcissism? The pressures of material reality are one, but not the only, factor in human development. The processes of distanciation from narcissism are more complex than a gradual disillusionment of the infantile orientation of omnipotence of thoughts. These processes involve cultural vehicles: language, ideals, and values that foster intra-psychic transformations. The reference to culture opposing narcissism underscores the effect of these forms in altering the orientation of the individual from being primarily drive-based and self-centered to acculturated, with all that this entails.

Totem and Taboo touches on essential problems related to the function of cultural forms fostering intellectual and ethical capacity. This recognition reappears throughout the text. For example, Freud asserts that "the mental life and cultural level of savages have not hitherto had all the recognition they deserve." Part of this lack of recognition is the application of the derogatory blanket categorization of superstition to complex psycho-cultural processes and formations. As Freud states, "even under the animistic system advancements and developments took place which are unjustly despised on account of their superstitious basis." The heart of the advancements experienced by the practitioners of animism is that "they have made an instinctual renunciation [*Triebverzicht*]."[63] Here, again, a major theme of *Moses and Monotheism* is indicated. In the later text the concept of renunciation comes to express a variety of interrelated psycho-cultural transformations involving modification of relational modalities. Thus in Freud's exposition the animistic worldview is welded to the constitution of a moral order in culture enabling the capacity to conceive and act in accordance with shared ideals and values. Freud's account discloses a different model for subjective development than that of the scientific myth of progress. It presents a more differentiated picture of cultural formation than can be subsumed under the rubric of reality-testing.

Freud's critical attitude toward animism and projection is connected with his method of revealing the latent content behind the manifest levels of given phenomena. In this respect he refers to a procedure of discerning "concealed reasons" behind the rationalizations of religious and cultural forms.[64] This one-dimensional application of a hermeneutics of suspicion is prominent in both *Totem and Taboo* and *Moses and Monotheism*. Freud's reductive analysis is like a hypostatized version of the procedures of dream interpretation. As applied to religious cultural phenomena, the latent is understood in the positivistic sense of an underlying material truth graspable in itself. Nevertheless, the manifest/latent mode is not necessarily reductive, and may be fruitfully employed in conjunction with theories of overdetermination and polysemy. Freud's text opens the question of how displacement and other creative symbolic processes are constitutive of culture and subjectivity. Yet, his overt level of questioning remains focused on the literal source and meaning of psycho-cultural productions. Issues concerning the symbolic are collapsed into the real, returning us to the problem of origins.

The sacrifice: from the real to the symbolic

In the fourth essay of *Totem and Taboo* Freud addresses the problem of how more comes from less – that is, how higher-order psycho-cultural formations emerge from beings essentially governed by the primary processes of the id. At the literal level of causal explanation, a peculiar type of event is required as the necessary transformative catalyst.

Once again, Freud argues against an innate horror of incest, for this would be equivalent to an innate sense of morality producing restrictions on drive activity. Freud's consistent anti-idealistic opposition to built-in moral capacity is expressed in passages such as the following from *Civilization and Its Discontents*: "We may reject the existence of an original, as it were natural, capacity to distinguish good from bad."[65] What *is* innate, in agreement with psychoanalytic findings concerning individuals and confirmed by the initial restrictions of cultural existence, is incestuous desire. To be sure, such arguments are connected with an overall picture of the human condition informed by a reductive, biologistic model. However, Freud's psycho-cultural inquiries repeatedly transcend the confines of psycho-biology. Symbolic forms, ethical capacity, and the formation of ideals can no more be *traced back* to innate psycho-biological tendencies than they can to innate spiritual principles. Their existence requires an interplay of inner and outer, indicating an ongoing constitution of subjectivity within culture. Thus Freud's anti-idealism leads him to pursue an *interpersonal* account of the emergence of an ethical sense within symbolic cultural worlds.

Freud returns to the question of how the symbolic structures that modify drive activity might have originated: "We are ignorant of the origin of the horror of incest and cannot even tell in what direction to look for it."[66] However, Freud proceeds to venture what he calls an "historical" response to the problem. Here, as well as in the more elaborated pronouncements of *Moses and Monotheism*, "historical" is synonymous with past events constituting the underlying latent content of religion and culture. These putative events explain both the *source* and the *meaning* of higher-order psycho-cultural developments. However, as I have indicated, it is more fruitful to understand Freud's hypotheses in *narrative* and even *mythical* terms. His histories represent an intertwining of literary, speculative, and scientific imagination. Approaching the material in this manner is compatible with Freud's own views concerning the intuitive psychological insights of poets, writers, and artists. Moreover, it is significant that Freud frequently evinced awareness of the role of myth-like formulations in scientific endeavors to grasp the unrepresentable.[67]

The very form of Freud's historical account in *Totem and Taboo* is constituted as a narrative composition employing material from several heterogeneous sources. We may recall that Freud himself retrospectively refers to this procedure as a *construction*. Indeed, the method of construction is not unlike the myth-maker's *bricolage* noted by Lévi-Strauss.[68] Further, there is a de-literalization of the constituent components of the Freudian account engendered by their recombination within a new context. In both *Totem and Taboo* and *Moses and Monotheism* some of the components appropriated by Freud may have historical significance, but recombination and recontextualization transform their nature and open new levels of meaning. They display a metaphorical disclosiveness relevant to psycho-cultural dynamics rather than a literal reference to events.

The first component of the *bricolage* is Darwin's theory of the primal horde. In this account the most incipient human organization is structured by the power of the dominant male, who monopolizes the females and keeps the less powerful males in a state of privation.[69] This construction is particularly congenial to Freud. It is founded on relations of libido and brute force, and it lends itself to Oedipal readings in terms of father and sons. Moreover, it shows a parallel with the laws of totemism because, as Freud points out with reference to the work of Atkinson, "the practical consequence of the conditions obtaining in Darwin's primal horde must be exogamy for the young males."[70] The mythic origin figuratively portrays a pre-humanized state in terms of the absence of social and symbolic structures. This condition falls under Lacan's category of the real as "beyond the symbolized." As one commentator notes, "in *Totem and Taboo*, this primary period of the Real is attached to the concepts of the primal horde, the primal scene, the primary process, primary repression, primitive man, primal words, and original sin."[71] The origin is empty, and points by contrast to the constitution of humans *as human* in a dynamic occurring within language, symbolization, and socialization. What is cultural, linguistic, and, ultimately, human is differentiated from – other than – the real.

On the literal level, the next requirement of Freud's account is that it logically explain the connection between Darwin's dominant male and the animal ancestors of totemism. We have seen that the mechanism of displacement has already been invoked in this respect, and extensively developed with reference to neurotic practices and fixations. Here Freud reinforces the coherence of his plot structure by introducing instances of animal phobia, as exemplified in the case of "Little Hans." This 5-year-old boy developed such a fear of horses that for some time he was hardly able to set foot outside the house.[72] Freud offers a general explanation of such phobias: "It was the same in every case: where the children concerned were boys, their fear related at bottom to their father and had merely been displaced onto the animal."[73] Again, the motive for displacement is seen to reside in the ambivalent feelings of the Oedipus complex: "The child finds relief from the conflict arising out of this double-sided, this ambivalent emotional attitude by displacing his hostile and fearful feelings on to a *substitute* for his father."[74] Analogously, then, and operating according to the same psychical mechanisms, the totem comes into being as a displacement of the primal father.

In invoking animal phobias, Freud's analogical procedure seems welded to the limited explanatory goals at the surface of his text. However, the psycho-cultural dimensions of his inquiry can be clarified by introducing Julia Kristeva's alternate analysis of the case of Little Hans. Kristeva de-literalizes a Freudian interpretation that simply replaces one object (the horse) with another (the father). She develops an understanding of phobia as designating and giving form to a *nameless* fear with a symbolic – or, more precisely, imaginary – object. As she states, "By means of the signifier of the phobic object, the 'horse,' it calls attention to a *drive economy in want of an object* – that conglomerate of fear, deprivation, and nameless frustration, which, properly speaking, belongs to the unnameable." Kristeva thus sees phobia as a "metaphor of want as such."[75] Symbols emerge in response to the inherent lack characterizing the level of the drive, the real. Their source is not a literal event, object, or person, but the unformed, unstructured, and hence potentially terrifying nature of the drive economy.

Kristeva introduces the term *abjection* to characterize the breakdown of meaning occasioned by threats to identity, system, and order. As she puts it, "the phobic has no other object than the abject."[76] This non-referent is not directly nameable, and hence requires indirect, displaced, symbolic expression. Symbolization can be pathologized, however, falling under the category of imaginary orientations that seek to fill or cover over lack and anxiety with a definite referent. Hence Kristeva describes "the phobic person as a subject in want of metaphoricalness," and relates this to "fetishist denial."[77] In fixating on a specific substitute object, fetishism represses the irreducibility of lack, and the open-endedness of both desire and symbolic activity. It inhibits a working-through of abjection by means of symbolic tools (such as metaphor) and welds the phobic individual to a fearful association with the substitute object. If we apply Kristeva's analysis to Freud's, the latter may be seen as tracing a process in which symbolic forms (including those characterized by imaginary, fixating tendencies) respond to emptiness on the level of the real as drive.

This de-literalized interpretation of animal phobias allows us to follow Freud's analogical procedure with added insight. Proceeding from the model of displacement from father to horse in the case of Little Hans, Freud postulates a parallel latent referent behind the manifest symbol of the totem animal:

> If the totem animal is the father, then the two principal ordinances of totemism, the two taboo prohibitions which constitute its core – not to kill the totem and not to have sexual relations with a woman of the same totem – coincide in their content with the two crimes of Oedipus, who killed his father and married his mother, as well as with the two primal wishes of children.[78]

But who is the father and what is the evidence of his murder? Answers to these questions occur with the final component in the mythic *bricolage*. This is taken from "Robertson Smith's hypothesis that the sacramental killing and communal eating of the totem animal, whose consumption was forbidden on all other occasions, was an important feature of totemic religion."[79] This hypothesis not only forms the link to the postulation of a desire to "murder the father," but provides a trace of just such an occurrence at the prehistorical origin.

Commenting on this hypothesis, Freud incidentally points out some of the relationships between *sacrifice* and acts of *renunciation*. However, these comments are rudimentary and are made secondary to another issue Freud wishes to emphasize. He refers to sacrifice as "the sacred act *par excellence*," and points out that the term "originally had a somewhat different meaning, however, from its later one of making an offering to the deity in order to propitiate him or gain his favor. (The non-religious usage of the word followed from this subsidiary sense of 'renunciation'.)"[80] The association between sacrifice and renunciation is reiterated later in the text. Freud notes that the original meaning of sacrifice and its connection to the totem feast were forgotten, and sacrifice "became a simple offering to the deity, an act of renunciation in favor of the god."[81] Here we can see two aspects of sacrifice. On one side, it is the victim who is sacrificed – that is, murdered. Conversely, it is the sacrificers who give something up, who undertake an act of renunciation. Something extant, some tangible thing, is relinquished in the name of a cultural ideal and law, and this is constitutive of a transformation in the psychical economy and topography of human subjectivity.[82] However, Freud bypasses the issue of psychical renunciation, which will be crucial to his analyses in *Moses and Monotheism* and is significantly developed in that text. Instead, Freud proceeds to highlight indications of a kinship between sacrificers and sacrificed – pointing to the imagery of a father-and-sons dynamic: "It can be shown that, to begin with, sacrifice was nothing other than 'an act of fellowship between the deity and his worshipers'."[83] The point is re-emphasized a few pages later: "In other words, the sacrificial animal was treated as a member of the tribe; the sacrificing community, the god and the sacrificial animal were of the same blood and members of one clan."[84] This emphasis on blood relations reinforces the claim that what is behind the representation is of the order of a family conflict. Preoccupation with analogies to the literally understood Oedipus complex and a focus on establishing causal origins obscure psycho-cultural insights of a different order.

By the time Freud produces his historical explanation it is tremendously overdetermined in its multiple sources and in its range of signification. The famous narrative construction of the primal parricide explaining the origins of totemism is created mainly by linking Darwin's primal horde with Robertson Smith's account of the totem meal. The plot structure is also governed by a panoply of psychoanalytically formulated observations and mechanisms:

> One day the brothers who had been driven out came together, killed and devoured their father and so made an end to the patriarchal horde. United, they had the courage to do and succeeded in doing what would have been impossible for them individually....Cannibal savages as they were, it goes without saying that they devoured their victim as well as killing him. The violent primal father had doubtless been the feared and envied model of each one of the company of brothers: and in the act of devouring they accomplished their identification with him, and each one of them acquired a portion of his strength. The totem meal, which is perhaps mankind's earliest festival, would thus be a repetition of the

criminal deed, which was the beginning of so many things – of social organization, of moral restrictions and of religion.[85]

Here the primal drives of love and hate are juxtaposed in the sons' relation to the father, indicating a typical Oedipal ambivalence: "They hated their father, who presented such a formidable obstacle to their craving for power and their sexual desires; but they loved and admired him too."[86] The suppression of the sons' sexual fulfillment by the father engenders hate; hence the eventual parricide. But the co-present love engenders feelings of remorse and ultimately of guilt. These emotions, the basis of a moral sense, create the need for some form of expiatory activity. Thus the "commemoration" represented by the totem meal is at once a displacement, a symbolic acting-out, and a ritual appeasement of guilty conscience.

The narrative of the primal father serves to gather together into a condensed mythic representation many of the key themes and insights of the preceding three essays of *Totem and Taboo*. It provides an explanation for the origin of the incest taboo, as well as for the emotional ambivalence present in relations to taboo objects. Its explanatory mechanisms function according to the principles of displacement (from father to totem) and projection (with guilt feelings acted out in relation to a realm of fantasy beings) found in animism and sympathetic magic. In describing creative cultural processes, Freud's account has recourse to the same productive mechanisms evident in both the dream work and in symptom formation – that is, condensation, displacement, representation or symbolization, and secondary revision. At the same time, numerous features problematize Freud's account as fact: its speculative quality, its assembling of heterogeneous fragments, and its formation according to psychoanalytic principles. The event loses its causal explanatory status by virtue of being constructed retroactively on the basis of the functions it seeks to explain.[87] Yet, failing as explanation, Freud's myth becomes instead a figure for the functioning of psycho-cultural processes that exceed cause and effect.

Even when it is analyzed as a myth, it bears noting that Freud's narrative is formulated in entirely male terms. The triangular relationships in the individual Oedipus complex are downplayed in favor of more dyadic relations. The role of women, except as sexual objects on the margins of a conflictual dynamic occurring between father and sons, is virtually eliminated. This restricts the symbolic range of Freud's pseudo-historical account. Nevertheless the narrative remains psychologically revealing. In some ways, the father takes over the roles of *both* mother and father (and this undifferentiated quality is indicative of his status as "pre-symbolic," that is, as representing the real). Noteworthy is the relation of ambivalence that includes both love and hate, attraction and repulsion, in relation to the sole figure of the primal father. Hence the father is both love object and competitor – a twofold status which in the standard model of the Oedipus complex is shared by mother and father.

Here, again, it is instructive to juxtapose Freud's imagery with Kristeva's related account of the breaking with the semiotic or maternal *chora*. The overarching dynamics expressed in the Freudian narrative are paralleled, and their psycho-cultural significance clarified, by Kristeva's analysis. In her version predominantly female imagery is used to designate the pre-symbolic condition represented by Freud's primal father. In conjunction, the two accounts de-literalize the male and female imagery and highlight a mutual reference to the pre-symbolic real. Thus Kristeva defines the *chora* as "a nonexpressive totality formed by the drives and their stases in a motility that is as full of movement as it is regulated."[88] The *chora* represents a psychical condition, inferred retrospectively but never known as a subjective position as such, "in which the linguistic sign is not yet articulated as the absence of an object and as the distinction between real and symbolic."[89] Acculturation requires distanciation, both intra- and extra-psychically, mediated by language and symbolic tools. Kristeva describes this formative process as "a series of separations...relating to fusion with the mother." These characterize "the struggle each subject must wage during the entire length of his personal history in order to become separate, that is to say, to become a speaking subject and/or subject to Law."[90]

Kristeva follows Freud in drawing upon anthropological observations to explicate psycho-cultural processes. Indeed, she extrapolates directly on Freud's formulations and explicitly associates the maternal *chora* with the primal father. Kristeva also develops the theme of a necessary distancing from the real and from relations of immediacy. She refers to the image of *murder* as expressing the "founding break" that constitutes the speaking subject within a symbolic order. "In all known archaic societies," she states, "this founding break of the symbolic order is represented by murder...Freud reveals this founding break and generalizes from it when he emphasizes that society is founded on complicity in the common crime."[91] Sometimes symbolized as "father," sometimes as "mother," sometimes as *chora*, what is in effect sacrificed is an undifferentiated relation to the real.

The psycho-cultural resonances developed by Kristeva clarify and amplify many aspects of Freud's narrative. For example, the transition from the real to the symbolic father engenders an *increased* power and value in the latter. In Freud's words:

> The dead father became stronger than the living one had been [*der Tote wurde nun stärker, als der Lebende gewesen war*]....What had up to then been prevented by his actual existence was thenceforward prohibited by the sons themselves, in accordance with the psychological procedure so familiar to us in psychoanalyses under the name of "deferred obedience" [*nachträglichen Gehorsams*].[92]

This graphically illustrates the displacement of the real by the *supplement* of symbolic, social reality with its formative ethical structures (that is, Lacan's Name-of-the-father). Symbols and ideals do not merely evade the harsh reality of material events, but are intrinsic to cultural processes constituting the speaking subject. In Kristeva's words, "sacrifice…indicates that all order is based on representation: what is violent is the eruption of the symbol, killing substance to make it signify."[93] Subjectivity remains undifferentiated without the intervention of some form of language, and in language experience of things is always distanced and mediated. The point is furthered by a Lacanian psychoanalyst, who states that "The Name-of-the-father represents the transcendence of the Symbolic order over the living existence of the real subject."[94] Thus Freud's "primal parricide" needs to be translated from the language of the real into that of the symbolic, and in these terms it expresses a psycho-cultural transition from a predominance of the real to that of the symbolic.

The *transcendent* status of the symbolic is indicative of a realm of values and ideals qualitatively informing psycho-cultural reality. Human existence is structured, quite literally, by that which *is not*. This theme has also been explored by Jean-Joseph Goux, who develops insights derived from Lacanian thought. He asks:

> What do we observe in the paternal register but that the mediation of the father is possible only to the extent that what functions as father is excluded from the world of other individuals, that is to say, is *killed*, functions only as the "dead Father," who rules only provided that he is departed from the group of people, that is, expelled into transcendence?[95]

Overall, Goux's arguments remain poised between an *historical* analysis concerning how cultures are formed – albeit one that is de-literalized in relation to Freud's formulations – and an account of how values and symbols *function* in culture. The latter dimension is emphasized here. It is precisely in not being "real," being distanced and dissociated from particulars, that values can function as universals. Goux elaborates the point in stating that "one element from the group is promoted to the role of exclusive and common mirror of values, arbiter of evaluations – the universal equivalent."[96] The primal father is an example of a particular that is displaced from its "horizontal" relations to other particulars in being elevated to the paternal metaphor, the Name-of-the-father. As Freud states, "it became possible for an ideal to emerge [*es konnte ein Ideal entstehen*] which embodied the unlimited power of the primal father."[97] While Freud seems to be arguing that the ideal is a *substitute* for the father, the ideal actually operates on a qualitatively different level and involves a different symbolic relation to reality. If we invert the cause-and-effect paradigm, the father becomes a *symbol* for cultural values.

What kind of views are discernible in the interstices of Freud's text, and to what degree are they antithetical to his manifest arguments? Certainly, even in discussing the cultural formation of ideals, values, and universals, there is no need to disavow Freud's anti-idealism in the strict sense of the term. Distancing from immediacy, from the real, is mediated by cultural structures governed by "universal equivalents" transcending particularity. These representations governing psycho-cultural transformations are not reflections of ideal entities existing in themselves. According to Goux, representations of ideals take shape in relation to the order of extant things, wherein particulars are symbolically elevated to the status of universal equivalents representing values. This is quite in accordance with Freud's general argument that ideals and values arise within contingent psycho-cultural dynamics, and that they therefore include *pathologized* features. One of the problems of cultural history becomes the literalization, fixation, and fetishization of the images associated with ideals. As Goux notes, when this occurs "the general equivalent becomes an alien medium, an independent third party." Goux connects this process of alienation, which traverses individual and cultural existence, with "the imaginary aspect of the reification of the symbolic."[98] This indicates how imaginary needs for closure and objectification continually reassert themselves in the psycho-cultural sphere. A universal, then, *fails* to function as such when it becomes a fixed, inflexible norm, frequently related to reified ideal entities disconnected from human experience. People become both attached to and conditioned by such ossified ideals, relinquishing critical, reflective, and transformative relations with cultural structures. In this regard, cultural values can become distorted by a combination of imaginary needs and power relations. The aggregation of these influences sustains closed, fetishistic relationships to symbolic forms.

The latent insights of *Totem and Taboo* may be supplemented by further clarifying the nature of psycho-cultural ideals and universals. An excellent discussion of the issue is provided by Luc Ferry and Alain Renaut. In their definition "the universal does not mean some norm...in the name of which violence is done to the particular." If, as they argue, the distinguishing feature of human beings "is nothing but freedom, if it is the ability to wrench free of multiple codes that constantly threaten to imprison individuals, the idea of universality is the horizon within which this wrenching occurs."[99] These arguments are quite compatible with Freud's and extend the meaning of the latent insights of his text. They forgo postulating fixed and reified transcendentals and universals, but indicate a *universalizing* capacity related to cultural ideals. These can have a liberating and transforming effect on human beings by generating symbolic mediation and distancing. This distanciation occurs in relation to both the real and the imaginary, with the latter being indicative of tendencies to literalize and fixate on particular symbolic constructs to the exclusion of others. As Ferry and Renaut summarize, "it is only through abstract universality that we can get away from all the particularisms whose absolutization in the form of *false universal* leads to the plan of exclusion."[100] The abstract universal uses specific symbols and terms to indicate shared ideals, whereas the false universal fixates on the specificity of the given symbolic media to the exclusion of others. Potentially, universals do not designate one particularized code among others, but form the reflective horizon against which particular claims to universality are measured. Symbolic forms can convey a movement toward universality, understood as a critique of closure and particularism associated with imaginary and ideological fixation. They can serve as guidelines for movement toward more encompassing, differentiated psycho-cultural perspectives with qualities of greater flexibility and inclusiveness.

In terms of the literally construed narrative, Freud has "explained" how morality, symbolization, and cultural structures come into being:

> Society was now based on complicity in the common crime; religion was based on the sense of guilt and the remorse attaching to it; while morality was based partly on the exigencies of this society and partly on the penance demanded by the sense of guilt.

However, beyond the more literal explanatory level, Freud's narrative describes how acculturation involves a transition from existence based on force and immediacy, to one informed by ideals. The theme of idealization is further elaborated with the image of the bonding of the brothers. This also expresses a movement away from incestuous closure, alienated narcissism, and relations of immediacy, to mediated symbolic, social relations. A chain reaction of supplementary idealization, in which more encompassing universals are formed, is also indicated:

> To the religiously-based prohibition against killing the totem was now added the socially-based prohibition against fratricide. It was not until long afterwards that the prohibition ceased to be limited to members of the clan and assumed the simple form: "Thou shalt do no murder."[101]

Beyond the explanatory hypotheses, what is indicated in Freud's account is the *status* of humanization or anthropogenesis (*Menschwerdung*) as necessitating symbolic forms that mediate a relation to values.

In this regard, Wallace notes the psychoanalytic view that socialization involves a diversion of libido from infantile to social aims. That is, socialization also involves intra-psychic transformations. The key process is the introjection of the ego-ideal represented by the patriarch. This is symbolized in the acts of slaying and "cannibalistic" consumption.[102] It should be emphasized that the formation of the agency of the super-ego, characterized by introjection of the ideal, is intrinsic to the capacity for sublimation. These themes will be extended in *Moses and Monotheism* with reference to capacities for idealization and renunciation. It is only in the later text that such insights into acculturation, far in excess of Freud's surface conclusions and seeming intentionality, will be further developed.

Totem and Taboo contains important constructive insights into psychocultural phenomena associated with religion. However, Freud's critical analyses of religious formations cannot be dismissed. One aspect of this appears in the following summation, which complements *The Future of an Illusion*'s focus on infantilism: "Totemic religion arose from the filial sense of guilt....All later religions are seen to be attempts at solving the same problem."[103] Freud's historicized explanation for specific cultural pathologies related to guilt and obsession may fail as such. Yet the expressed links between authority, infantilism, and guilt remain psychologically illuminating. Indeed, constructive critique is an essential dimension of the psychoanalytic contribution to understanding cultural forms and processes. The question that arises concerns the *nature* and *goals* of that critique. Freud's concerns with traumatic experience, and with related manifestations of guilt, anxiety, and infantilism, are not predicated on the literal truth of his historical constructions. Rather, his arguments address core problems in psycho-cultural formation and development, appearing as imaginary closure and related obsessional activity. When Freud's account is *de-literalized*, it points insightfully to the trauma of symbolic distancing, to the fetishization of symbolic media, and to personal and cultural pathologies related thereto.

A more questionable component of Freud's critical analysis emerges from his reiterated emphasis on the events underpinning cultural production. Significantly, the attempt to remain on a literal, causal-mechanistic level of explanation necessitates one of Freud's most outlandish hypotheses, the postulation of a collective mind with inherited transmission of memory.[104] This problem reappears in *Moses and Monotheism*, and I will discuss it in that context as indicating a lack of clarity concerning social reality and cultural transmission of traditions and worldviews. Toward the end of *Totem and Taboo* Freud raises the possibility that the factors behind cultural displacements involve wishes and psychical reality, and concern psychical trauma related thereto. Nevertheless he concludes with an insistence on the literal deed.[105]

The text depicts a qualitative transformation from relations to the real unmediated by cultural reality, to psycho-cultural formation within symbolic structures. This is portrayed in pseudo-historical terms but has reference to the status of the individual developing within a cultural dynamic. The latter is constituted in displacements, supplements, symbolism, and idealization. Freud's attempts to "reconstruct the real" actually provide a narrative scaffolding for psycho-cultural inquiry. These views coalesce with Lacan's arguments that the real is only an inference, something which is posited as originary but is itself meaningless. Only when the real, representative of immediate presence and external force, is *sacrificed* (displaced, de-literalized, supplemented, and symbolized) do the language and laws constitutive of human culture and human psychological reality become internalized. The point is not to escape the circular relation of individual and culture by positing an origin, as Freud seeks to do, but to enter into the circle, as Hans-Georg Gadamer might say, to understand its significance. This concerns the status or function of culture in the experience and shaping of reality along lines that involve ideal and ethical components. Hence we move from the problem of *origins* to that of *origination*, i.e. to the processes of becoming within which human existence takes shape. These are the first indications of how questions concerning the nature of religion and morality, and how they function in human existence, become manifest in covert and unexpected ways in Freud's accounts.

Chapter 4

Moses and Monotheism
The trauma of symbolization

Unluckily an author's creative power does not always obey his will: the work proceeds as it can, and often presents itself to the author as something independent and even alien.[1]

More originary hypotheses

Totem and Taboo provides an originary myth that, while failing to explain how cultural symbol systems arise, illustrates their formative and, indeed, humanly constitutive qualities. Within the terms of Freud's inquiry, acculturation occurs by means of processes of displacement, projection, and symbolization. Thus the cultural world-building found in animism, magic, and religion provides vehicles for far-ranging differentiations and transformations of the personality. These include an ethical orienting of subjectivity governed by structures mediating differentiated relations along lines of value.

In certain ways, *Moses and Monotheism* constitutes a structurally parallel, supplementary narrative that reflects on the input of monotheistic religious forms (i.e. symbolically articulated worldviews, ideals, ethical systems) into acculturation. On the surface *Moses and Monotheism* still conceives of the question of origins literally and historically. It renegotiates this theme with respect to "the origin of monotheist religions in general."[2] In this endeavor Freud draws upon hypotheses taken from Breasted, Sellin, and others. Of course, the ensuing reconstruction, or narrative myth, has more points of intersection with history than do the constructions of *Totem and Taboo*.[3] This has led to ongoing controversy regarding the historical accuracy of the theories and, most particularly, Freud's personal attitudes toward Judaism.

Especially problematic are Freud's hypotheses concerning the Egyptian heritage of Moses. These postulations have elicited the outrage evident in Martin Buber's lament: "That a scholar of so much importance in his own field as Sigmund Freud could permit himself to issue so unscientific a work, based on groundless hypotheses, as his *Moses and Monotheism*, is regrettable."[4] More recently, W. W. Meissner has summarized the scholarship related to the historical emergence of Judaism. He concludes that the hypothesis of a pure Egyptian monotheism imposed on the Jewish people "cannot be maintained in the face of contemporary views of biblical history."[5] Similarly, Yosef Hayim Yerushalmi notes that *Moses and Monotheism* "has been rejected almost unanimously by biblical scholars as an arbitrary manipulation of dubious historical data and by anthropologists and historians of religion as resting on long outmoded ethnological assumptions."[6]

While agreeing with critiques of *Moses and Monotheism* as an historical work, Yerushalmi concurs with the present analysis in arguing that the text is best approached on *alternative* levels. For him, however, this new approach entails "treating the book as a psychological document of Freud's inner life...."[7] In undertaking this task, Yerushalmi has amassed evidence of a lifelong positive relation to Judaism on Freud's part. However, Yerushalmi's work makes little headway in providing a detailed rereading of *Moses and Monotheism* itself. He chooses instead to reflect on the text indirectly, through insights gathered from other, primarily biographical, sources. This extra-textual material augments the present reading, insofar as it indicates tensions and qualifications occurring between the surface postulates of *Moses and Monotheism*, and other evidence from Freud's life and thought.

In a different vein, Jan Assmann has discussed *Moses and Monotheism* as part of an ongoing tradition in Western thought, in which Moses is addressed as "a figure of memory" rather than a figure of history.[8] He notes that, while there is evidence to support Moses's Egyptian background, his own concerns are with the *role* of this image in cultural memory. Thus Assmann argues that Freud's postulating the Egyptian origin of Moses served to "deconstruct the murderous distinction" between Jew and non-Jew.[9] According to this argument, in the face of rising anti-Semitism in central Europe in the 1930s, Freud's postulation of an Egyptian Moses sought to undermine the special status of the Jews that made them an object of perverse hatred.

However, the present inquiry is not primarily concerned with the history of religions, with biography, or with cultural memory and imagination. Rather, my hermeneutical concerns are directed towards more strictly psychoanalytic issues. The focus is the yield of the text *in its depiction of the nature and function of religious dimensions of psycho-cultural existence*. While this theme intersects with analyses of specific, exemplary religious forms, its referent is *psychodynamic* rather than historical. Freud's text portrays human subjectivity as necessarily interlinked with cultural forms characterized as religious (that is, as offering resources for modifying existence in relation to symbols and ideals). Therefore, in bracketing historical concerns my guiding question becomes "what does the text signify?" rather than "what is its signified?" In taking this approach, I argue that surface intentional preoccupations with historical signifieds mask psycho-cultural insights of a different order.

A precedent for my approach has been established by Julia Kristeva, who also notes the problematic nature of the historical scholarship on which Freud's manifest formulations are predicated. She therefore sees the main value of the text as residing in its status as "a narrative construction, a story, a fiction created by Freud himself."[10] This fictive dimension stands apart from historical truth, the level with which Freud remains manifestly preoccupied. Unfortunately, Kristeva does not proceed very far in developing the possible fictive meanings of the text. However, further clues concerning the nature of this fictive dimension are offered by Lacan. In commenting on "the astonishing work that is *Moses and Monotheism*," he refers to the "duplicity of its reference." The second-order or fictive level of reference is not systematically elaborated by Lacan. However, he provides a guiding thread in pointing to this as concerning "the No/Name-of-the-Father in its signifying function." Additionally, Lacan connects this symbolic function with "a structuring purpose that appears to be a sublimation."[11] Later in the same work, Lacan offers further comments that cast additional light on the second-order significance of Freud's text. Lacan notes that both *Moses and Monotheism* and *Totem and Taboo* have a mythic quality, and that they are thematically connected. He then indicates the nature of this shared theme in stating that "the function of the Father is a sublimation that is essential to the opening up of a spirituality that represents something new, a step forward in the apprehension of reality as such."[12] In other words, Lacan indicates the relevance of Freud's speculations to issues of qualitative psycho-cultural transformation. With the detailed interpretations of the text developed in this and the following chapter, Lacan's somewhat impressionistic remarks will increase in significance.

Moses and Monotheism contains a great deal of technical metapsychological material. However, many of the relevant psychological insights occur in narrative and symbolic form. The interplay between metapsychological theory and narrative construction makes the text an especially rich (if challenging) resource for psychoanalytic cultural reflection. Psychoanalytic views of subjectivity predicate psycho-cultural formation and transformation upon temporal dynamics. Hence a narrative form is well suited to portraying subjective development as dynamic, interactive, and unfolding within cultural structures. There is no need, however, to conflate the narrative with literal events occurring in historical time. This should be kept in mind in engaging Freud's postulate – offered as "a first historical foothold" but cleverly constructed from bits of etymological evidence, current speculation, and psychoanalytic deciphering – that Moses was an Egyptian.[13]

Assmann may very well be right in linking Freud's postulation of the Egyptian origin of Moses with a desire to undermine anti-Semitism. However, in my view Freud's hypothesis also serves a clear *narrative* function. Freud seemed to think in terms of options between material and historical truth (as is articulated later in his text). If the self-understanding of a divine, revelatory origin of religious postulates is not literally (or, to use Freud's term, materially) true – and Freud insists that it is not – then the option for him seems to be a causal-reductive origin with a material basis. The theory of Moses's Egyptian origin reflects an ongoing desire to postulate material, non-ideal bases for psychical and cultural higher-order developments. Here, once again, there is a definite convergence with the manifest goals of *Totem and Taboo*.

The hypothesis of Moses's Egyptian heritage serves to link the great patriarch to a prior ideal structure – the original monotheism of the Aten religion. This is described as "a strict monotheism, the first attempt of its kind, so far as we know, in the history of the world."[14] The Aten religion is the fruition of tendencies at work among the Egyptian priesthood "in the direction of developing the idea of a *universal* god and of emphasizing the *ethical* side of his nature."[15] Freud highlights the connection of this god with the ideal principles of *truth* and *justice*. The transition from a magical polytheistic universe to a religious one, as postulated in the first two stages of the developmental scheme of *Totem and Taboo*, is here encapsulated and explained within a particular historical-cultural situation. Thus in summarizing the three main features of the Aten religion Freud notes its profound contrast with the prevalent Egyptian polytheistic and magical cults: "In the first place, everything to do with myth, magic, and sorcery, is excluded from it." Second, all representation of the deity is reduced to the single prosaic image of "a round disk with rays proceeding from it," which was a first indication of monotheistic iconoclasm. Third, "there was complete silence about the god of the dead, Osiris."[16] Each of these transformations expresses a shift from a primarily *imaginary* to a more *symbolic* psycho-cultural modality.

In tracing the origins of monotheism back from Judaism, via Moses, to the Egyptian Aten religion Freud is potentially involved in an infinite regress. However, as with the marvelous *bricolage* of *Totem and Taboo*, Freud makes use of available hypotheses to construct a coherent narrative, if not a convincing history. The origins of Aten monotheism are explained by Egyptian imperialism and the Pharaoh forming the actual basis for models of a sole, dominant, ideal father figure. The authority of this figure also borders, in terms of the experience of the people under his sway, on an uncontested universality: "In Egypt, so far as we can understand, monotheism grew up as a by-product of imperialism: God was a reflection of the Pharaoh who was the absolute ruler of a great world-empire."[17] This is another manifestation of Freud's empiricist orientation. Ideals are imprints or ectypes of original, external, material realities. As with the primal father of *Totem and Taboo*, though on a more complex level of social organization, the authority of the Pharaoh is based on material force. The spiritual representation of this force and authority in a single God is but a displaced copy of the original worldly power. Again, the imprint of a particular great individual is found in this process: Amenophis IV, who was later called Akhenaten.[18]

As he elaborates upon the connections between Egypt and Judaism, Freud points out that the only people known to have practiced circumcision prior to the Jews were the Egyptians, adding another link to his argument:

> If Moses gave the Jews not only a new religion but also the commandment for circumcision, he was not a Jew but an Egyptian, and in that case the Mosaic religion was probably an Egyptian one and, in view of its contrast to the popular religion, the religion of the Aten, with which the later Jewish religion agrees in some remarkable respects.[19]

Interestingly, the Freudian account involves an initial rejection of monotheism by the Egyptians:

> It is not to be wondered at that these measures [e.g. repressing the plurality of deities] taken by Akhenaten provoked a mood of fanatical vindictiveness among the suppressed priesthood and unsatisfied common people, and this was able to find free expression after the king's death.[20]

The ethical ideals of monotheism are portrayed as too lofty and unattainable. Its iconoclastic exclusiveness and intolerance are insupportable by the common people, with their needs for imaginary gratification through the graphic illusions of magical and polytheistic religious worldviews.

In Freud's account Moses becomes the key transitional figure between the Aten religion and Judaism. To a certain extent Moses (originally known by an appellation such as *Tuthmosis* in Freud's reconstruction) is a messenger or mediator. He transposes an extant set of ideals from one cultural milieu to another. However, as the narrative unfolds, Moses's status transcends this mediatory function. He is described by Freud as being "in a high position and a convinced adherent of the Aten religion, but, in contrast to the meditative king, he was energetic and passionate." This character analysis is an important part of Freud's fantasies concerning Moses as a "great man" and is also intrinsic to the narrative movement of Freud's construction. With the collapse of Aten, Moses seeks a second people as recipients and vehicles of monotheistic ideals: "Under the necessity of his disappointment and loneliness he turned to these foreigners [a Semitic tribe] and with them sought compensation for his losses. He chose them as his people and tried to realize his ideals in them."[21] Thus there is a further set of links established in the process of "imprinting" ideals. A specific personality is part of the transmission and, ultimately, the formation of the tradition. In Freud's psychodynamic narrative Moses's personality is operative both in the shaping of monotheistic ideals and in their assimilation or introjection:

"Nor can the possibility be excluded that some of the character traits which the Jews included in their early picture of their God – describing him as jealous, severe and ruthless – may have been at bottom derived from a recollection of Moses."[22] Here Freud accentuates Moses's volatile personality. The latter is important for the *affective* dimensions involved in the introjection of ideals (that is, Moses is both feared and admired; he makes a powerful impression on his followers on more than one level). The portrayal of Moses as passionate also takes on greater significance through his capacity to *channel* that passion. Ultimately, Moses represents capacities for renunciation and sublimation that are, in Freud's view, essential psychological effects of monotheism.

In Freud's account a series of causal connections is established: imperialism, Pharaoh, Aten religion, Moses, monotheistic God of the Jews, and subsequently of the Christians and Muslims. Ultimately, the primal father is also invoked as another precursor, so that, strangely, there is an inherent, recollected prototype of an empirical imprint from primeval times that accompanies and supplements the secondary Egyptian ectopia. This pluralization of originals is not without significance; it further undermines the literal, linear presentation of the narrative and indicates its symbolic, overdetermined dimensions. Although Freud's own relation to Judaism was complex, and perhaps ambivalent, the postulation of the Egyptian origins of Moses serves a definite purpose in the narrative argument and has little to do with disparaging the Jewish religio-cultural achievement. (The irreducible psycho-cultural value of this achievement is, as we shall see, repeatedly emphasized by Freud.) In narrative terms, on the diachronic level the alien origin of monotheistic ideals allows Freud to introduce a profound, disruptive, and traumatic tension in the psychodynamic, interpersonal, and cultural processes by which Hebraic monotheism emerged. Synchronically, the narrative describes processes of acculturation involving an intrusion of the ideal and symbolic into the real and imaginary. This intrusion creates an ongoing tension and trauma resulting from living *between* matter and spirit, or between drives and ideals. There is tension in the interplay between the alien religion, of which Moses is the vehicle and exemplar, and the Hebrew people in their pre-monotheistic condition. This account illustrates both the higher-order processes of idealization, renunciation, and sublimation, and some pathological by-products of their implementation.

Textual and psychological vicissitudes

At the end of the second book of *Moses and Monotheism* Freud undertakes a discussion of textual distortion. An inquiry that has so far been developed by juxtaposing historical information and speculative hypotheses is now augmented by a more characteristically psychoanalytic endeavor. The biblical texts are read like dreams or symptoms, subject to the same mechanisms of distortion and the same split between manifest and latent contents. Again, however, the governing interpretive assumption is that what is latent has the status of historical truth or fact: "The Bible narrative that we have before us contains precious and, indeed, invaluable historical data, which, however, have been distorted by the influence of powerful tendentious purposes and embellished by the products of poetic invention."[23] This interpretive approach incorporates Freud's insistence on the "facts" of the primal father and parricide. Similarly, he emphasizes that the reconstructive, retrospective discovery of these facts forms the most significant yield of his analysis. The proclaimed value of the inquiry is restricted to historical data, to the material facts behind the textual distortions. Yet these facts are never directly available, but must be reconstructed from details and insights derived from divergent realms.

Despite the controlling paradigm of an underlying factual truth, Freud's analysis of the Bible employs fascinating and provocative interpretive strategies. Indeed, Freud's approach has repercussions for the interpretation of texts generally, including his own. One such insight is the possible significance of the non-homogeneity of texts, the *meaningful* co-presence of conflicting elements: "The text, however, as we possess it to-day, will tell us enough about its own vicissitudes. Two mutually opposed treatments have left their traces on it." Freud understands these opposing forces as primarily constituted by two attitudes among the biblical redactors: "On the one hand it has been subjected to revisions which have falsified it in the sense of their secret aims, have mutilated and amplified it and have even changed it into its reverse." This revisionism, however, comes into conflict with "a solicitous piety" that has "sought to preserve everything as it was, no matter whether it was consistent or contradicted itself." Freud is unclear as to whether the two motivations were at work in the same or different individuals, but in any case his exegesis highlights textual fault lines produced by conflict: "Thus almost everywhere noticeable gaps, disturbing repetitions and obvious contradictions have come about – indications which reveal things to us which it was not intended to communicate."[24] Significantly, this conflictual model parallels the psychological dynamics Freud indicates, somewhat later in the text, in a discussion of the ego's defense mechanisms. The ego represses, covers up, and seeks to eliminate, while the unconscious or id preserves memory traces. Hence tensions, symptoms, and clues emerge as meaningful by-products of intra-psychic conflict.[25] Similarly, gaps, contradictions, and other textual vicissitudes are not simply accidents of historical transmission and the oversights of numerous exegetical hands. Like dreams, parapraxes, and symptoms, they disclose hidden (or new) meaning irreducible to either of the conflicting agencies.

Freud's discussion of textual vicissitudes opens the possibility of reading a text beyond itself – that is, in excess of its surface arguments. He thus anticipates the deconstructionist articulation of processes of *dehiscence* and *dissemination* as features of meaning production. In addition to having some applicability to the biblical writings, it is quite fascinating that Freud provides a model of how we may read his own work. Tensions and conflicts are not simply dismissable as extraneous, accidental features of a text. They can indicate alternative readings and levels of meaning, and can overturn the predominance of literally understood surface elements. This interplay between psychological and interpretive models also has important implications for understanding relationships between subjectivity and language.

The possible insights emerging from parallels between texts and subjectivity reflect meaningfully on Freud's overall analyses of religion. However, once again this potential is curtailed by Freud's quest for literal, causal explanation. He turns in this direction by privileging a specific literary genre that governs his interpretive reconstruction of events: "In its implications the distortion of a text resembles a murder: the difficulty is not in perpetrating the deed, but in getting rid of its traces."[26] Whether intentionally or not, Freud's exegesis mimics the structure of a typical murder mystery. Freud applies an analogy that is itself modeled on the key hidden fact or deed he will ultimately discern behind the textual distortions. In some ways this analogy is more revealing than he intends. It represents how the potential of his interpretive model becomes closed and truncated, even as Freud seeks to unravel hidden levels of meaning.

Freud notes minor distortions and displacements that ensue from the desire that "every trace of Egyptian influence was to be disavowed." As part of this task, "the man Moses was dealt with by shifting him to Midian and Kadesh, and by fusing him with the priest of Yahweh who founded the religion." In addition, the rite of circumcision was detached from its Egyptian origin.[27] Of all these suppressed and repressed events, however, "one stood out, the suppression of which was enjoined by the most immediate and best human motives. This was the murder of Moses, the great leader and liberator." The murder of Moses re-enacts the rejection of Aten by the Egyptians. In addition, and more specifically, it reads into the biblical narrative a re-enactment of the original murder of the primal father: "The same thing happened in both cases: those who had been dominated and kept in want rose and threw off the burden of the religion that had been imposed on them." The Egyptians, however, waited for the death of the Pharaoh, while "the savage Semites took fate into their own hands and rid themselves of their tyrant."[28] Here Freud does not allow the text, in its heterogeneity, to signify beyond itself. It is made to refer back, if indirectly, to the causal event of parricide. In accordance with the radical empiricism operative at the surface of Freud's analyses, profound psycho-cultural transformations seem inexplicable without some intruding force originating on the level of the real. This necessitates positing an underlying primal parricide, with the ensuing trauma producing repressions and displacements. Thus, instead of elaborating upon the symbolic *death of the real*, Freud maintains the postulation of a *real death*.

What textual evidence does Freud offer to support his hypothesis of a murderous deed? Interestingly, his main reference is to the biblical narrative of the golden calf and the breaking of the tablets. Freud's interpretive argument is confined to a straightforward reversal of meaning. He asserts that "by an ingenious turn, the breaking of the tables of the law (which is to be understood symbolically: 'he has broken the law') is transposed on to Moses himself, and his furious indignation is assigned as its motive."[29] In other words, Moses's fury is an inverted projection of the murderous fury of the Hebrew people. In some ways this is the most questionable type of psychoanalytic reading, interpreting a symbol or myth by simply inverting statements into their opposites. This procedure operates along the lines of the principle that if something is denied it must be true. This approach can, of course, yield insight within the contextualized discourse of analytic practice, but it is highly problematic when applied in a routinized manner to texts.[30]

At the same time, Freud offers ideas that exceed a reductive and codified implementation of psychoanalysis to the biblical story. Indeed, while this episode seems to offer little support for Freud's manifest reconstruction, it actually displays symbolic resonances with some of his *underlying* themes. Freud had previously devoted an essay to an artistic rendition of precisely this event, "The Moses of Michelangelo." Though undeveloped, this analysis contained an important insight of a different order, one that coalesces with some of the greater themes of *Moses and Monotheism*. Thus, in discussing Freud's essay on Michelangelo's Moses, Jean-Joseph Goux notes that the key insight of the analysis concerns Moses's "checked fury."[31] That is, the depiction of Moses provides a prototype for sublimation. Goux adds another important point: there is a symbolic connection of the golden calf with the Egyptian Isis, and with mother goddesses generally. Therefore he notes that "it is strange that [Freud] does not make explicit the connection that appears to me so tremendously illuminating, between the Judaic prohibition against worshiping images and the prohibition against incest with the mother."[32] In other words, the biblical episode actually symbolizes a major psycho-cultural theme of both *Totem and Taboo* and *Moses and Monotheism*: distanciation from immediacy by means of ideals.

The golden calf story may be seen, among other things, as a prefiguration of transformations from the real (represented by gold, tangibility, fertility), through the imaginary (represented by the immediate gratifications and consolations of idolatry) to the symbolic (represented by iconoclasm and law). These transformations and conflicts were expressed mythically in Freud's analysis of the incest taboo, indicating movement away from the real, the id, and states of self-enclosure. Similarly, the image of Moses railing against idolatrous worship of the golden calf symbolizes a conflict between the requirements of universal law, and more immediate libidinous and imaginary gratifications. However, the brief analyses of "The Moses of Michelangelo" actually take the issues a step further than this. Freud argues that the sculpted figure of Moses, as rendered by the great artist, embodies not only a denunciation of idolatry, but *a further mastery of the anger accompanying outrage*. In Freud's words:

> the giant frame with its tremendous physical power becomes only a concrete expression of the highest mental achievement that is possible in man, that of struggling successfully against an inward passion for the sake of a cause to which he has devoted himself.[33]

Again, as in the primal parricide of *Totem and Taboo*, we find scattered insights into the problem of the "break with the real," intersecting with themes of sacrifice and renunciation. Such issues lead directly to concerns with higher-order cultural formations and the accompanying transformations of subjectivity. These matters become quite explicit, and are significantly developed, in the penultimate sections of *Moses and Monotheism*.

I must bypass issues of the overall textual and historical accuracy of Freud's constructions, and their sensitivity or violence to the biblical writings. Most significant for my purposes is Freud's appropriation of traditional resources in narrativizing a psychodynamic cultural process. Again, this narrative is not nearly so dismissive of religion – understood in relation to cultural and psychological existence – as the causal-mechanistic conclusions at its surface might indicate. Even in the preliminary formulations of *Moses and Monotheism* (before he develops the key themes of *Geistigkeit* and renunciation), Freud points to a special *quality* of monotheistic ideals. Whatever the nature of the "events" Freud seeks to discern behind these cultural transformations, he nevertheless understands them to be essentially meaningful and constructive:

> The Egyptian Moses had given to one portion of the [Hebrew] people a more highly spiritualized notion of god [*eine andere, höher vergeistigte Gottesvorstellung*], the idea of a single deity embracing the whole world, who was not less all-loving than all-powerful, who was averse to cere-monial and magic and set before men as their highest aim a life of truth and justice.[34]

Most significantly, the institution of these ideals becomes a source of strength and guidance in facing further existential vicissitudes. As Freud emphasizes, ideals can function powerfully and constructively in historical and personal existence: "No one can doubt that it was only the idea of this other god that enabled the people of Israel to survive all the blows of fate and that kept them alive to our own days."[35]

Trauma and the return of the repressed

Having noted the powerful *effects* of religious ideals, Freud yet remains preoccupied with the question of their underlying factual basis. In *Moses and Monotheism* the oppositional categories of manifest/latent appear most strikingly in Freud's distinction between material and historical truth, with which the text concludes. This dichotomy elaborates the theoretical and methodological underpinnings to positing primal traumas as the cause of psycho-cultural symbolic displacements. *Material* truth actually signifies the *false* literal postulates of religion, for example its claims to represent the eternal verities of a divine being. Freud refers to such claims as the "pious solution" – that is, to the problem of the abiding power of religious traditions. He continues: "we too believe that the pious solution contains the truth – but the *historical* truth and not the *material* truth."[36] In effect, Freud here juxtaposes *two forms of literalism*: that of religion, or onto-theology, and that of the scientific disciplines, positivistically construed. In this direct confrontation within a restricted framework, science undermines religion.

Nevertheless, while keeping in mind the force of these critical arguments, my concern is to explore the truth of the psycho-cultural formations (i.e. ideals) outlined in Freud's inquiry. This truth will be seen to function on a level that cannot be collapsed into either of the dichotomies within which Freud tends to confine his manifest arguments and conclusions. It resonates with narrative truth, with the strangely neglected category of *psychical reality* discussed by Freud in the *Introductory Lectures on Psychoanalysis*, with overdetermined readings of trauma, and with the interstitial status of illusion.

As noted in the previous chapter, even in earlier works on religion such as "Obsessive acts and religious practices" and *Totem and Taboo*, Freud is aware of how cultural constructs inform and mediate individual experience of reality. This awareness is more pronounced and well articulated in later works such as *Civilization and Its Discontents*.[37] The stark dichotomy between illusion and reality breaks down when the culturally constructed dimensions of human experience are acknowledged. Thus the focus of psychoanalytic cultural inquiry becomes interstitial, because its temporal and dynamic analyses cannot be collapsed into prior, given entities or forces. A similar orientation, expressed in different terms, is offered by Gianni Vattimo: "It is certain that the human world of ethics and politics at least cannot be drawn back to 'given' laws, but only to what humanity, as free, makes of itself."[38] Freud's text provides a figurative account of such open-ended formation as intertwined with ideals and symbol systems. This analysis also conjoins free and deterministic elements. Subjective agency is not relinquished; indeed, the task of psychoanalytic theory and practice (at least in principle) is to augment the reflective awareness necessary to autonomy. However, subjectivity is shown to be interconnected with both libidinal psychodynamics and the formative influence of contingent experiential factors.

Culture does not reflect a priori structures – although in a psychoanalytic view it is predicated on some innate force such as *Eros* and the tendency toward representation that characterizes psychical processes. These inner potentialities are open-ended, however, and they are empty without the interpersonal and cultural dynamics symbolized in the Oedipus complex and its Totemic and Mosaic variants. Subjective formation and acculturation always occur within relations to the Other. Freud's analyses, however, do not have precise formulations of the distinction between interactions *with objects* and *within cultural systems of meaning* at their disposal. Quite often, formative interrelations, best understood within the second category, become constricted by a more two-dimensional, rectilinear model.

Processes of acculturation are not merely ideational, but involve what may be termed, following Lacan, a dialectic of desire. These libidinal, interpersonal dimensions are evident in the dynamics of the primal horde, revolving around the ambivalence of love and hatred for the patriarch. They reappear in the emphasis on Moses's volatile personality, with parallel consequences of attachment and rejection. The affective dimension of meaningful, constitutive relations is also evident in Freud's accounts of *Eros* as a force of culture-building presented in *Civilization and Its Discontents*. In these analyses Freud argues that love and emotional bonding are as intrinsic to social formation as are utilitarian concerns. Thus the dialectic of desire occurs within intersubjective encounters that also involve contingency on numerous personal and cultural levels. Relations with particular others mediate acculturation to a significant degree, providing the actual basis for symbolic identifications. However, the inescapable contingency of these relations can contribute elements of conflict and dissonance.

Characteristically, Freud's analysis accentuates pathology. Although cultural ideals are not entirely pathologized, dissonant and dysfunctional elements are discerned in their formation and influence. These appear because culture and the acculturated subject are not givens, but developmental tasks accomplished in the face of both external and internal resistance. In terms of an inquiry into the nature and function of religion, this point is significant beyond Freud's inclination to view religion as a prime expression of pathological aspects of culture. The obsessive dimensions of religion are connected with a deeper sense of trauma inherent in psycho-cultural formation. Even in a narrative portraying the origin of ideals as imprints from an originally external, material source, their internalization and integration is conflictual. The imprint is not passively received, because we are affective beings mired in imaginary fixations. We seek to respond to emotional needs with immediate libidinous and narcissistic gratification. The ensuing fixations impede the development of an ability to defer, distanciate, renounce, and reorganize desire within cultural vehicles.

Hence there is a dimension to the engagement with ideals that is disruptive of stasis and inertia, and may be described as traumatic. In *Totem and Taboo*, Freud focused on the murderous break with the order of force, the real, as represented by the primal patriarch. Related to this break are the ambivalence and guilt that haunted the perpetrators of the crime, as well as the symbolic displacements that ensued from emotional conflict. In *Moses and Monotheism* Freud retains a mutation of these narrative elements, but supplements the analysis by elaborating on their psychically and culturally constitutive results.

We have seen that the pivotal historical truth unearthed by Freud is *the murder of Moses*. As a consequence of this act, Freud further postulates that "one portion of the people had an experience which must be regarded as traumatic."[39] The link between trauma and symbolic break with the real, also portrayed in *Totem and Taboo*, is again conflated with an actual event. The evidence Freud offers to substantiate the hypothesis of a traumatic event is what he calls "the most striking fact about Jewish religious history." This is the "yawning gap between the law-giving of Moses and the later Jewish religion – a gap which was at first filled by the worship of Yahweh, and was only slowly patched up afterwards."[40] According to Freud's findings, the Mosaic monotheistic ideals and doctrines, combined with iconoclasm and a strict ethical code, exerted their effects only after a long interval had elapsed. Thus Freud asks: "How are we to explain a delayed effect of this kind and where do we meet with a similar phenomenon?" This question leads Freud to the analogy – which ultimately approaches identity – with traumatic neuroses.[41] The intention here is to find in the temporal gap a clue that discloses its secret only in the light of psychoanalytic knowledge. The clue points to an actual historical trauma, i.e. the murder of Moses, paralleling traumas in individual experience. Despite this fixation on causal explanation, however, more complex formulations concerning trauma theory appear in Freud's analysis. Indeed, psychoanalytic inquiries into the problem of trauma are developed in significant ways. The presence of these reformulations in a text that also adheres to literal postulates that are regressive in light of psychoanalysis itself yet again points to tension and ambivalence in Freud's grappling with issues of cultural formation.

Some of Freud's theories of trauma and the etiology of the neuroses were discussed in Chapter 1. It was noted that Freud did not deny the profoundly damaging effects of traumas based on childhood seduction and abuse. However, Freud developed a position that sought to account for the general vicissitudes of human development and that transcended the original cause-and-effect trauma model. These issues become particularly relevant on the psycho-cultural level, because Freud's construction of historical traumas strives to achieve closure unrealized on the individual level of inquiry. However, the questionable status of these constructions confounds literal explanation and further highlights the symbolic significance of the account.

Important transformations and de-literalizations of the notion of the traumatic event are developed within Freud's analysis of monotheism. These appear in the postulate of a *supplementary* or *complemental* series (*Ergänzungsreihe*), "in which two factors converge in fulfilling an aetiological requirement."[42] In fact, there is no need to remain confined to two factors. Rather, the complemental series expresses the dynamics of inner and outer realities, each of which has multiple constituent features and variants. As with his earlier reformulations of trauma theory, Freud takes a middle ground that includes a spectrum of possibilities. He particularly emphasizes, however, instances in which there is an "unusual, abnormal reaction to experiences and demands which affect everyone, but are worked over and dealt with [*die...verarbeitet und erledigt werden*] by other people in another manner which may be called normal."[43] The event is constituted by a series of factors, both subjective and objective, working to supplement each other. The difference here is not between an event and its absence, but between modes of apprehension and response. The crucial theme of "working over" overlaps with the more common technical expression *working-through* (*Durcharbeiten*). Both indicate a capacity for grappling with and responding meaningfully to problems and conflicts.

The discussion of the complemental series is connected with a pluralization of the nature and meaning of traumatic experience. Freud discusses how in the paradigmatic instances of infantile trauma amnesia can occur with respect to the actual traumatic events. Substitute, displaced formations – "screen memories" – appear in their stead. These "relate to impressions of a sexual and aggressive nature, and no doubt also to *early injuries to the ego (narcissistic mortifications)* [*narzißtische Kränkungen*]."[44] This is a crucial point which might go unnoticed. It indicates a radically different *type* of trauma, one that relates to the ego's identity as fixed within an imaginary orientation. Of course, this point may be taken simply to indicate hurtful events that damage one's sense of self. But the very language of narcissistic mortifications, particularly in a text of which a major underlying theme is the possibility of *trans-narcissistic self-development*, indicates something more intricate. It highlights necessary components of pain and disruption in psychological growth. These ensue from conflicts between the self-enclosed narcissistic ego and possibilities that exceed and challenge it. It is important that such conflictual experiences are primarily interpersonal, yet they should be differentiated from abusive events *per se*. The latter take us into the realm of specific instances of psychopathology related to personally damaging experiences. The more general issue of personality development, however, involves traumatizing encounters with ideals derived from the Other. This is a key underlying theme of Freud's reflections on religion.

Freud expands on the issue of narcissistic mortifications with a brief portrayal of the problems of the *defense ego*. This aspect or quality of the ego is not compatible with the reality-testing function; rather, it comes into conflict with external reality because of its protective, narcissistic self-enclosure. These are the features leading to Lacan's association of the ego with the imaginary register and hence with resistance to subjective transformation. Freud portrays the problem of narcissistic mortifications as a wounding and scarring of the ego, leading to a defensive constitution too rigid and inflexible to respond meaningfully to ongoing existential encounters:

> The reactions and alterations of the ego brought about by the defense now prove a hindrance in dealing with the new tasks of life, so that severe conflicts come about between the demands of the real external world and the ego.[45]

Here Freud clearly indicates the way in which rigidity and closure inhibit creative responses to life experience. His analyses point to a need for *disruptions*, *displacements*, and *decenterings* of the ego as part of continuing psychological growth. On this level the problem is not avoiding a trauma or curing the consequences of a psychical trauma in a manner modeled after physical illness. Rather, the issue is that of possible meaningful responses to traumatizing dimensions of human existence. A defensive reaction takes the path of closure and fixation. A progressive response takes the form of symbolizing, creatively appropriating, and transforming the organization of the personality. As the Lacanian analyst Bruce Fink states, "Trauma implies fixation or blockage. Fixation always implies something which is not symbolized, language being that which allows for substitution and displacement – the very antithesis of fixation."[46] These two paths, regressive fixation and progressive symbolization, are seen by Freud to be simultaneously present in monotheistic religion, just as they were in totemism. They express two aspects of culture and two modes of being of the subject-in-culture.

In Freud's historical narrative the trauma ensues from the murder of Moses. This crime is itself a reaction against the *imposition of ideals*, and this point alerts us to the underlying symbolic significance of the narrative. That is, the trauma is related to a psycho-cultural break with the orders of the real and the imaginary. The need for an external force, an Other, to catalyze the developmental dynamic that generates religion, culture, and morality also involves positing a traumatic relation to that Other. This functions like Freud's modified trauma theory, incorporating an interplay of experience and symbolization. It also displays an Oedipal dynamic, encapsulating a process involving a crisis resulting from resistance to cultural authority. In effect, Freud's reflections mix trauma and Oedipal theories concerning vicissitudes of libido in relation to cultural authority figures. This mixture conjoins these theories concerning the etiology of the neuroses into something more complicated. In *Moses and Monotheism* the traumatic experience is constellated by a dynamic of *psychical* oppression (Moses imposes ideals that are too lofty), rejection and repression (symbolized by the slaying of the paternal figure and the forgetting or covering over of this crime), and return of the repressed (the displaced emergence of cultural ideals modeled after the teachings and the personality of the "great man" as cultural vehicle), accompanied by pathological formations such as guilt and compulsiveness.

Moses and Monotheism takes up aspects of *Totem and Taboo*'s narrative and replays them in a different context. In so doing, the later text extends and develops psychoanalytic insights of the earlier. What poses as an independent set of historical events is better understood as furthering a symbolic narrative, reflecting the developmental intersections of psychology and culture. One key moment in this repetition and extrapolation is the slaying of the patriarch. This is portrayed as an actual event that reduplicates a previous actual event:

> Fate [*das Schicksal*] had brought the great deed and misdeed of primaeval days, the killing of the father, closer to the Jewish people by causing them to repeat it on the person of Moses, an outstanding father-figure. It was a case of "acting out" instead of remembering, as happens so often with neurotics during the work of analysis.[47]

The invocation of "fate" is a particularly telling transgression of causal explanation. It masks the rather obvious presence of narrative repetition. The myth of the primal horde and the slaying of the primal father acts as a paradigm informing the narrative model for the slaying of Moses. Yet, resisting de-literalization, Freud asserts the reality of the primal parricide as the "phylogenetic source" of the later repetition.

In the course of his discussion Freud notes two groups of effects of traumatic experiences, which he categorizes as *positive* and *negative*. This description has nothing to do with qualitative evaluation, but highlights features of *presence* and *absence* in the pathological consequences of trauma. Thus positive effects "are attempts to bring the trauma into operation once again – that is, to remember the forgotten experience or, better, to make it real, to experience a repetition of it anew." These effects are summarized under the headings of "fixations to the trauma and as a compulsion to repeat."[48] By contrast, "the negative reactions follow the opposite aim: that nothing of the forgotten traumas shall be remembered and nothing repeated." This reaction manifests itself in compulsions such as avoidances, inhibitions, and phobias.[49] In each case a compulsive form of behavior becomes prevalent in the group or individual. Internal psychical factors become determinative of experience of the external world, the most extreme form of this being psychosis. It is important to note, following Freud, the role of the defensive ego in instituting repression, and the understanding of symptoms as the return, in distorted and displaced form, of that which the ego has repressed.[50] This supplements Freud's discussion of "narcissistic mortifications." It points toward Lacanian associations of the ego with imaginary closure – that is, with blocked personal development.

Freud offers the following formula to summarize the pattern evident on both individual and cultural levels: "Early trauma–defense–latency– outbreak of neurotic illness–partial return of the repressed."[51] The collective version of this model of the etiology of neuroses and psychoses is the basis for some of Freud's most critical assessments of religion. The analogy between the cultural experiences indicated by the textual and other proffered clues, and obsessional neuroses related to trauma allows Freud to assert that "we believe that we can guess these events and we propose to show that their symptom-like consequences are the phenomena of religion."[52] There is no point in attempting to refute Freud's arguments that there are symptom-like, pathological elements to the variegated phenomena of religion. Indeed, we shall follow Ricoeur in affirming that Freud's critical, iconoclastic stance is crucial to a contemporary, demystified understanding of religion.[53] Still, emphasis on a material event that causes pathology obscures creative processes of displacement and symbolization in the formation of culture and subjectivity.

The murder of the *present* or actual patriarch represents a breaking with the real and with imaginary orientations. This engenders the institution of something displaced, deferred, different, difficult: symbolically mediated ideas, ideals, and values. In commenting on the text, Kristeva argues that "the Freudian narrative...exists to give meaning, motivation, and plausibility to certain 'universals' that recur throughout this narration: *alterity, strangeness, disavowal of identity, separation and murder.*" As she somewhat cryptically concludes, "the murder of the father is thus inscribed within the linguistic sign."[54] As in *Totem and Taboo*, the phenomenon of an augmented deferred effect comes into play. After the murder/rejection, in Freud's words, "the *tradition* of it remained and its influence achieved (only gradually, it is true, in the course of centuries) what was denied to Moses himself."[55] Freud sees the emergence of cultural ideals as akin to neurotic repression and the return of the repressed. However, like his earlier emphasis on the enhanced power of the "dead father," this analysis also shows that linguistic and ideational forms take on a life of their own, becoming independent of material sources and forces. Ultimately, Freud's account indicates how symbolic systems are more psychically effective and important than is the order of the real. Their *truth* resides in the ethical quality of their formative effects, rather than in conformity with facts.

Freud's analysis of traumatic experience is overdetermined and, indeed, unnecessarily confused and misleading. It actually takes two paths, of which the misleading one tends to be highlighted. The two paths in the analysis of the trauma are: (1) the mixture of psychical and existential factors in constituting traumatic experience (the complemental series); and (2) the positing of a phylogenetic trauma that leaves memory traces. This indicates the co-presence of the cause-and-effect, deterministic thinking characteristic of the first trauma theory and the later interactive or dynamic view involving creative psycho-cultural activity. Tensions between the seduction and Oedipal theories, and within the spectrum of meanings of the Oedipal model itself, are never decisively resolved. We may recall that the Oedipus complex represents a structural universal with innumerable cultural and individual variables. It is necessarily open-ended because it involves particular relations, both interpersonally and culturally. Yet the search for explanatory primal scenes, modeled after the initial seduction theory, persists. In this regard, Jean Laplanche notes that "throughout the whole of Freud's work, an endless series of oscillations concerning seduction and, more generally, the reality of primal sexual scenes may be discovered."[56] Indeed, Freud could not relinquish the goal of grounding psychical processes in some historical or material reality – the origin or primal scene. As Laplanche summarizes, "despite the incessant oscillation between such terms as *reality, pure imagination, retrospective reconstruction*, etc., Freud will reaffirm with increasing insistence the *fact* of seduction."[57] This recurring emphasis on etiological fact appears in analyses of individual case histories, most emphatically that of the Wolf Man, as well as throughout the cultural-historical analyses. It is, however, almost always in tension with counter-tendencies qualifying and subverting the literalism of Freud's postulates.[58]

Tensions between literalism and acknowledgment of the creative psychical processes, found in the theory of individual neurosis, are also evident in Freud's approach to cultural issues. For example, in the *Introductory Lectures*, after discussing the importance of psychical reality, Freud immediately proceeds to introduce "primal phantasies." These are the result of a "phylogenetic endowment" derived from primeval collective experiences, related to a "prehistoric truth."[59] Here psychical reality attains a status equal to physical reality in individual existence, only to become predicated upon an original physical trauma (projected on to the mythical prehistoric time of *Totem and Taboo*). By proposing an explanation based on definite events inscribed on the mind and transmitted hereditarily, Freud is led to embrace highly problematic theories. In *Totem and Taboo* this takes the form of the hypotheses concerning the biological transmission of learned experience.[60] In *Moses and Monotheism* the inheritance of experience based on the primal parricide is retained, with other questionable historical hypotheses concerning Moses's Egyptian origins, the murder of Moses, and so forth, grafted on to it. That is, the pattern of the phylogenetic trauma resurfaces in several forms, necessitating deeds based on the same paradigm to stimulate further progress in displacement, symbolization, and idealization.

After indicating that the transformative effects ensuing from the murder of Moses are linked to its traumatic component, Freud re-enacts the dilemmas of the early years of psychoanalysis by taking the trauma literally. Indeed, he intermixes this analysis with the theory of the neuroses, engaging in the following hypothesis, which is regressive in relation to psychoanalytic theory:

> When we study the reactions to early traumas, we are quite often surprised to find that they are not strictly limited to what the subject himself has really experienced but diverge from it in a way which fits in much better with the model of a phylogenetic event and, in general, can only be explained by such an influence.[61]

Here the insights into psychical reality, fantasy and narration, vicissitudes of the developmental process, and the conflictual interactions of Oedipal dynamics disappear in favor of pre-psychoanalytic views. The crude temporal extension of the literally understood trauma necessitates the insupportable positing of phylogenetic transmission of memories. This line of thought is summarized in Freud's assertion that "men have always known (in this special way) that they once possessed a primal father and killed him."[62]

The arguments concerning phylogenetic transmission are obviated by attention to the *cultural transmission of ideational and symbolic forms*. This option, avoiding the simplistic extremes of idealism and materialism, highlights the latent issue of the function of symbolic realms in constituting and mediating human experience. However, Freud appears to be quite attached to the "firm ground" offered by the postulation of inherited memory. He actually attempts to rule out the explanatory viability of cultural transmission with the following argument:

> A tradition that was based on communication could not lead to the compulsive character that attaches to religious phenomena. It would be listened to, judged, and perhaps dismissed, like any other piece of information from outside; it would never attain the privilege of being liberated from the constraint of logical thought.[63]

This argument entirely misses the point that culture and tradition shape and inform the subject's sense of self and reality long *before* the formation of autonomous critical faculties.

Indeed, the constitutive qualities of tradition, whatever their constraining and delimiting features, also enable the formation of a rational self that may ultimately reflect critically on particular cultural forms, such as religious ones. Tradition embodies the legacy of existing cultural realities formative of the subject and preceding the development of rational capacities. Its contents may later be subjected to rational critique, but it has already taken hold on a deeper level. This begins, at the very least, with the identifications of the mirror phase. Cultural worldviews enter more deeply and intricately into subjective existence with the acquisition of language, as illustrated in the introjection of super-ego functions on the basis of affective dynamics. In negative terms, this deep-rootedness of tradition contributes to the persistence of seemingly irrational and outmoded culturally supported worldviews. Interestingly, this is a point Freud himself develops at length, and persuasively, in *The Future of an Illusion*, where it is used to support the elimination of early religious indoctrination.[64] By contrast, Freud's later argument against the power of tradition not only hypostatizes reason and grants to it a self-transparency that psychoanalytic findings severely qualify. His argument also neglects fundamental psychoanalytic insights concerning the primacy of the drives, and the secondary emergence of the ego and rational faculties within interpersonal, culturally mediated processes.

Literal trauma was found by Freud to be a possible, but not the sole or a necessary factor in the etiology of individual neuroses. This is because psychical reality is a mixture of experience and representation, with subjectivity being linguistically formed and engaging events within frameworks of meaning. On the cultural level, the hypothesis of specific traumatic events associated with symbol-formation is gratuitous. Yet, just as individual fantasies have a psychological, if not a literal truth, so too does Freud's account. The insights which follow from postulating a traumatic event are not vitiated by shifting to a model of overdetermined, relational processes, in accordance with the complemental series. On one level, Freud's analysis posits the retroactively constructed event to explain specific anomalies, such as contradictions and lacunae in the biblical texts and the temporal gap in the institutionalization of Mosaic ideals. Yet other features of religion are drawn into the orbit of this explanatory mechanism, and these are actually of greater interest. The wider issue concerns the existence and function of psycho-cultural ideal forms and, accompanying them, pathological features such as compulsive behavior and extreme, unwarranted guilt. Illustrating that traumatic moments occur within processes of acculturation related to distanciation from immediacy furthers our understanding of *both* dimensions of religion and culture.

De-literalizing the traumatic event releases its possible symbolic meanings in relation to issues of distanciation in psycho-cultural existence. Even without the normative judgement that culture is pathologized, Freud requires the traumatic element in his theory of origins. This is because something more than a constant pressure of authority seems necessary for the development of culture. That is, a break, an absence, a negation, indicative of displacement of immediacy, is operative in the emergence of ideas and ideals. Again, these accounts symbolically depict temporal cultural processes on a generalized or abstract level, but they also speak to issues of the formation of individual psychology *as* psycho-cultural. The trauma becomes indicative of a rupture with an existing state of affairs, a loss of a certain type of problematic yet reassuring mode of relation. Identity on an imaginary level is comforting and safe, yet also confining and repressive. For subjectivity to develop, the initial identity must be displaced, must, as it were, *die*. We can understand this in terms of phylogenetic or ontogenetic development, but again the point is that it tells us something about the function of symbolic systems in human existence.

In *Totem and Taboo* the primal father represents the hegemony of the real. His displacement on to the symbolic father represents cultural processes such as exogamy, totemism, symbolization, and also the internalization of moral authority (the super-ego). There is a partial transition to the symbolic, mediated by the imaginary, indicated here. The literalization of the totem, the fixations and compulsions analogous to phobia, the recourse to the wish-fulfilling, fetishistic practices of magic indicate imaginary residues akin to both illusion and ideology on psycho-cultural levels.

By comparison, Moses is far more of an ideal figure. In Freud's reconstruction he represents a transition from imaginary modes of being to a more rigorous institution of the symbolic order both culturally and psychologically. The second narrative is predicated upon the first, which may be part of Freud's need to invoke phylogenetic memories. In any case, *Moses and Monotheism*, failing as and irreducible to historically accurate reconstruction, discloses the vicissitudes of higher-order psycho-cultural development: renunciation, idealization, and sublimation.

Chapter 5

Moses and Monotheism
The psychodynamics of *Geistigkeit*

The great man and the symbolic order

Throughout *Moses and Monotheism* Freud remains preoccupied with causal-mechanistic explanations for the remarkable transformative power of ideals. In this, his skepticism concerning the autonomy of intellectual, ethical, and creative capacities is quite evident. Nevertheless, meaningful ruptures in the reductionistic program continue to appear, leading to further articulation of latent themes concerning psycho-cultural development.

There is a peculiar moment when Freud aligns himself with *mytho-poetic* views of the origins of culture and religion, in opposition to "modern scientific views." Freud notes that his focus on the singular activities and effects of Moses as the "great man" (*der große Mann*) verges on the mythicization of cultural origins in the deeds of paradigmatic figures. As Freud asks, "Is not a hypothesis such as this a relapse into the mode of thought which led to myths of a creator and to the worship of heroes?" By contrast, Freud points out that "the modern tendency is rather towards tracing back the events of human history to more concealed, general and impersonal factors ....Individuals have no other part to play in this than as exponents or representatives of group trends."[1] Here it is precisely the mechanistic leveling of human existence into anonymous forces to which Freud objects. Though he sounds defensive, Freud nevertheless remains adamant in his departure from "scientific" approaches to these psycho-cultural issues. To substantiate his position, he invokes the principle of *overdetermination*. Freud emphasizes that "each event seems to be overdetermined and proves to be the effect of several convergent causes."[2] This approach indicates complex mixtures of forces, experiences, and potentialities at play in cultural formation, cultural reality, and individual existence. Overdetermination allows us to understand the influence of singular individuals in conjunction with "the importance of the general and impersonal factors." As well, overdetermination relates to overinterpretation, indicating the plurality of methods and models that may shed light on different aspects of these phenomena.

Freud's characterization of the "great man" as a vehicle of cultural formation supplements the symbolic dynamics clustered around the images of the primal parricide, sacrifice, and renunciation in *Totem and Taboo*. Thus, like the primal father, Freud's Moses is more an overdetermined symbol than a portrayal of a distinct historical individual. He is, nevertheless, a very *human* figure, and this quality resists the impersonal and deterministic perspectives Freud wishes to avoid. A relevant discussion of such mythicization or symbolization, with specific reference to the figure of Moses, is offered by Paul Ricoeur. In *The Symbolism of Evil* Ricoeur employs the expression "Mosaic fantasy" to describe idealizations of the figure of Moses as the embodiment of "the law for all times and all men."[3] Ricoeur indicates how an outstanding historical figure becomes a condensed symbolic referent for highly valued personal and cultural qualities. Freud may be seen to offer a psychoanalytic version of a Mosaic fantasy. In this, what is most significant for the present inquiry is not the way in which Freud may be projecting fantasies of an idealized father figure on to Moses. Rather, I am interested in the way the image of Moses becomes a paradigm for religious dimensions of acculturation. He is both a cultural representative and a subjective embodiment of the highest cultural forces.

In extrapolating from Moses to the effects of culturally significant individuals, Freud uses outmoded patriarchal language for expressing pivotal interpersonal relations within symbolic forms. We might equally well speak of "great women," or substitute the gender neutral "towering individual," to more adequately characterize those who enter significantly into processes of psycho-cultural formation. Therefore, without neglecting the specific qualities of Moses as a religious and cultural founder, it is the symbolic features transcending particularity that I wish to emphasize. That is, the Freudian image of Moses is also a paradigmatic representative of all significant individuals connected with acculturation along religious and ethical lines.

Freud refers to his present investigations as demonstrating "the transcendent influence of a single personality."[4] This influence occurs on two interrelated levels: establishment and modification of cultural forms and internalization of these forms in subjective acculturation. On the historical level, a multifaceted, inclusive view of psycho-cultural developments connected with religious formations is indicated. Such a view would respect and incorporate the findings that have appeared in textual, archeological, historical, and other areas of inquiry. Yet in its sensitivity to the distinctly human and interpersonal features of the phenomena of symbolic and cultural formation, an overdetermined view resists reductive, cause-and-effect explanations. This complexifying orientation appears in Freud's insistence that "thus we reserve a place for 'great men' in the chain, or rather the network [*Netzwerk*], of causes."[5] The image of a network has a different quality than does a linear deterministic paradigm. It indicates multiple overlappings that require, but supersede, their constituent elements.

In this case the great man emerges as a singular force in the creation of Hebrew monotheism. As a key component in cultural networks, towering individuals absorb influences and transmute them to a higher order of cultural development. In Freud's portrayal the two factors constitutive of the great man are his personality, and the ideas and ideals he conveys.[6] Here we might build on Ricoeur's comments concerning the Mosaic fantasy as a condensed representative of the symbolic order. In similar terms, Jacques Derrida describes such a paradigmatic cultural figure as a "man of the law;" one, indeed, who represents "the law itself, the law above other laws," that is, "a law beyond legality."[7] In her or his ideas and personality, the great person embodies the law, associated with symbolic modes of being in Lacan's sense. This *law* is irreducible to codification in fixed, particularized terms, and operates on the level of what may be called "cultural universals." These take the form of ideals, such as justice, that act as resources for transcending not only motivations governed by immediate ends, but also the dead letter of legalism. The ideal of justice, for example, does not exist in itself but becomes a question directed at particular codes and actions claiming to be just. The ability to act as a vehicle for cultural structures, conjoined with individual reflection and questioning within specific variable circumstances, is what constitutes the great person. Such people become living instantiations of symbolic realities and possibilities.

As his portrait of Moses takes shape, Freud also makes passing reference to the pluralization of paradigmatic individuals at work in the formation of monotheism. The Pharaoh Akhenaten is invoked as a precursor to Moses, and the Jewish Prophets are mentioned as successors who furthered the tasks that will subsequently be described as the advance in *Geistigkeit* and the capacity for drive renunciation.[8] These pluralizations do not detract from Freud's admiring portrayal of Moses, but they tend once again to indicate networks and overdeterminations. The transcendent dimension embodied in the great man resists and qualifies explanation on the level of causal links and influences. Yet neither does Freud invoke notions of the "genius" standing outside of cultural processes. Thus this transcendent quality is manifest beyond singular individuals as such, in ongoing cultural interaction to which many contribute and within which they themselves are formed.

Freud supplements the characteristic of embodying and conveying ideals and values (that is, *law* in the broader sense shared by Lacan, Ricoeur, and, it would seem, Derrida) with references to what he calls the *paternal* qualities of great men. He highlights the features of authority, decisiveness of thought, strength of will, and, above all, autonomy and independence.[9] Needless to say, all of these qualities are attributed to Moses, joined by a further reference to "his wrathful temper and relentlessness." There is, in this Freudian Moses, a peculiar combination of lofty ideals and all-too-human emotions. Far from being incompatible, however, these combined features reflect psychoanalytic insights into the necessary mediating function of emotion-toned, interpersonal relations in processes of acculturation. These human relations provide the basis for symbolic identification.

Thus Freud's recognition of the force of ideals is complemented by a more characteristically psychoanalytic emphasis on the concrete impact of particular human influences on personality formation. This point indicates the relevance of Freud's reflections for more general issues of cultural transmission of ideals in the acculturation of subjectivity. Interactions with significant others provide the medium within which ideals and values can be *emotionally engaged*. In this view, individuals who embody values allow for identifications with and internalizations of cultural forms through interpersonal communication. That is, acculturation occurs in a living manner, in which there is a possibly transformative dynamic at the deepest affective as well as cognitive levels of the personality. In Freud's non-idealistic view, values arise and are transmitted within human relations, and so, at least potentially, they remain in play, subject to critique and comparison. This serves to offset tendencies to fix them as abstract, frozen universals.[10]

Freud conveys a sense of relations to cultural representatives as catalyzing capacities for idealization involving symbolic forms. An interpersonal dynamic is configured around the great person as the embodiment of ideas and ideals. The great person indicates how inner potentiality becomes manifest and intra-psychic differentiation occurs through interpersonal relations. It must be emphasized that such relationships are of a different order than encounters with objects or things. (Use of the term "object-relations" to describe formative interactions with persons is unfortunate in this regard.) Even when indicating the formative influence of individuals encountered directly in daily life, the great person's reality is not so much physical, material, literal, of the order of the real or fact, but already psychically complex, and culturally informed and transformed. Symbolic features, such as law and value, are brought to presence in such individuals. What is important is the force and quality of personality, and its interconnection with the ideas and ideals conveyed.

The overdetermined notion of the great man indicates, all at once, the contributions of singular individuals to cultural transformation, their role as vehicles of cultural transmission, and serves as a figuration of the symbolic orders of given cultures. In traditional cultures, at least, these processes and the ideational forms they engender appear within the framework of religious structures and the individuals who represent them. In these religious dimensions of culture, symbolic and ideational realities enter into the formation of acculturated human personalities. In a contemporary context, this religious dimension also has broader manifestations within secular artistic, philosophical, and other terms. That is, the religious function need not be restricted to the cultural forms classified as religious *per se*. The cultural features that find classical representation in the religions become at least partially translated and diversified in contemporary existence. The abiding quality encapsulating these cultural variables is the ability to influence personality development in ways including meaningful symbolic and ethical dimensions. Moreover, many of the formative influences in contemporary culture occur through communicative media, rather than through direct contact with persons. Many issues emerge from this point, but one comment can be made in the present context. That is, just as the *embodiment* of ideals in great persons provides a vehicle for identification and introjection, so too might the *tactile* and *sensory* aspects of media. In other words, the problem of acculturation extends beyond cognitive assimilation of norms and values. These are points that are particularly germane to Kristeva's work, and I will return to them in the final chapter.

Freud's reflections on the great man illustrate the interplay between affective relations, identification, and the formation of super-ego functions. Relationships with others in the deepest, formative sense elide the strict demarcation between inner and outer. Identity is mediated by otherness that involves shared, interpersonal, cultural, and symbolic space. This is quite different from the simple, erroneous mixing up or category error found in states of delusion, and attributed by Freud to animism and religion. Again, this is also a very different dynamic process from that of ego, representative of *Logos*, encountering external reality in the form of *Ananke*. In this regard, Freud's analysis supplements some of the latent insights of *Totem and Taboo*. It reveals creative projections and introjections – mediating inner and outer – to be involved in acculturation. These processes foster *symbolic remove* – that is, distanciation from immediacy through language. These are issues that become paramount in the culminating sections of Freud's text. Thus there are intrinsic connections and resonances between the formulations concerning the great man and subsequent arguments, wherein key psycho-cultural contributions of monotheism are traced under a variety of rubrics and concepts.

The realm of *Geist*

The crucial section of *Moses and Monotheism* on "The advance of intellectuality" (*der Fortschritt in der Geistigkeit*) further articulates distancing from embeddedness in materially determined existence (the real) through symbolic processes. This distancing is described in various ways, but in each instance it is precisely deterministic relations of immediacy that are offset by cultural symbolic forms.

One instance of symbolic distancing occurs in a further discussion of the self-understanding of the Hebrews as chosen people being independent of material and empirical confirmation. Thus Freud questions "why the people of Israel, however, clung more and more submissively to their God the worse they were treated by him."[11] Actually, two different issues are conjoined in this question, both of which preoccupy Freud over the remaining course of the book. One issue concerns pathological manifestations of excessive, unrealistic guilt related to a "punishing super-ego." The other point, more directly germane to the present inquiry, concerns the formation of a semi-autonomous spiritual-intellectual psycho-cultural realm. One facet of this latter development is that the reality and power of ideals become partially detached from direct evidential support. Material rewards, tangible proofs and gratifications, are not required to sustain the identity of the people and their faithfulness to their God. Freud has previously mentioned the survival value of this self-understanding, linked as it is to the ideals of monotheism. A crucial point emerging here is that distanciation from material confirmation is correlated with a sense of self and world, and a capacity to act based on *principles* rather than on responses to sensory stimuli. This theme is repeated and augmented by the following focal points of Freud's analysis.

Freud highlights *Mosaic iconoclasm* as the most prominent vehicle for superseding modes of existence oriented by immediacy. In discussing this injunction, Freud indirectly offers an alternative interpretation of the golden calf story, contrasting it with his previous analysis. "Among the precepts of the Moses religion there is one that is of greater importance than appears to begin with. This is the prohibition against making an image of God – the compulsion to worship a God whom one cannot see."[12] The psycho-cultural implications of this prohibition are profound:

> For it meant that a sensory perception was given second place to what may be called an abstract idea – a triumph of intellectuality [or spirituality] over sensuality or, strictly speaking, an instinctual [or drive] renunciation with all the necessary psychological consequences [*einen Triumph der Geistigkeit über die Sinnlichkeit, streng genommen einen Triebversicht mit seinen psychologisch notwendigen Folgen*].[13]

The transformations linked with *Geistigkeit* are not merely based on externally imposed prohibitions. They are simultaneously transformations in worldview and in psychological modality; these exhibit a more encompassing range than can be conveyed by the English term "intellectuality." On the other hand, a hypostatized notion of spirit, as opposed to matter, does not capture the sense of the psycho-cultural processes Freud traces.

The conjunction of *spirituality* with a capacity for drive renunciation indicates something beyond merely *relinquishing* specific forms of drive satisfaction. It expresses an ability to withstand the lure of the tangible and immediate by virtue of *meaningful abstractions*. The capacity for renunciation is a crucial instance of the intersection of culture and psychology. It is fostered by cultural vehicles such as ideals, principles, and values, articulated within symbolic media. It engenders and is sustained by psychological consequences – that is, essential alterations in the very structure of the personality. There is also more at issue here than a demarcation of mental and physical realms. The lure of immediacy includes not only material objects, but concrete images and narcissistically gratifying fantasies; that is, immediacy includes all that constitutes the order of the imaginary in Lacan's sense. Therefore the advance in *Geistigkeit* and drive renunciation indicates alterations in subjective orientation far more subtle and constructive than can be subsumed under the categories of asceticism or world denial.

In pondering the link between religion and modified relations to phenomenal immediacy, Freud recalls his earlier treatment of "omnipotence of thoughts" in *Totem and Taboo*. Once again the repetitions within, and the narrative and thematic intersections between, the two texts are highly significant. In the previous discussion of the issue of omnipotence of thoughts, I noted that Freud tended to emphasize the *narcissistic* dimensions of this phenomenon. In particular, he highlights its overestimation of mental processes and its factually unrealistic relationship to external material forces. Yet Freud's analysis of animism and magic also indicated that omnipotence of thoughts, linked with the activity of projection, contributed to symbolic cultural world-building. Now, in portraying the advances of iconoclasm in modifying psycho-cultural ideas and ideals, Freud makes even stronger reference to the constructive dimensions of phenomena associated with animism. He emphasizes that in these cultural worldviews "*ideas, memories, and inferences* became decisive in contrast to the *lower psychical activity* which had direct perceptions by the sense organs as its content."[14] Symbolic forms and religious ideals, unprovable on the level of correspondence with material reality, are essential aspects of "the path to hominization [*der Weg zum Menschwerdung*]."[15] Thus these forms have an enormously important psycho-cultural function; they constitute *human* worlds that include some form of value. Acculturated human existence includes a "transcendent" dimension of ideas, ideals, and symbolic and narrative constructs overarching and informing existential relations. Furthermore, and most importantly, *these forms contain conceptual features resisting reification and regression to (imaginary) immediacy*. The iconoclastic prohibition is paradigmatic of this resistance.

Freud's discussion of iconoclasm is also supplemented by reference to paternity (a hypothesis based on thought processes) superseding maternity (linked to confirmation by the senses).[16] Here the point made by Goux concerning the movement from the real to the symbolic in the golden calf narrative is paralleled and supplemented by Freud's explication of a significance of the institution of patrilineage. Of course, the narrow patriarchal tenor of these arguments and illustrations is obvious. Nevertheless, the crucial point, whatever the conditioned terms and images used to illustrate it, remains that of distanciation through symbolic remove. Mediated relations to reality are intertwined with transformations of personality evinced in capacities for intellectualization or spiritualization. Freud is asserting in yet a third way the irreducible value of that which is *not* of the order of matter, fact, or empirical reality. The empiricist model of imprinting external events upon the mind is qualified and counterbalanced by awareness of creative, non-empirical dimensions of psycho-cultural realities.

At this point in the text, Freud undertakes a further discussion of animism. This religio-cultural form now takes on renewed significance in light of Freud's concerns with *Geistigkeit*. Here it becomes increasingly clear that he recognizes invaluable psycho-cultural transformations occurring in conjunction with religious projections: "Human beings found themselves obliged in general to recognize 'intellectual' [*geistige*] forces – forces, that is, which cannot be grasped by the senses (particularly by the sight) but which none the less produce undoubted and indeed extremely powerful effects."[17] Symbolic constructs, such as those of animism and other religious world-views, provide a framework, a language, for ethical and ideational activity. Symbol systems constitute a transitional realm intersecting psyche and culture. Such symbolic worlds foster the independence of mind and intellectual inquiry that reaches its paradigmatic form, for Freud, in Western science: "This too led to the discovery of the mind [*Seele*] as that of the intellectual principle [*geistiges Prinzip*] in individual human beings."[18] However, the psycho-cultural developments Freud outlines cannot be confined within a narrow rationalism, as his rendition of the process graphically illustrates. Meaningful overdeterminations of language are quite evident in the conjunctions of *mind* and *soul, intellectual* and *spiritual*.

In addition, Freud's text indicates more than one type of process occurring here. Diachronically, he reflects on the development of cultural realms or worlds of symbols, codes, ethical precepts and ideals (although this eludes the causal-mechanistic explanation Freud pursues). Synchronically, these realms are seen to be constitutive of, and inextricable from, human existence. That is, with cultural worlds there comes into being – and is affirmed as essential to our humanity – an inner realm of intellect, ethical capacity, and aesthetic and representational ability. These faculties are correlated with a scope and sense of self not equivalent to the reality-testing adaptive ego. Thus Freud strains his vocabulary to give expression to this set of faculties and capacities. The complementary terms spirit, soul, and intellect, brought into partial conjunction with the overdetermined ethical agency of the super-ego, indicate *non-reifiable and ultimately non-localizable dimensions of subjectivity*.

Is Freud's quasi-religious discourse indicative of a lapse into metaphysical postulations, antithetical both to psychoanalysis generally and to the surface components of his texts? He seems, rather, to be struggling to articulate a psycho-cultural dimension that cannot easily be incorporated into either of the oppositional categories of spirit or matter, superficially defined. Just as the realm of the real is inadequate to explain psycho-cultural existence, so too is the invocation of hypostatized, a priori spiritual factors. The tension in Freud's discourse ultimately indicates a formative interplay of forces in the constitution, and reconstitution, of cultural and psychological existence. The tension actively delineates a between space. Thus *Geistigkeit* is something of an umbrella term. It functions much as does the notion of the subject-in-process, existing within language and the symbolic, common to Lacan and Kristeva. That is, it indicates an interplay of cultural and psychological developments, incorporating and exceeding the discrete psychoanalytic agencies of ego, id, and super-ego. The text appropriates the language of religion and metaphysics, in a non-hypostatized, de-literalized form, to convey the dynamic relations mutually constitutive of symbolic systems and subjectivity. In so doing, whether intentionally or unintentionally, Freud once again opens doors to much more penetrating psychoanalytic insights into the nature of religion than those presented at the surface of his inquiry.

Yet the intermediate, symbolic domain that continually emerges in the interstices of Freud's analyses tends to be collapsed by narrower, empirically oriented arguments. It is somewhat ironic that these seemingly tougher-minded explanations are much less capable of embodying, reflecting, and illuminating the complexities of psycho-cultural existence. It is yet another manifestation of the tension in Freud's thought and writing that insights subverting narrowly reductionist orientations are offered as, ultimately, being themselves of the nature of "historical truth."

Freud's penchant for grounding his inquiries in historical explanation is partially related to his awareness of regressive and pathological features in religio-cultural developments. Here again the analyses reflect back on those of *Totem and Taboo*: concomitantly with the emergence of symbolic worlds, there are established superstitious imaginary worlds in which spirituality is hypostatized. Spiritual dimensions of existence are literalized and concretized, for example, as places populated by beings responsive to human wishes. Thus, having noted the overlapping of cultural ideals and the awakening to mental/spiritual forces, Freud returns to the "category error" of animism: "Now, however, the world of spirits [*Geisterreich*] lay open to men. They were prepared to attribute the soul [*Seele*] which they had discovered in themselves to everything in nature. The whole world was animate [*beseelt*]."[19] This passage indicates some of the connections between the realm of spirituality-intellectuality and the belief in independently existing anthropomorphized spirits. On the level of cultural history it may be that such concretizations are the necessary imaginary vehicles of psycho-cultural formation. This would parallel the way that, on the level of subjective development, imaginary identifications form the basis for symbolic introjections. Ideally, of course, the tendencies toward fixation characteristic of these imaginary constructs would be offset by the gradual assimilation of symbolic resources, providing tools for reflective and critical capacity.

Freud's analysis tends to focus on the pejorative features of imaginary religious formations as abiding, regressive impediments to psychological maturation. Spiritual – that is, symbolizing, idealizing, and ethical – concerns are projected on to the realm of nature, becoming reified into entities called *spirits*. This confusion leads to superstitious orientations that create delusional restrictions in relations to reality. These, of course, are the problems addressed by critical and scientific thought. However, rather than seeking to eliminate symbolic forms in the name of a presumed objective engagement with reality, the task of critical thinking is altered in light of the culturally mediated experience of reality. It becomes one of sorting out the progressive and regressive aspects of these cultural forms. Thus the function of symbol systems enabling capacities for ethically informed relations requires extrication from closed imaginary representational frameworks.

In regard to the issue of constructive critique, it is significant that Freud makes a point of contrasting "spirituality" (*Geistigkeit*) with "faith" (*Glauben*). The former term seems to designate a sensibility that includes, but exceeds, intellectuality *per se*, involving, as we have seen, symbolic and ethical capacities formed within acculturation. The term *faith*, on the other hand, is viewed by Freud as "a very puzzling emotional phenomenon," which he immediately characterizes in terms of Tertullian's *credo quia absurdum*.[20] Granted, Freud offers a rather narrow view of faith, assimilating it to uncritical, naive belief. Nevertheless, the contrast between *Geistigkeit* and *Glauben* highlights the point that Freud's differentiations are more nuanced than are simplistic contrasts between religion and reason, or myth and reality. It is clear that, here as well as in *The Future of an Illusion*, mentally constricting types of psycho-cultural formations are the main object of Freud's criticism. To extrapolate: literalistic, superstitious, and imaginary orientations inhibit maturation because they weld reflective capacities to rigid and closed *false universals*. Religious symbol systems function in an imaginary mode when their language is conflated with descriptive reference to factually extant entities and forces. However, this problem is not restricted to the realm of religion *per se*. Whenever cultural worldviews become exclusive and immutable, as for example in extreme forms of nationalism, a similar problem of ideological closure occurs. The issue is less a matter of failure to correspond to empirical reality than a fixation at the level of collective identity.[21]

Psychoanalysis provides conceptual resources for pursuing the task of critically distinguishing between progressive and regressive psycho-cultural modes. However, Freud's tools become blunted when directed towards the features of religion he finds restricting, infantile, and falsifying. He asserts that "science, which came so much later, had plenty to do in divesting part of the world of its soul once more; and indeed it has not completed that task even today."[22] Granting that Freud's critical concerns remain valid, we may yet ask what does it mean to *divest the world of its soul*? Is human reality reduced to the engagement with *Ananke*, with the real? In any event, to fulfill its task adequately, science must include something like psychoanalysis. This is because differentiating and evaluating modes of culturally informed subjectivity are as important as inquiries into empirical reality. This task of psycho-cultural critique comes to the fore in Freud's analyses of religion. The question, to which I shall return, is the extent to which Freud's work on religion remains cognizant, in its critical orientation, of its difference from empirical science. Relatedly, how consistent is Freud in remaining aware of the constructive, psychologically enhancing components of *Geistigkeit* embodied in religious forms?

Especially in his summary formulations, the critical orientation modeled after natural science tends to obscure Freud's deeper, more nuanced and intricate insights. Because of the interpretive closure fostered by Freud's sweeping positivistic conclusions, the more variegated psychoanalytic attitude toward *spiritual* developments needs repeated emphasis. Throughout *Moses and Monotheism* one finds interlinking arguments and insights that reveal an appreciative attitude toward Judaism in particular, and the function of religion-like cultural ideals and universals in general. For example, returning to the topic of iconoclasm, Freud notes that "the Mosaic prohibition [*das mosaische Verbot*] elevated God to a higher degree of intellectuality [*auf eine höhere Stufe der Geistigkeit*]."[23] Here Freud connects the de-reification of cultural representations of God with an elevation of intellectual-spiritual faculties and accomplishments. Freud's appreciation of such developments appears in the following reflections:

> The pre-eminence given to intellectual labours [*geistige Bestrebungen*] throughout some two thousand years in the life of the Jewish people has, of course, had its effect. It has helped to check the brutality and the tendency to violence which are apt to appear where the development of muscular strength is the popular ideal.

Freud notes further that, while the "ideal harmony" of intellect and physique envisioned by the Greeks has been denied the Jews, "their decision was at least in favour of the worthier alternative."[24] In such passages Freud's respect and admiration for these intellectual, spiritual, and ethical accomplishments is strikingly evident.

Drive renunciation and subjective transformation

The section of *Moses and Monotheism* on "Renunciation of instinct" (*Triebverzicht*) extends the insights and heightens the tensions in Freud's analysis of *Geistigkeit*. In particular, it further analyzes the formation and functions of the dimension of subjectivity characterized by the agency of the super-ego. Drive renunciation, as Judith Van Herik indicates, is not a standard technical term in psychoanalytic theory "and cannot be unequivocally defined in terms of the psychical dynamics that underlie it." She further notes that renunciation may be connected with or connote processes of repression, suppression, or sublimation, and that it may be a conscious or unconscious process.[25] Again, the use of a term encompassing various possibilities, both developmentally creative and pathological, is indicative of the new psycho-cultural terrain into which Freud was venturing.

Freud opens this section of the text by recapitulating some of the multiple dimensions of the advance in *Geistigkeit*. It has as its concomitants a "set back to sensuality" and a raising of an individual's or people's self-regard. He argues that this advance "seems to presuppose the existence of a definite standard of value and of some other person or agency which maintains it."[26] Freud again highlights the intrusion of a qualitative dimension, occurring by means of symbolic identifications, into psycho-cultural existence. Specifically, drive renunciation is closely connected with the agency of the super-ego, and this agency also reveals a broad spectrum of functions and manifestations spanning sublimity and pathology. Indeed, the super-ego emerges as a highly overdetermined, multifaceted component of subjectivity. Internally or intra-psychically, it reflects many of the tensions and polarities contained in the cultural formations related to religion.

Freud's account discloses relationships among psychology, religion, and culture, in both their constructive-creative and pathological-compulsive forms. Here again, the limits of the ego as the core of subjectivity, and as a reality-testing agency, are indicated by Freud. As he states, given the existence of pressing instinctual demands, "the simplest and most natural thing is that the ego, which has the apparatus of thought and the muscular apparatus at its disposal, should satisfy the demand by an action."[27] One implication of this is that the ego is partially governed by the pleasure principle. Throughout Freud's writings there appear points of rupture which indicate interdependencies between the discrete agencies. One such area of intersection is that between id and ego. For example, in his essay "On narcissism" Freud indicated that the ego could become the object of the libido in states of self-love and that this made it difficult to differentiate ego instincts clearly from libido.[28] Later, in *Civilization and Its Discontents*, Freud argues "that the ego, indeed, is the libido's original home, and remains to some extent its headquarters."[29] By this time he has thoroughly revised his instinct theory, having introduced the aggressive (death) drives alongside the erotic drives. Each can become manifest in ego-activities, so that the ego is a vehicle for acting out irrational impulses. Furthermore, each drive can take the ego itself as object, so that the ego is affected by narcissistic self-love or, conversely, melancholic self-loathing. For our present purposes the dual instinct theory is less relevant in itself than are Freud's qualifications of the pre-eminence of ego functions.

In elucidating the effects of the pleasure principle on the ego, Freud further addresses the function of restricting and modifying forces that enable drive renunciation. Here it is quite evident that the ego, with its narcissistic orientations, is an insufficient and inadequate resource for this resistance. In light of this, *Moses and Monotheism* outlines two factors that may lead the individual *not* to act upon drives. The first is renunciation of an instinct because of an external danger or hindrance, the prime instance of "obedience to the reality principle." The second source of renunciation, however, is not directly related to reality-testing. It involves more abiding, far-ranging transformations of personality. Freud continues: "instinctual renunciation can also be imposed for other reasons, which we correctly describe as *internal*."[30] That is, renunciation is enabled by the internalization *and appropriation* of cultural ideals in the formation of super-ego functions. In Freud's words:

> in the course of an individual's development a portion of the inhibiting forces in the external world [is] internalized and an agency is constructed in the ego which confronts the rest of the ego in an observing, criticizing and prohibitive sense. We call this new agency the *super-ego*.[31]

Here the super-ego is associated with what can be termed, following both Winnicott and Lacan, a third, intermediate realm that intersects inner (psychical) and outer (cultural) realities. Thus the super-ego represents inner differentiation, utilizing the pluralized resources of language and culture. As Steven Marcus states, "for Freud the super-ego brings into being the higher and 'supra-personal' side of human nature."[32] This perspective offsets tendencies, especially evident in some versions of post-Freudian ego-psychology, to locate human development within the parameters of the adaptive ego.

The differentiations within subjectivity, unassimilable to the ego *per se*, qualify depictions of the super-ego as merely an internalized agency of parental and cultural authority. As regulated by differentiations within the structure of the personality, renunciation cannot be understood simply as a forced response to imposed restrictions. Nor is it synonymous with repression, in which drive activity is split off from consciousness, remaining unconscious, unaltered, and psychically dangerous. Renunciation seems rather to indicate possible *transformations in the nature of desire as a component of subjectivity*. That is, the internalized "hindrance" does not leave the overall psychical topography and modality unaltered. This intermediation refers to a different order of psychical dynamics, one also connected with processes of sublimation. As subjectivity is transformed by internalizing and assimilating ideals, so too is the nature of what is valued and desired. These transformations extend beyond the rational, reality-testing features of the ego, indicating a more differentiated view of subjectivity.

As might be expected, indications of the transformative nature of psycho-cultural processes related to the super-ego are obscured by reified, energetically oriented models. Freud focuses on the issue of substitute satisfaction in such a way as to highlight economic exchanges in sources of pleasure connected with approval or affirmation by an authority. Instinctual renunciation based on recognition of and acquiescence to external forces is mainly unpleasurable. However, "when it is for internal reasons, in obedience to the super-ego, it has a different economic effect."[33] The substitute satisfaction providing the ego with pleasure, of a sort, from internally motivated renunciations, stems from "pleasing" the internalized agency of cultural authority: "The ego feels elevated; it is proud of the instinctual renunciation, as though it were a valuable achievement."[34] The point here is not to dismiss Freud's arguments concerning the mechanisms whereby renunciation is supported by substitute satisfactions. However, the language of internalized authority also limits Freud's insight into transformations in the very structure of subjectivity. When the super-ego is construed merely as a mimetically internalized authority alien to the ego, the significance of each agency as representing *constitutive dimensions of developing subjectivity* can be overlooked.

It is not surprising that Freud does not seem entirely satisfied by his own account. He returns to the image of the "great man" and asserts that "he is precisely the authority for whose sake the achievement is carried out...in group psychology the role of the super-ego falls to him."[35] Yet the status of the patriarch is itself *dependent* on cultural advances involving intellectualization and distanciation from immediacy. As Freud states:

> the father...is only elevated into being an authority by the advance itself. Thus we are faced by the phenomenon that in the course of the development of humanity sensuality is gradually overpowered by intellectuality [*daß die Sinnlichkeit allmählich von der Geistigkeit berwaltigt wird*] and that men feel proud and exalted by such an advance. But we are unable to say why this should be so.[36]

In terms of establishing an empirical, cause-and-effect explanatory model, Freud is correct in assessing the disappointing results of his inquiry. But perhaps his portrayal of the formation of meaningful symbol systems that alter both culture and subjectivity has obviated the question of origins. Functionally, *der Fortschritt in der Geistigkeit* encompasses processes whereby relations to the external world and to internal drives become mediated by symbolically transmitted ideals. Thus spiritualization and renunciation conjointly designate attributes and capacities constituting a mediating realm that is both psychological and cultural.[37]

At this point in the text the theme of iconoclasm returns. Within this theme, distancing from material influences is further associated with distancing from determination by the drives. These links are indicated in numerous places. For example, Freud notes that "the religion which began with the prohibition against making an image of God develops more and more in the course of centuries into a religion of instinctual renunciations."[38] This association reinforces the significance of both iconoclasm and renunciation for the theme of symbolic distancing. Freud is at pains to emphasize that these psycho-cultural developments clustered about the theme of renunciation are "most intimately connected" with religion.[39] To develop these themes, Freud once again renegotiates some of the core findings of *Totem and Taboo*, particularly those that link totem worship, exogamy, and symbolic displacements. In discussing the background narrative to *Moses and Monotheism*, Freud further emphasizes the crucial feature in the nexus of formations he is analyzing in monotheistic religion. This is the link between the restrictions and renunciations of religion and "the first beginnings of a moral and social order."[40] Symbolic constructs related to cultural forms are key factors in the twin displacements (internal and external) constitutive of ethical subjectivity.

Freud also offsets the focus on mimesis of paternal authority by noting that "two different motives are at work here." *Some* prohibitions seem to carry on the will of the father; that is, they reproduce and sustain extant cultural authority. Yet the "third command" noted by Freud, the "granting of equal rights to the allied brothers – disregards the father's will." Freud refers to this as a "new order," whose symbolic structures and regulations prevent a "relapse into the earlier state."[41] *This is the antithesis of a mere repetition of the same.* It is a significantly new qualitative cultural-ethical development irreducible to a simple translation of the original authority into another form. Displacement, seemingly describing the eluding of repressing forces, actually signifies something more complicated. It relates to transformations in value connected with symbolic, ethical, and intellectual processes. Most importantly, as in the discussions of iconoclasm, cultural displacements exhibit features resisting regressive tendencies toward developmentally earlier psycho-cultural orientations. Thus displacement is again described in terms indicating correlations with sublimation.[42]

The theme of sublimation is discussed in *Civilization and Its Discontents*, where Freud more explicitly connects two key processes outlined in the pseudo-historical narratives. The first is the "replacement of the power of the individual by the power of a community," which he calls "the decisive step of civilization." The second is a "rule of law," to which all have contributed "by a sacrifice of their instincts [*durch ihre Triebopfer beigetragen haben*]."[43] Freud tends to describe this process in terms of individuals forcibly relinquishing innate drive dispositions. This, of course, is one of the overt themes of the text, in which the more intricate formulation of renunciation appearing in *Moses and Monotheism* is not as well articulated. Both texts, however, address the related theme of the formation of ideals. In this process justice, for example, emerges as an ideal with formative and transformative power. This ideal expresses and embodies orientations to the other incorporating empathy, equality, and freedom. Again, what is most clear about such ideals is that they deflect subjective motivations away from more immediate impulses and gratifications such as pleasure, aggression, and self-ishness. Such ideals, underpinning ethical principles, are predicated on acculturation. They are actualized beyond codified implementation by subjective transformations indicated in the functions of the super-ego.

Freud's inquiries also indicate that there is no exact correspondence between justice, as a regulative ideal, and any *extant* form of social order. This raises the critical issue of ameliorating existing societies, which Freud approaches in terms of *tensions* between a society and its members. According to Freud, individuals may exhibit both *regressive* and *progressive* tendencies in relation to the symbolic order and cultural ideals of their society. Freud argues that each of these tendencies creates an existential dissonance that can serve to offset societal closure:

> What makes itself felt in a human community as a desire for freedom may be their revolt against some existing injustice, and so may prove favourable to a further development of civilization; it may remain compatible with civilization. But it may also spring from the remains of their original personality, which is still untamed by civilization.[44]

These comments show how Freud's approach to the relations between psychology and culture contains potential for ethical critique. Excluded dimensions of subjectivity react upon the rectilinear structurings of socio-cultural forms. The dis-ease engendered by repressed drive activity can provide a catalyst for transformations of symbolic orders, and not merely become manifest as destructive, regressive overflow. The difference hinges on the possibility of conjoining the excess of the real with the pluralized repre-sentational resources of the symbolic. I will explore these issues further in Chapter 6.

Toward the end of the section of *Moses and Monotheism* on drive renun-ciation Freud makes a final point related to the intertwined processes of acculturation and the supersession of immediacy in both drives and ego. Freud interprets Moses's introduction of the custom of circumcision in light of the need for "painful instinctual renunciation" intrinsic to acculturation. In what seems to be a strange leap in the argument, Freud concludes that

> circumcision is the symbolic substitute for the castration which the primal father once inflicted upon his sons...and whoever accepted that symbol was showing by it that he was prepared to submit to the father's will, even if it imposed the most painful sacrifice on him.[45]

While the introduction of the primal father seems like a gratuitous *non sequitur*, it intervenes in the text in two antithetical ways. On the one hand, recalling the primal father sets the stage for the final statements of the brief sections concluding the book. In these sections Freud seeks to bring his argument to closure on a literalized, historicized, cause-and-effect level. In Lacanian language, he attempts to *suture* his text, to control its symbolic proliferation and occlude its multiple resonances.

Still, circumcision as *symbolic castration* need not lead us back to the primal father, to the transmission of his deeds and threats through acquired memory, and to the irresolvable difficulties of these formulations. Thus, in contrast to his obsession with phylogenetic transmission, Freud has indicated a symbolic connection that further illuminates the issue of acculturation and psychical transformation. However, to articulate this level of meaning Freud's analysis must be subjected to a symbolic reading of castration. In at least one place in his writings Freud formulates just such an extended, symbolic understanding of castration imagery. In *Inhibitions, Symptoms and Anxiety*, in a pattern that should now be familiar to the reader, Freud, while attempting a reductive analysis of the problem of anxiety in terms of "castration anxiety," nevertheless subverts his more limited arguments with the following statement: "Just as the father has become depersonalized in the shape of the super-ego," he argues, "so has the fear of castration at his hands become transformed into an undefined social or moral anxiety."[46] Here, while attempting to find a definitive reference point for anxiety in the threat of castration, Freud actually de-literalizes the concept. Castration anxiety becomes indicative of the conflicts involved in ethical acculturation.

Lacanian readings of castration extrapolate significantly upon such openings in Freud's thought. Richard Boothby, for example, notes that "acceptance of castration means abandoning the narcissistic dream of absolute self-adequacy and submitting to an original being-at-a-loss."[47] Lacan himself, however, offers a more complex formulation. He argues that "castration means that *jouissance* must be refused, so that it can be reached on the inverted ladder [*l'échelle renversée*] of the Law of desire."[48] In other words, castration symbolizes more than a *relinquishing* of desire. For Lacan, it signifies a transformation or sublimation of desire within the structures of the symbolic order. The Lacanian view indicated here is predicated on psychoanalytic insights into the originally unformed, and hence open-ended and relational, nature of subjectivity. The first, formative, response to this occurs as the narcissistic, imaginary closure of the ego. As we have seen, Oedipal dynamics symbolize processes whereby the subject is transformed in relations with particular others as a cultural being. Lacan takes up the related theme of castration and, in accordance with his symbolic reading of Oedipal dynamics, interprets it as relinquishing illusory narcissistic omnipotence. This renunciation is necessary to becoming acculturated – that is, a speaking being. This latter point emerges in Boothby's analysis, as he further summarizes: "For Lacan, castration is the pivotal moment in which the child effects the transition from a predominantly imaginary mode of functioning to a predominantly symbolic one."[49] It is a symbol of entry into the symbolic order, the Name-of-the-father, as opening subjectivity to symbolic mediation and otherness. Freud's statement concerning symbolic castration, i.e. circumcision, as "submitting to the father's will" may therefore be understood in relation to the major theme he had been pursuing: renunciation and sublimation as intrinsic to acculturation.

At a manifest level, Freud resists these and other such figurative interpretations. As previously noted, *Moses and Monotheism* closes with an assertion of "historical truth," which is contrasted with the "material truth" characteristic of literal self-understandings of religion. Interestingly, Freud's suturing of the text appears explicitly in relation to the problem of controlling the psycho-dynamic power – and, indeed, mystery – of the phenomena discussed. He notes that "there is an element of grandeur about everything to do with the origin of religion, certainly including the Jewish one, and this is not matched by the explanations we have hitherto given."[50] Something extraordinary must lie behind these developments, seemingly leading Freud to choose between two explanatory options. The "material truth" postulated by religious self-understanding, in which the idea of a single god effected an enormous influence on humanity because of its direct reflection of eternal truth, is rejected as resting on an unacceptable "optimistic and idealistic premise."[51] The explicit alternative to this literal idealism, as we know, is confined to the order of actual events, so that we are brought full circle to the constructions of *Totem and Taboo*: "When Moses brought the people the idea of a single god, it was not a novelty but signified the revival of an experience in the primaeval ages of the human family." Once again, Freud's quest for material grounding and closure leads to the assertion that this primeval event "had left behind it in the human mind some permanent traces, which can be compared to a tradition."[52]

With the dichotomization of truth into material and historical types, the category of psychical reality, and its interrelationship with cultural realities, is forgotten. As Jean Laplanche states, Freud

> failed to render explicit what is, nevertheless, present in the notion of "psychical reality," something which would have all the consistency of the real without, however, being verifiable in external experience, a category which might, on first approach, be designated as the "structural."[53]

Psychical reality does not designate an innate, ideal realm, but is intermeshed with the symbolic (or, in Laplanche's terms, structural) sphere. Both *Totem and Taboo* and *Moses and Monotheism*, released from the project of literal etiological explanation, offer narrative constructs providing symbolic accounts of the status and function of these intermediate psycho-cultural dimensions.

Whatever his manifest intentions, Freud's work on religion illustrates that subjective formation necessarily occurs within culturally constituted ideational matrices. These writings articulate the function of symbolic and ideal features of culture, by which capacities for renunciation and sublimation are stimulated and heightened. The psychological transformations related to this dynamic are encapsulated in the formation of the super-ego but reflect changes in the total personality. These transformations involve participation within a symbolic order intrinsic to becoming an ethical, speaking subject. We find, then, *two interrelated latent interpretations of religion* enmeshed within Freud's historical narratives. *Religion embodies aspects of cultural symbol systems serving as bearers of ideals, and it concerns the transformations of subjectivity fostered by such ideals.*

Chapter 6

Psycho-cultural inquiry from Freud to Kristeva

Issues of critique and transformation

Given the benefit of a close reading, Freud's writings on religion offer remarkably profound resources for ongoing cultural and metapsychological reflection. The main features of the psycho-cultural model emerging from these writings can be summarized as follows:

- Subjects are open systems existing in and through language.
- Cultural symbols and ideals play a necessary role in the formation of ethically informed subjectivity.
- Meaningful, ethical subjectivity is pluralistic; it includes functions classified as id and super-ego as well as ego.
- The culturally fostered capacities for renunciation and sublimation indicative of an advance in *Geistigkeit* express subjectivity as informed by ideals.
- There are both constitutive and traumatic effects of acculturation in the distancing from relations governed by immediacy (understood in terms of the materiality of the real and the fixed images of the imaginary). This traumatization is partially responsible for tendencies to literalize and fixate upon cultural constructs.

The last of these points reminds us of the *critical* features of Freud's analyses, particularly those emphasizing regressive tendencies in religion. However, beyond overt critiques of religion as illusion and delusion, and as the by-product of traumatic historical experience, Freud raises other concerns related to acculturation. Primary among these is the abiding issue of *regulative cultural ideals as intrinsic features of subjective formation*. The main problem that arises in relation to this issue is that of formulating, within divergent, fluctuating, finite cultural and historical contexts, guiding orientations for ethical maturation.

Because subjectivity is culturally formed, the task of critical reflection on cultural ideals emerges as all the more significant. These issues relate not only to the religions as such, but to the worldviews and attitudes embodied, both overtly and covertly, by all cultural forms and communicative media. While the necessity of acculturation has been emphasized throughout the previous chapters, it must be remembered that cultures are necessarily formed under specific finite determinants. They are shaped by historical, geographical, economic, political, and other factors. Therefore their capacity to embody and actualize regulative ideals is in any instance highly particularized, if not compromised. This point accords with Mark C. Taylor's comment that "consciousness is inevitably mediated by structures of awareness that are historically relative and culturally conditioned."[1] The *constituted*, as well as *constitutive*, nature of cultural realities affects their ability to foster capacities for self-reflection within differentiated relations, and so to actualize ideals such as freedom, equality, and justice.

The closure of cultural worlds can be understood as a collective manifestation of imaginary fixation, such as occurs in the form of ideology.[2] Paul Ricoeur, discussing the work of Louis Althusser (who is influenced by Lacan), elucidates the matter succinctly in stating that "an ideology is both lived *and* imaginary, it is the lived *as* imaginary."[3] Like imaginary ego formations on the subjective level, ideology as the cultural imaginary serves, in Ricoeur's words, to "preserve a certain order."[4] While necessary, this preservation occurs at the cost of obscuring and repressing alternative views and possibilities. Such delimiting influences condition subjectivity as powerfully as do more idealized, constructive cultural universals. As Kaja Silverman puts it, "although it constitutes itself through speaking, the Lacanian subject is always simultaneously spoken."[5] *Being spoken* here reflects being informed by stereotypical ideological constructs that reinforce, rather than counteract, imaginary tendencies. This problem, endemic to cultural existence, disrupts facile associations of progressive symbolic modalities with any *given* form of society. The intrinsic imperfection that is the correlate of conditionedness indicates the need for ongoing ameliorating modification of psycho-cultural structures. It is not surprising that Freud, acutely aware of individual and societal imperfections, emphasized the *pathological* components of culture, and that he was concerned to formulate critical analyses in relation to them.

However, in Freud's historical treatments of religion, constructive cultural critique is curtailed by a predominant explanatory model positing fixed empirical causes underlying cultural distortions. A reductive approach, governed by a medical paradigm of eliminating pathology, is conjoined with a naive-realist epistemology oriented toward discovering an explanatory bedrock of forces and events. Yet the preceding chapters illustrate that many elements of Freud's analyses of religion and culture subvert naive realism and positivism. The realm of facts-in-themselves, the Lacanian real, is shown to be *outside* of symbolically constituted modes of psycho-cultural existence. One cannot rely on purely empirical criteria for evaluating and modifying cultural forms. Nor does a leveling-down of cultural constructs to a utilitarian engagement with the real offer an adequate response to critical issues.

In contrast to the empiricist orientation, there are also subjective reference points for critique and transformation appearing in psychoanalytic theory. Freud's work is often associated with what can be termed an *ethic of the pleasure principle*, in which well-being requires the release of repressed sexual energies. In some early writings, Freud addressed the issue of sexual repression in modern culture as a fundamental problem in the interface between psychology and society.[6] This theme persists, and appears as one of the dominant elements in the series of tensions between individual and culture discussed in *Civilization and Its Discontents*. On this level, Freud speaks as advocate for the id, for liberation from an overly restrictive "civilized sexual morality." These arguments indicate elements of a "psychological hedonism," concerned with actualizing the pleasure principle, within a psychoanalytic ethic.[7] Even if it is inadequate in itself, this orientation contributes to a pluralized analysis of psycho-cultural existence, insofar as it offsets realist and rationalist criteria.

Focusing on the forces of the id partially engages issues of expressive and creative dimensions of psychical reality. However, as framed within the parameters of a drive-based model, these arguments cannot in themselves offer an adequate developmental reference point. The "tension-reduction" paradigm, describing relations among the id, the other psychical agencies, and cultural forms, is simply too limited to address meaningful human development. In some ways, Kristeva's analyses of the *semiotic* dimensions of the drives (discussed below) incorporate and modify this feature of Freud's thinking. Kristeva retains the view of individuals as desiring beings, existing in tension within the regulating structures of culture. However, she augments and extends Freud's insights with a more nuanced analysis of these non-rational, primary-process dimensions of human existence. Specifically, she develops issues of the *representational* features of the drives, and dynamically links this semiotic dimension to issues of acculturation and ongoing subjective transformations within culture.

By contrast, the arguments of *The Future of an Illusion* are *antithetical* to those prioritizing libidinal gratification. Freud critiques indulgence in infantile tendencies, with associated fixation to illusory (imaginary) forms such as a wish-gratifying paternal God. These infantile tendencies, rooted in the id, are non-sexual manifestations of the pleasure principle. Yet Freud argues that they are regressive and in need of modification. Human maturation is linked with capacities for renunciation and rational, ethical self-transformation. Despite popularizations of psychoanalysis as advocating gratification of the pleasure principle based on a mechanistic vision of the human condition, rationalist views are given equal measure in Freud's discourse. The arguments for rational ethical development of *The Future of an Illusion* accord with the cultural analyses later developed in *Moses and Monotheism* but are more narrowly conceived. In the earlier work Freud scarcely attends to the wider psycho-cultural dynamics of renunciation and sublimation, focusing instead on the ego as the seat of rationality. Although the task of this ego-based maturation explicitly incorporates ethical transformation, this tends, at least overtly, to be restricted by something like a utilitarian model. This is because Freud's rationalist developmental model emphasizes adaptation to a positivistically understood reality. It thus neglects direct engagement with issues on the level of the structuring function of cultural symbol systems.

Freud continuously oscillates between stressing attributes associated with one or the other side of polarities such as freedom and determinism, drives and ego, individual and culture. Each of these co-present orientations proves only partially adequate for shaping ongoing inquiry into the formation and development of subjectivity. Yet the dynamic interplay engendered by these polarities reveals more complex and inclusive psychoanalytic views than does any single set of extreme perspectives. One area where polymorphous analyses appear is in Freud's affirmation of multiple, often contradictory, super-ego functions. In their non-pathologized forms these outline a middle ground reducible neither to id/drives/pleasure principle nor to ego/reason/reality principle. In the super-ego, Freud states, "the two processes, that of the cultural development of the group and that of the cultural development of the individual, are, as it were, always interlocked."[8] Thus this agency, or dimension of subjectivity, is exclusively neither psychological nor cultural, but occurs at the intersection of the two.

In the overview, a pluralistic orientation to psycho-cultural dynamics emerges from Freud's analyses. The multiple perspectives emerging from these inquiries create a space of play, resisting explanatory closure. This also reflects a complexified psychoanalytic model of subjectivity as interlinked with linguistic and symbolic factors. In other words, the overdetermined quality of the writings themselves expresses, in a way that might be termed *performative*, the multifaceted vision of human existence they disclose.

The latent insights emerging from Freud's work provide a differentiated model for addressing issues of psycho-cultural transformation. They indicate that cultural critique must be undertaken *within*, and by means of, symbolic cultural resources. These make possible the expressive and reflective capacities that foster critical and transformative interactions. As cultural resources become internalized, they are also appropriated and integrated into the personality in a way that is individualized. Thus culture, when subjectively mediated, potentially provides the tools for offsetting cultural closure. It is therefore crucial, with respect to critical possibilities, that this interface between psyche and culture is not seamless. These points have significant implications for reconceptualizing religious or religion-like cultural phenomena. Since these represent dimensions of culture connected with ideals and ethics, they are intrinsic to the formation *and re-formation* of subjectivity.

Displacing the ego and opening to the Other

Issues of constructive psycho-cultural critique lead to the following question: "Can the psychoanalytic topographical model accommodate issues and insights related to ethical self-transformation?" I have illustrated that Lacan's contributions are helpful in this respect. The registers of imaginary, symbolic, and real provide a means of extending and refining Freudian inquiries into psycho-cultural dynamics. This topography, conjoined as it is with a non-reified model of the subject-in-process, also offers resources for clarifying the meaningful pluralization of psychical agencies evident in Freud's work. These resources from Lacanian thinking, enhanced by Kristeva's innovations, can be employed to amplify Freud's inquiries into psycho-cultural development.

As was noted in Chapter 2, Lacan's approach to subjective transformation is initiated by a critical interrogation of attributes and functions associated with the ego. This critique parallels those found in religious philosophies throughout history, although it has no definite metaphysical underpinning. I believe this contiguity with religious thinking is most important for understanding the Lacanian subject. In both cases, a critique of the *given*, under the psychological heading of ego, is undertaken in pursuit of a potentially more advanced condition of the personality. When this sense of a progression beyond mere adaptation, conformity, and reality-testing is lacking, Lacan's arguments are sometimes construed in terms of a pessimistic and regressive dismissal of the qualities of reason and autonomy associated with the ego.[9] However, the ego's formation within the register of the imaginary indicates that, for Lacan, it represents a specific mode of consciousness, and a specific correlative organization of the personality. Thus the movement from ego to subject is best understood as a *qualitative transformation of modes of consciousness*.

Lacanian thought extrapolates on splits, tensions, and overdeterminations in the understanding of the ego occurring throughout Freud's work (one instance of which was noted in the discussion of *Civilization and Its Discontents* in Chapter 2). The meaning and status of the ego in psychoanalytic theory are complicated, and often confused, because of these varying trends in Freud's writings. These provide at least two major definitions of the ego as agency, as well as various approaches to the locatedness of that agency within the wider range of subjectivity.

Jean Laplanche has discussed the ego's relation to a more encompassing and differentiated psychoanalytic topography. He notes that "within Freud's work there is a tendency to distinguish two quite different meanings of the 'ego.'" One meaning is based on the common use of the pronoun "I," so that the term ego "designates simply the individual." Distinguished from this non-technical usage, however, is the more "properly psychoanalytic meaning in which the ego, this time, is taken as part of the totality and no longer the totality itself, as an 'agency,' and, for that reason, as one of the protagonists in the conflict splitting the individual."[10] Laplanche argues that a term technically designating a *subsystem* has been appropriated by some schools of psychoanalysis to designate the totality – that is, a self or subject. Interestingly, this appropriation is not unlike a metonymical process. A part has come to represent, to substitute for, the unarticulated but assumed whole. This " 'metonymical conception of the ego' represents the prevalent theoretical tendency within psychoanalysis concerning the problem of the ego."[11] A gap in theory has been covered over, and certain issues and insights obscured, following a logic unconsciously governed by quasi-linguistic processes.

Expanding the ego to designate the person is associated with an emphasis on adaptive and reality-testing functions. However, Freud also sees in the ego regressive, fixating characteristics, as found in its features of *defense* and *narcissism*.[12] A crucial split therefore appears in Freud's accounts of the ego's function of reality-testing. Lacan argues that, in the topographic model that associates the ego with the system perception-consciousness, "the ego takes sides with the object." That is, it is characterized as the agency related to objective knowledge of the external world. Conversely, however, "the ego takes sides against the object in the theory of narcissism."[13] In this view, equally central to Freud's model, the ego exhibits tendencies toward self-enclosure that condition relations with the external world.

The issues concerning the ego's status as part or whole and concerning its capacity to engage alterity intersect. Freud's portrayal of the ego as part of a wider personality structure highlights issues of splitting and self-deception. In its narcissistic-defensive modes, indicative of self-enclosure, the ego's relationship to the "inner other" – that is, to the wider range of subjectivity connected with the primary process and the other agencies – is characterized by resistance and disavowal. The defended, narcissistic ego encapsulates tendencies toward exclusion, resistance, and repression, in pursuit of control and continuity. As Samuel Weber has shown, a critique of systematizing, fixating ego tendencies, similar to Lacan's, is explicitly present in some of Freud's own formulations. For example, in critiquing the Adlerian "system" Freud states that the dream material is "viewed purely from the standpoint of the ego, reduced to the categories with which the ego is familiar, translated, twisted and – exactly as happens in dream formation – misunderstood."[14] Here, Freud views tendencies toward the systematizing of experience, in a manner controlled by fixed interpretive standpoints and a need for mastery, as *narcissistic*. This is clearly both unhealthy and restrictive of understanding.[15] As Weber points out, these arguments establish a series of connections among the ego, narcissism, repetition, and the perpetuation of familiarity under the rubric of "the Same."[16]

Connections between the ego as informed by the pleasure principle, as narcissistic, and as manifesting a quality that can be termed *hating* are indicated in the following passage from Freud, quoted by Leo Bersani. Freud is discussing the formation of the ego, and notes that

> the external world, objects, and what is hated are identical. If later on an object turns out to be a source of pleasure, it is loved, but it is also incorporated into the ego; so that for the purified pleasure-ego once again objects coincide with what is extraneous and hated.[17]

Commenting on this passage, Bersani notes that "the ego, then, far from having any original aptitude for dealing with reality, is in a state of radical hostility to the external world."[18] Thus rejecting otherness acts as a means of consolidating a fixed sense of identity.

In response to such issues, Lacan formulates a model of the subject-in-process at once more *differentiated* and more *encompassing* than those structured around the ego. The Lacanian critique of establishing the ego as a developmental reference point addresses the problem of spiritual loss, or the loss of *Geistigkeit*, produced by closure and conformity. This emerges in his stating that "it is clear that the promotion of the ego today culminates, in conformity with the utilitarian conception of man that reinforces it, in an isolation of the soul [*un isolement de l'âme*] ever more akin to its original dereliction."[19] Lacan's use of the term *soul* evokes Freud's many references to *Seele*. In each case, the term seems to characterize subjectivity-in-process as irreducible to a central controlling agency, and this usage clearly overlaps with and complements the use of the term *Geistigkeit*. Loss of soul therefore ensues from entrenchment within an imaginary, ego mode.

Lacan insists that "the ego is an imaginary function, it is not to be confused with the subject."[20] His sense of the developing subject is frequently delineated in negative terms, by a contrast with and critique of the ego. Rather than being the agency through which self-development occurs, the ego is characterized by a *refusal* of the dynamic which, for Lacan, constitutes the subject in pursuit of truth:

> We call the ego that nucleus given to consciousness, but opaque to reflection, marked by all the ambiguities which, from self-satisfaction to "bad faith" [*mauvaise foi*], structure the experience of the passions in the human subject; this "I" [*moi*] who...opposes its irreducible inertia of pretenses and *méconnaissances* to the concrete problematic of the realization of the subject.[21]

Lacan's delineation of *le sujet* does not entail positing a fixed "higher self" or determinate spiritual agency contrasted with the ego. This would repeat the errors of objectification and reification that characterize the ego's resistance to the dynamic of subjectivity. Hence, while Lacan shares with C. G. Jung a psychodynamic model in which the ego is decentered in favor of a wider "individuating" process, Lacan occasionally criticizes Jung's concept of the self as a reification that re-establishes centralization and totality.[22] Any such totalized spiritual agency becomes an alternative ego construct conditioned by the viewpoints and presuppositions characterizing notions of a dominant center. By contrast, the Lacanian subject is a mode of relation based on communicative interplay. As such, it is not representable, as it were, in Newtonian terms. Hence there is a need for literary and linguistic strategies, both within the analytic process of reading the traces of subjectivity through gaps in the defenses of the ego, and to convey the subject-in-process on a theoretical level.

Lacan works with the inherent incompleteness of our being, associated with *un manque à être*, as a resource for fostering ongoing development. Discontinuities in self-awareness, evident in meaningful slips (parapraxes) and overdeterminations, are exploited to foster a self-reflective movement beyond the imaginary. Lacan argues that in these phenomena psychoanalytic inquiry encounters "something of the order of the *non-realized*."[23] Opening to alienated potentiality motivates the developmental process that Lacan calls the "dialectic of desire." As Mark C. Taylor expresses the matter, "by refusing to transform desire into need, the subject consents to its own incompletion."[24] This is not a passive consent to existing inadequacy, but an embracing of existence as always unfinished and hence open to possibility. Within imaginary orientations, however, open-endedness creates anxiety. The "want of being" impels an imaginary "want to be," leading to attempts at *filling* lack, which is misconstrued as "a *deficiency* that one must strive to overcome."[25] The objectification of lack as something to be filled according to demand is the correlate of the objectification of the subject (as ego) in imaginary identifications. If we follow Lacanian thinking, the task is not to satisfy psychological needs and demands arising from longing for a "lost plenitude of being." Rather, transformations of subjectivity involve bringing desire into communication within the symbolic.

In an overdetermined statement, Lacan emphasizes that "the unconscious is the discourse of the Other (with a capital O)."[26] Incorporated into this comment is an argument that acculturation is not confined to the ego, but involves the wider personality, the subject. Therefore language, as the paramount factor in the formation of subjectivity within cultural worlds, is not merely a tool controlled by the ego. In exceeding the utilitarian procedures of fixed communication, language discloses meaning that exceeds or offsets ego intentionality. Lacan states:

[The] passion of the signifier now becomes a new dimension of the human condition in that it is not only man who speaks, but in man and through man *it* speaks (*ça parle*), that his nature is woven by effects in which is to be found the structure of language, of which he becomes the material, and that therefore there resounds in him, beyond what could be conceived by a psychology of ideas, the relation of speech.[27]

This play on the Freudian topography indicates that *das Es*, the id, *le ça*, forms an active and expressive dimension of subjectivity, rather than a quasi-biological instinctual ground. Lacan's playful writing of *jouissance* as *jouis-sens* gives expression to this conjunction of desire and signification, while illustrating the *working* of language in displaying multiple meaning.[28] The ego and its inner other, the unconscious as including id and super-ego, are formed within the Other of language and the symbolic.

The supersession of the ego within linguistic practice is the key to the realization of the subject-in-process. This occurs, as it were, in two interrelated directions: by means of decenterings occasioned by unconscious expression and through the pluralized resources of symbolic cultural forms. In each interrelated instance, language is a vehicle liberating subjectivity from the alienation of the ego. In Lacan's words:

> It is therefore always in the relation between the subject's ego [*moi*] and the "I" [*je*] of his discourse that you must understand the meaning of the discourse if you are to achieve the dealienation of the subject [*pour désaliéner le sujet*].[29]

The key here is the play between manifest and latent, creating in their tension new levels of meaning that displace closed subjective orientations. Interconnections between subjectivity and language offer resources for transformation and development, because language exceeds the delimitations of the imaginary:

> In order to free the subject's speech, we introduce him into the language of desire, that is to say, into the *primary language* [*langage premier*] in which, beyond what he tells us of himself, he is already talking to us unknown to himself, and, in the first place, in the symbols of the symptom.[30]

The disclosure of unseen and often unwanted insight, as can occur in the analytic session, dislodges the ego's claim to control meaning and to constitute the totality of subjectivity. This displacement is fostered by forms of discourse that expose the literal and the familiar to possibility. Boothby notes, for example, that "metaphor announces a complexity and ambiguity incapable of expression in the register of the imaginary."[31] Indeed, emergent subjectivity parallels in its off-centering itinerary, the action of linguistic processes such as metaphor and metonymy. Actualizing desire as potential subjectivity is, in Lacanian terms, a symbolic process. This emerges when Lacan refers to the Other (*Autre*) as being for the subject "the locus from which the question of his existence may be presented to him."[32] This Other is, at one and the same time, language, culture, and the unconscious dimensions of the personality.

In relation to subjective development, Lacan formulates two modes of language use, which he terms empty speech (*parole vide*) and full speech (*parole pleine*). The former operates within prestructured and habitual frames of reference. For Lacan, "empty speech is the discourse of the ego, in which the resources of the symbolic have been drawn into the orbit of imaginary formations."[33] Empty speech is narcissistic, because in it one always finds one's viewpoints intact and unchanged. By contrast, "full" speech is not complete, but ex-centric and excessive. It surpasses and relativizes the closed views of the ego, occurring in the interstices between ego and other/Other (as inner and outer). The dialogical and metaphorical forms of full speech engender transformations of subjective stances. Full speech may also be described as "performative" because it acts upon and effects changes in the ego's orientation. This occurs, for example, in linguistic figures such as irony, paradox, and *double entendre* that frustrate immediate recognition and control. Thus, speaking of metaphorization, Gilbert Chaitin argues that "without it the subject would have remained tied to the object, reified in an inescapable because too proximate meaning."[34] Freud's texts on religion, liberated from interpretive closure on the literal level, can function in this metaphorized manner.

The links between the intra-psychic transformations expressed in full speech, the realization of the subject, and the extra-psychic formations of the symbolic order are partially instantiated in the intermediate status of the Freudian super-ego. The functions associated with the super-ego augment ego functions and, in pluralizing subjectivity within cultural resources, subvert closed-system models. This configuration within the agency of the super-ego of inner- and outer-directed pluralization and open-endedness is lucidly summarized by Samuel Weber:

> The superego defines the aporetic identity of the subject: it represents both the ideal toward which the ego strives, and the interdictory limit it can never attain. As such, the superego embodies the indispensable and irreducible element of alterity, in which both intrapsychic and metapsychic moments converge.[35]

This passage conveys the status of the super-ego as superseding reduction to internalized (and frequently pathologized) parental and cultural authorities. An inner/outer dynamic involving ideas, ideals, and systems of symbols locates subjectivity within wider cultural processes. Hence the inner other resists assimilation to the *narcissistic* ideal ego; multi-perspectives offset the ego mono-perspective. This counteracts refusal to acknowledge contexts and associated tendencies toward closure and reduction to familiarity and sameness. Thus the super-ego represents a set of essential attributes within the dynamic open system of decentered subjectivity.

Just as the differentiated quality of subjectivity disrupts closure intra-psychically, so too it is related to cultural transformation. This may be seen in Lacan's statement that "the super-ego is at one and the same time the law and its destruction."[36] The subjective internalization and appropriation of cultural forms, of law, feeds into a dynamic interplay acting back upon specific cultural constellations. The key to this critical feedback is not reference to given ideals or universals, but the *universalizing* capacity to think and imagine beyond the given. Differentiation and communication, both intra-psychically and interpersonally, are essential to the realization of the subject. Here it bears emphasis that, as a differentiation of subjectivity occurring within the communicative and expressive resources of culture, *decentering* should not be confused with *disassociation*. The former is broadly *dialogical*, necessitating intra-psychic and extra-psychic communication, whereas the latter seems to involve communicative breakdown within the subject.[37]

These transformative processes, intersecting psychology and cultural resources, are prefigured in the concepts of renunciation and *Geistigkeit*. Furthermore, Freud's use of multiple terms to describe these faculties and capacities is quite compatible with the Lacanian refusal to totalize the subject. Metapsychologically, it is not a matter of naming the totality, correctly grasping the person as a "whole."[38] Indeed, these orientations are part of the problem whereby the dynamic, decentering insights of psycho-analysis are lost. Of particular significance to the psychology of religion is the relation of emergent subjectivity to symbolic and semiotic processes that decenter the ego. It is particularly important that the ego is more than an intra-psychic agency; it also represents internalized, culturally formed norms and assumptions. Granting that subjectivity is formed through symbolic forms and ideals, we must pursue issues of critical transformation within psycho-cultural dynamics. In this, the contributions of psychoanalysis as a hermeneutic of suspicion may be conjoined with reflections on subjective development.

The unconscious structured like a language

A differentiated psycho-cultural model may be further developed by illustrating that meaningful aspects of subjectivity occur outside ego functions. A crucial area where manifestations of meaningful unconscious expression are discerned is the analysis of the dream work. We have seen that Freud's interrogations of dreams reveal creative representational processes akin to (but not identical with) linguistic ones. Each of the features of the dream work isolated by Freud – condensation, displacement, symbolization, and secondary revision – involves remarkably complex signifying processes. Moreover, their appearance during sleep extends the range of meaningful subjectivity because they occur without the awareness of the conscious personality.[39] A lucid presentation of this side of psychoanalytic theory, influenced by Lacan, is found in Kaja Silverman's *The Subject of Semiotics*. Drawing primarily on *The Interpretation of Dreams*, Silverman explicates primary-process or unconscious activity occurring in the dream work as displaying quasi-linguistic characteristics. Wishful impulses, characteristic of unconscious processes, are inseparable from "unconscious discourse...those signifying formations motivated by the unconscious, such as dreams, parapraxes, daydreams, neuroses."[40] The dream work's distortions and displacements, its disguised, oblique, and overdetermined forms of expression, are marvelously unraveled in the numerous examples of *The Interpretation of Dreams*. These occur as a result of repressions by the system preconscious-conscious, symbolized in the image of the "censorship." Thus primary-process signification cannot simply be understood as interpretable *in itself*. Meaning occurs on multiple levels in the interplay between the systems of the personality.

In critiquing mechanistic models of the primary process, Silverman nevertheless resists attributing *innate* higher-order qualities to the unconscious. She opts instead for an interpretive model that follows Lacan in seeing unconscious components of subjectivity as also formed by cultural influences: "We cannot attribute to the unconscious a prelapsarian or 'archaic' status; preconscious and unconscious develop through mutual tension, a tension which is introduced through language and which reflects the larger cultural order."[41] Thus Silverman develops a dynamic view of subjectivity along several lines. Intra-psychically, there are at least two interactive levels of signification forming the subject. As Silverman notes, "Freud stresses that neither the primary nor the secondary process is alone capable of signification; it is only through their collaboration that discourse occurs, and that the subject is constituted."[42] This collaboration is indicated in the need to engage interpretively the manifestations of unconscious levels of personality, in dreams, symptom formations, and other phenomena, in order to foster therapeutic working-through and self-knowledge. In this respect, Silverman also notes Freud's early emphasis on "facilitations" or connecting representations between primary and secondary process. Both primary and secondary processes are culturally constituted and display overdetermined, culturally informed signifying activity. The internalization of cultural forms, especially language, is the *sine qua non* of personality formation. This occurs across the spectrum of conscious and unconscious levels.

Silverman argues that in Freud's second topography insights into the dynamic, interstitial nature of subjectivity are obscured by the more fixed agential terminology. She notes that the agency of the id differs from earlier formulations concerning the unconscious in several respects. For example, "it lacks the latter's signifying capacities, seeming to be little more than an area of instinctual anarchy."[43] Furthermore, the relationship between id and ego is portrayed in adversarial terms, as indicated in Freud's famous analogy of a rider on horseback struggling to control the unruly beast: "This relationship contrasts strikingly with the notion of 'facilitations'...used by Freud to explain the interactions of the primary and secondary processes. It brings together brute strength and superior wisdom instead of two equally complex signifying systems."[44] However, granting Silverman's points concerning some neglect of earlier insights, it is also the case that Freud's late work offers alternative formulations counterbalancing mechanistic portrayals of the id. For example, the poetic and mythical language of *Eros* conveys creative, open-ended dimensions of desire that overlap uneasily with the realm of the id.[45] The tension between antithetical readings of the primary process comes to expression in a doubling of terminological designations. The aspects of subjectivity linked with *Eros* are closer to the mysterious powers of love than to a mechanistically construed pleasure principle. They also intertwine with representational and aesthetic components of psycho-cultural existence. As we have seen, Freud's most elaborate treatment of these aesthetic and symbolic processes appears in the intersecting discussions of love, beauty, art, and culture in *Civilization and Its Discontents*.

Silverman presents psychoanalysis as pluralizing signifying modes, and as extending meaningful subjectivity beyond the ego and the secondary process. These issues can be further developed with reference to Kristeva's formulations concerning the *semiotic* and the *symbolic*, a differentiation occurring within the general category of signifying expression.[46] The term symbolic, following Lacanian use, indicates socially constituted communicative forms. Kristeva emphasizes that the symbolic prioritizes the secondary-process activity of the ego and is therefore restricted in expressing other, non-rational dimensions of subjective experience. In response to this issue, Kristeva expands the range of meaningful communicative activity to include less formalized modes of expression characterized as semiotic (these are also described in terms of *signifiance*, in contrast to the *significance* of the symbolic). In Kristeva's definition, the semiotic describes modes of expression more closely related to the body, the drives, and the primary process. Kristeva's analyses, illustrated by numerous clinical and cultural examples, reveal non-conscious dimensions of subjectivity to be irreducible to mechanistic terms. She speaks of a "distinctive mark, trace, index, precursory sign" connected to a "precise modality of the signifying process." She continues: "This modality is the one Freudian psychoanalysis points to in postulating not only the *facilitation* and the structuring *disposition* of drives, but also the so-called *primary processes* which displace and condense both energies and their inscription."[47] Semiotic expression can appear in the gaps and contradictions within formal discourse (that is, what Freud terms "faulty acts" or parapraxes). It also characterizes communication in the form of gestures, tears, or moods, and thus might assist in releasing repressed levels of affect. In addition, semiotic modes play a role in more refined expressive forms such as art and poetry. Manifest in a variety of figures of speech in literature, or in the use of color, texture, perspective, and other devices in painting, it appeals to a broad spectrum of emotional and sensory experience, and serves to convey multiple levels of meaning. Thus Kristeva's model of language includes tactile, rhythmic, and imagistic forms.

Extending meaningful communication beyond one-dimensional instrumental language intersects with an expansion of meaningful subjectivity beyond the ego. Just as Silverman emphasizes the interstitial nature of subjectivity as located "between" primary and secondary processes, Kristeva illustrates that subjectivity involves both semiotic and symbolic modes.[48] Kristeva explicitly defines her model of subjectivity as including, as taking account of, the Freudian unconscious. This differentiates the subject from what Kristeva calls the "transcendental ego" – that is, from a mode of consciousness that views itself as fully autonomous and transparent.

One feature of Kristeva's differentiated model of language is that the dynamic between discursive modes provides a critical check upon cultural symbol systems. *Signifiance* creates a conduit between inner experience and cultural representation, simultaneously linking self and other, and altering the stasis of the Other. As Kristeva states, "instinctual operation becomes a *practice* – a transformation of natural and social resistances, limitations, and stagnations – if and only if it enters into the code of linguistic and social communication."[49] The heterogeneity of the semiotic disrupts potential closure and totalization of communication by means of individualized, multifaceted, and polysemous forms of expression. Freud's insight that the inexhaustible residues of drive activity react against the full absorption of the individual into culture are here taken to a more detailed level of analysis. Kristeva's work also adds a critical element often seen to be lacking in Lacan's formulations concerning the symbolic. The semiotic harnesses resources within subjectivity that counteract ossifying (imaginary and ideological) tendencies within cultural systems. When specific qualities of symbol systems become entrenched in this manner, they are not simply more limited and inflexible. In addition, they become dirempted from and closed to the variability of existing subjects. As this occurs, symbolic forms become restricted in their ability to relate meaningfully to individual experience. They lose the ability to respond to personal crises and to guide maturation.

In Kristeva's work the latent level of Freud's inquiries – in which psycho-cultural existence is understood to be necessarily informed by symbolic vehicles – is brought into greater resolution with his more overt concerns with cultural critique. In other words, critical inquiry now focuses on the psycho-cultural efficacy of symbolic forms, in terms of their ability to foster differentiated and reflective subjectivity accommodating the variables of individual psychodynamics. These issues are further addressed in Kristeva's inquiries into *failures* of symbolic mediation, as exemplified in conditions of melancholia.

Kristeva on melancholia, art, and religion

A prominent theme in Kristeva's work is the revolutionary impact of semiotic forces on the symbolic orders and worldviews of given cultures. In her earlier writings this revolutionary dimension is explored primarily in relation to artistic production, which she describes as "the flow of jouissance into language."[50] One should note the conjunction of pleasure, desire, and meaningful creative overflow in the term *jouissance*. Art comes into being at the interface of *jouissance* and culture. It functions in a transformative manner by opening existing symbolic structures to repressed and unrealized experiential dimensions. Aesthetic production allows for an influx of innovative subjective experience into the communicative realm, and thus into culture. This point extrapolates on Freud's insight into the potentially transformative effects of drive representations in relation to culture. This becomes a meaningful challenge and transformation, however, only if *jouissance* is brought to articulation within the symbolic, and especially in relation to cultural ideals. The movement into cultural communication indicates a dynamic process occurring between the semiotic and the symbolic.

Kristeva's *Black Sun* represents an important shift in the relationship between art and religion that had been formulated in her *Revolution in Poetic Language*. In the earlier work religion was seen in a more strictly conservative light, as supporting existing social-symbolic orders by prohibiting and controlling *jouissance*. (Kristeva discusses Freud's analyses of exogamy in this respect.) This regulating function was contrasted with the challenging and transformative semiotic productions of art.[51] With *Black Sun*, a twofold complementary view is developed. On one side, semiotic expression in art itself has a *religious* dimension, because it can effect a meaningful reconfiguring of worldviews. Reciprocally, religious forms such as sacred writings, symbols, and rituals incorporate and utilize semiotic modes of expression that resist semantic closure. Thus religion and art converge from two directions. In this, the key psychological consideration is that semiotic forms provide a means of articulating and grappling with deep traumatic levels of experience and crises of meaning. Because subjectivity is not confined to cognitive activity but includes the drive-based activity explored by psychoanalysis, semiotic forms are essential to self-expression, self-understanding, and self-transformation.[52] The interface between religion and aesthetics is articulated in the following summary of *Black Sun*'s overall line of argument:

Aesthetic and particularly literary creation, and also religious discourse in its imaginary, fictional essence, set forth a device whose prosodic economy, interaction of characters, and implicit symbolism constitute a very faithful semiological representation of the subject's battle with symbolic collapse.[53]

Kristeva's definition of religion has expanded to include representational modes fostering psychological *transformation*. Religion overlaps with art, in that each provides vehicles for multi-tiered expression and reflection. This interpretation takes us to a level where the psychology of religion refers to ongoing subjective development within symbolic structures. Thus Kristeva's psycho-cultural model is explicitly dynamic and dialectical. It transcends possible conflicts and antitheses such as those between tradition and innovation. Her work articulates a creative middle ground that both speaks to individual developmental needs and emphasizes the necessary social-symbolic components in meaningful ethically oriented modalities of subjectivity.

Kristeva offers a deepened understanding of the psycho-cultural nature and function of religion. Her work thematizes latent and marginalized insights of Freud's explorations of culture, ethics, and human development. Moreover, her analyses remain sensitive to the specificity of individual and cultural contexts, resisting any imposition of fixed symbolic codes. Kristeva opens the way to approaching artistic and religious imagery in ways that transcend the Freudian split between these forms of "illusion" and the experience of reality. In discussing religion, Kristeva stresses that "the function of the psychoanalyst is to reawaken the imagination and to permit illusions to exist."[54] Here illusion articulates the mediating symbolic space by which the subject experiences being as meaningful. Indeed, the commingling of subjective and objective in representational forms infuses existence with human meaning. This creative interplay is also evident in art and literature. For example, in Kristeva's discussion of the work of Georgia O'Keefe she uses the expression *subjectivement objective* to convey the aesthetic reinscription of passion and intimacy into the experience of reality.[55] Rather than positing a developmental ideal of a strictly objective relation to reality, Kristeva consistently argues that both religion and art serve essential psycho-cultural functions by fostering a creative interplay that includes subjective experience.

Black Sun explores intersections between symbolization and subjectivity by focusing on the problem of severe depression and melancholia. This inquiry overlaps with the concerns of the previous chapters in several ways. In discussing *Totem and Taboo* and *Moses and Monotheism*, the problem of traumatization appeared in relation to distanciation from immediacy. This symbolic break, with its attendant pathologies and advances, was seen to be intrinsic to subjective formation within language and symbolization. On a more detailed, more explicitly individual level, *Black Sun* also explores the problem of psychical trauma. This is approached through depressive states requiring renewals of symbolic articulation and mediation. Kristeva illustrates, in effect, the pathological consequences of the *dysfunction* of mediating symbol systems. Also, the forms of melancholia traced in *Black Sun* indicate psychological processes whereby opportunities for symbolic renewal might occur. Kristeva demonstrates a need for *personal* engagement with the affective and somatic dimensions of being, often initiated involuntarily by crises and the breakdown of meaning. These arguments and illustrations augment Freud's analyses of psycho-cultural formation. *They show that extant symbol systems, unless meaningfully integrated with and renewed by personal experience, become closed and static and hence void of psychological efficacy.*

Because acculturation involves distancing from inner and outer immediacy, there is a perpetual risk of *disconnection* and *alienation*. This point highlights the counter-side to the constitutive function of symbolic forms disclosed in Freud's writings on religion and culture. That is, symbolic and ideal constructs can become reified and subject to fixation under the psychocultural mode of the imaginary. Individuals contribute to this reification, perhaps because of anxiety engendered by conceptual freedom and the possibilities for creatively reconfiguring worldviews and modes of existence. Cultures, more obviously, tend to perpetuate themselves by "absolutizing" their worldviews. Ironically, when ossified psycho-cultural forms resist change, a process ensues in which these forms become less and less able to speak effectively to issues of meaning and value. Reification reflects the inability of symbol systems to develop in accordance with other cultural changes and to reflect subjective experience. The circuit between subjectivity and symbolic systems is arrested and a dilemma ensues: subjects can take on cultural structures at the expense of individuality, or subjectivity can become disconnected from symbolic resources. Possible outcomes of this alienation are subjects becoming truncated, stunted, disillusioned, disoriented, or depressed.

Kristeva addresses these issues by exploring the interface between subjectivity and culture as both fissured and creative. Her work extends our knowledge of the relationships among sense of self, experiences of trauma and suffering, and semiotic and symbolic expression. In this, she clarifies some of the key points of intersection between religion, aesthetics, and subjective transformation. Like Freud, Kristeva uses pathological extremes to illuminate more general psychological issues. Everyday occurrences such as dreams and parapraxes reflect the same compromising of the ego's hegemony as do, in a more forceful way, overwhelming moods or symptoms. Building explicitly on the Lacanian critique of the ego, Kristeva explores such compromising moments as possible openings to subjective transformation. The intersecting issues concern psychical suffering, the mediating function of representational forms, and the possibility of psycho-cultural renewal.

The religious dimensions of Kristeva's inquiry are indicated in her comments that "the depressed person is a radical, sullen atheist [*un athée radical et morose*]."[56] Later she defines atheistic as "deprived of meaning, deprived of values."[57] Thus loss of personal meaning intersects with an ontological loss of meaning. In these remarks, theological language is de-literalized, and is employed to address issues of a sense of self and world as meaningful and value-laden. Here the atheist is not one who disbelieves in the existence of a specific being, but one for whom *being as such is devoid of value*. Both psychotherapeutically and ontologically (that is, in terms of cultural representations of being), however, the issue should not be reduced to one of individual fault or inadequacy. Kristeva's analyses illustrate multiple sides to the interplay between suffering and symbolization. Experiences of suffering and trauma may rupture symbolic worlds; suffering may ensue from the dysfunction or inadequacy of symbolic worlds; suffering becomes traumatic without the mediation of symbolic worlds; and suffering may catalyze a process leading to the renewal of symbolic worlds. Thus in Kristeva's analyses breakdown and traumatization are not exclusively confined to individual experience. Her concerns are with the viability of extant symbol systems and social modes of discourse, especially in their ability to respond to life issues that pressure subjective identity and that may give rise to traumatic moments. Here a critical and transformative space is opened that extends psycho-cultural inquiry beyond the limits established by both Freud and Lacan.

Kristeva illustrates that melancholia is not only a depressive state enveloping one's sense of self and world. It simultaneously involves the inhibition, or breakdown, of both interpersonal relations and the capacity for self-expression. These interrelated aspects of melancholia appear in Kristeva's definition: "I shall call *melancholia* the institutional symptomatology of inhibition and asymbolia."[58] She further describes melancholia as involving "a common experience of *object loss* and of a *modification of signifying bonds*."[59] Melancholia and depression graphically illustrate interconnections between states of mind, relations to others and the external world, the capacity for self-expression, and the necessary mediation of these relations within language and cultural structures. Melancholia is at one and the same time a mood, an inability to relate and to discern meaning in relations, and an inability to speak meaningfully, articulately to connect one's self and experience to an other. It forms the antithesis to the psychodynamics of love explored in *Tales of Love*, where Kristeva writes that "the psyche is one open system connected to another, and only under those conditions is it renewable."[60] In melancholia the connection to the other is lost or becomes impossible. The psyche closes in on itself and renewal is denied.

Crises of meaning are, of course, endemic to human existence in many ways. They result from the contingency, variability, and open-endedness of the human condition. This constitutional vulnerability is exacerbated by specific traumatic experiences (as indicated in Freud's notion of the complemental series). Kristeva's notion of the semiotic responds to these issues by giving expression to dimensions of subjectivity that are, strictly speaking, pre-linguistic. The semiotic does not quite conform to Lacan's imaginary (a term which Kristeva also employs), but it overlaps with it in referring to pre-symbolic formation. Thus, in emphasizing the constructive and curative dimensions of semiotic expression, Kristeva also indicates a constructive dimension of imaginary formations. She speaks of "primary identification," which refers in Lacanian theory to the initial imaginary formations of the ego associated with the mirror stage. This identification "secures the subject to another dimension, that of imaginary adherence, reminding one of the bond of faith, which is just what disintegrates in the depressed person."[61] When these underlying identity formations become destabilized, the ability to locate oneself within social-symbolic worlds is compromised. Rather than *covering over* this fissure, in what might be termed a *manic* response, Kristeva points to the need to return and reconnect with the foundations of subjectivity. Semiotic modes provide the means for accomplishing this.

Drawing on her clinical experience, Kristeva describes the speech of depressed people as "repetitive and monotonous...they utter sentences that are interrupted, exhausted, come to a standstill...sinking into the blankness of asymbolia."[62] This breakdown of language indicates a splitting and alienation within the personality as well as in external relations. The level of surface communication is dissociated from the deeper, troubled emotional core. The accompanying loss of interest in and involvement with others is manifest in dysfunctions of symbolic capacity. If speech is not completely inhibited, it becomes lifeless and fragmented, incapable of meaningful communication with others. Kristeva refers to the "wounded speech" (*parole blessée*) of her analysands; this includes resonances and nuances to which the analyst must carefully attend.[63] The wounds and gaps in discourse are usually incommensurable with the ego's intentional level of meaning. Because of this, wounded speech can become the occasion for semiotic expression, which, in turn, can open into the full speech described by Lacan. As this occurs, *significance*, connected to deep levels of affect and crisis, slips through defenses and resistances.

However, the inability to articulate traumatic experience contributes to withdrawal from meaningful communication. In a more recent work Kristeva discusses these problems under the rubric of "new maladies of the soul." She describes the "patient's inability to symbolize his unbearable traumas."[64] These experiences impinge on our sense of self and world, yet cannot be fully or directly rendered in language. In *Black Sun* Kristeva uses the image of the gravitational pull of a black sun to describe the compelling void into which the depressed person sinks. Kristeva designates this mute internal realm as "the Thing," which she describes as "an imagined sun, bright and black at the same time [*la Chose est un soleil rêvé, clair et noir à la fois*]."[65] Images of the Thing and of the black sun as anti-objects build both on Kristeva's earlier discussions of *abjection* and on Lacan's idea of the *real* as that which resists symbolization.[66] Thus Lacan, similarly, speaks of the real in terms of the image of the Thing, stating that "*Das Ding* is that which I will call the beyond-of-the-signified."[67] For Kristeva, attachment to the Thing coincides with rejection of actual, symbolized relations. The Thing represents regression to the maternal *chora*; it is an affective core without signification, unnameable, sustaining the state of asymbolia. In this condition desire is internalized such that the loss and pain of interpersonal relations is offset, indeed prevented, by an attachment to an imagined totality. This totality is all-absorbing, mute, deathly. Kristeva cites one of her analysands who described herself as feeling "as if I were dead but I do not even think of killing myself, nor do I desire to do so, it is as if it had already been done."[68] Another "would speak of 'anesthetized wounds,' 'numbed sorrow,' or 'a blotting out that holds everything in check.'" As Kristeva summarizes, "the whole depressive identity was organized around this nothingness. Such nothingness was an absolute."[69] Hence the Thing is like a totalized *anti-ideal*; rather than fostering relations to the other, it denies relation.

The Thing represents what Kristeva calls the denial of negation (or, more literally, the denial of de-negation) (*le déni de la dénégation*).[70] Language is predicated on negation, because it creates a symbolic space that both separates one from the immediacy of objects and allows reference to that which is not present. Within the terms of her inquiry, Kristeva notes that

> signs are arbitrary because language starts with a *negation* [*Verneinung*] of loss, along with the depression occasioned by mourning....Depressed persons, on the contrary, *disavow the negation*: they cancel it out, suspend it, and nostalgically fall back on the real object (Thing) of their loss, which is just what they do not manage to lose, to which they remain painfully riveted.[71]

Immersion in the Thing, in the asymbolic depressive state, *represents the inverse of the symbolic break explicated by Freud*. Melancholia highlights the significance of distanciation from the real in the constitution of the speaking subject within symbolic orders. Severely depressed persons do not distance themselves from loss by moving from direct object-attachment to symbolic articulation. They cling to the illusion of immediacy in an internalized, fantasized form.

The presence of the Thing bypasses the need for authentic speech, sustaining the condition of asymbolia. Reconnecting with others and with the world involves relearning to speak meaningfully, which is also (and this is a crucial point) to speak one's own meaning. In so doing, one participates in the linguistic and symbolic processes of negation, which involve not only mourning, but also renunciation in the Freudian sense. In Kristeva's words, "Speaking beings, from their ability to endure in time up to their enthusiastic, learned, or simply amusing constructions, demand a break, a renunciation, an unease at their foundations."[72] Renunciation expresses the ability to relinquish attachment, in this case to the encompassing emptiness of the depressive space. This facilitates distancing and freedom from the Thing. Kristeva articulates two related components to the transformative and curative process: "the mourning gone through for the lost object (and in its shadow the mourning for the archaic Thing)" and "the subject's acceptance of a set of signs (signifying precisely because of the absence of object)."[73] In light of these psychotherapeutic issues, it becomes evident that the *real*, the non-symbolized, cannot serve as a touchstone for psychocultural transformation. Language, which removes us from the fantasized, illusory plenitude of immediacy, is also the resource for renewing meaningful, symbolically mediated existence.

In accordance with the insight that meaningful existence is constituted within polysemic linguistic and symbolic expression, Kristeva reformulates the psychoanalytic definition of sublimation. Like Freud, Kristeva understands sublimation as involving modified expression of the drives, yielding culturally valued creative production. However, sublimation, for Kristeva, is not simply a model for the transformation of sexual energy into higher mental processes. In addition, sublimation involves translating and connecting the *form* of signification evident in primary process or semiotic expression (*signifiance*) to secondary-process symbolization. In *Powers of Horror* Kristeva summarizes her model by stating that "sublimation…is nothing else than the possibility of naming the pre-nominal, the pre-objectal."[74] *Naming* here indicates a process of bringing into language that reconnects the individual to alienated strata of subjectivity, and hence to otherness and to others. It is in this respect a feature of working-through. Referring to this possibility of reconnecting with others as one articulates deep, disconnected dimensions of subjectivity, Kristeva states that "sublimation is an attempt to do so: through melody, rhythm, semantic polyvalency, the so-called poetic form."[75] The extended communicative resources categorized as semiotic have a closer proximity to the somatic, the tactile, and the affective. Because of this, they connect with and allow expression of troubled emotional cores that elude direct designation.

Sublimation is a process of symbolizing and speaking the affective core in a manner enabling communication and understanding: "Sublimation's dynamics, by summoning up primary processes and idealization, weaves a *hypersign* around and within the depressive void."[76] Sublimation, then, conjoins emotion and expression to establish connections with the inarticulate realm of affect. This allows alienated aspects of subjectivity to be brought to articulation in the interpersonal realm. Giving symbolic expression to the semiotic reconnects self and world as a shared meaningful world. For Kristeva, this is nothing less than "an ethical option, for *named* sexual desire insures securing the subject to the other and, consequently, to meaning – to the meaning of life."[77] Sublimation indicates a religious dimension to both therapy and art, insofar as they involve meaningful transformation of modes of subjectivity, including interpersonal relations. This religious dimension appears in the explicit connections between symbolic tools, healing, and processes of self-transformation involving both meaning and ethics (i.e. relations to others guided by values). Here religion has an innovative, and not only a conservative, function. The new constellations produced by sublimation alter the constituent elements brought into conjunction, as the semiotic impinges upon and disrupts the symbolic. Thus there are parallel, interconnected modifications of subjectivity, communicative media, and social-symbolic reality.

The intimacy between religion and art, indicated in Freud's use of the term *illusion* to designate both realms, is brought to a more comprehensive thematic articulation by Kristeva. She develops constructive resonances of the association, providing a reformulated understanding of the psycho-cultural functions of religious forms. Problems of meaning are understood as religious issues (to which the historical religions may be seen to respond in a variety of ways). *Black Sun* integrates religious dimensions of self-understanding and self-development with aesthetic expression in its manifold forms. In this respect, art displays religious qualities, regardless of its connection with traditional religious themes and images. This broadly religious function appears in the potential for aesthetic activity to contribute to the resolution of personal crises through representational renewals of worldviews and of relational modalities.

The severely melancholic condition illustrates the counter-side to the interplay between psyche and culture. That is, cultural existence is renewed on an individual level through processes of breakdown, reconnection with the affective levels of the primary process, and a return to speech utilizing the resources of the semiotic. Kristeva's imagery draws upon Freud's figuration of acculturation, or movement into the symbolic, as involving the "death of the real." Here the process is reproduced on the individual level of breakdown and renewal, potentially leading to personal transformation rather than cultural formation.

Such cycles of death and renewal might be initiated voluntarily, for example through ritual or contemplative practice. They might also occur *involuntarily*, when personal identity and modes of existence suffer disruption and come to be questioned and destabilized. Indeed, with the decline of culturally instituted (religious) practices providing resources for initiatory destructuring and restructuring, involuntary forms of psychological descent appear to proliferate. The task then becomes providing means of responding constructively to these crises. Because of this, the therapeutic concerns of psychoanalysis are raised to the level of subjective transformation in Kristeva's inquiries into art and religion.

Artistic experience can occur somewhere at the intersections of these voluntary and involuntary modes of descent, and this is one reason why it has special significance for Kristeva. For example, concerning the *The Body of the Dead Christ in the Tomb*, painted by Hans Holbein the Younger in 1522, Kristeva writes:

> *[A] melancholy moment* (an actual or imaginary loss of meaning, an actual or imaginary despair, an actual or imaginary razing of symbolic values, including the value of life) summoned up his aesthetic activity, which overcame the melancholy latency while keeping its trace.[78]

The artist is here seen as, in a certain way, being inspired by depression. Artistic expression can provide symbolic resources for grappling with the destruction of meaning and for turning it towards a reconstruction, potentially effecting psycho-cultural renewal. As Kristeva states: "In returning, through the event of death, toward that which produces its break; in exporting semiotic motility across the border on which the symbolic is established, the artist sketches out a kind of second birth."[79] This indicates a cross-fertilization of psychoanalysis, religion, and art that highlights the interplay between symbolization and subjectivity. It may be seen that, while Kristeva ultimately offers a constructive interpretive approach to traditional religions, she points beyond them to the possible transformative function they share with art. Hence she argues that "the artistic experience...appears as the essential component of religiosity. That is perhaps why it is destined to survive the collapse of the historical forms of religion."[80] This point speaks to the issue of discontinuities between traditional modes of symbolization and cultural changes affecting individual experience. It is not so much an issue of whether or not art can replace religion. Rather, the underlying point is that symbol systems, however necessary to the structuring of human existence, must also remain fluid and responsive enough to address both individual variations and cultural changes.

It may therefore be seen that Kristeva's work is explicitly concerned with the problem of reification and closure of cultural forms, including the religious ones. Thus a critical and iconoclastic dimension informs her vision of psycho-cultural renewal. Semiotic upwellings conjoin with the infinite play of symbolic resources in a reconfiguration of cultural representations. This is the point where religion and art overlap in a way that alters our understanding of each. For Freud, the association of art with beauty tends to make it something of a cosmetic gloss. It serves the need for consolation and satisfaction of personal fantasy but impinges only minimally on shared lived

experience. Often, however, art is characterized by an unsettling and challenging *transfiguration of vision*. Thus, for example, Karsten Harries has
argued, with reference to the surrealistic movement, that much of this art
"has as its goal the descent to a more immediate level of experience by
means of a destruction of our superficial understanding of what is real."[81]
Clearly, this goal intersects with religious models of initiatory destructuring
and restructuring. The reality-altering effects of art are further clarified by
Gianni Vattimo's statement that "aesthetic experience leads us into other
possible worlds, and we are made to realize the contingency and relativity of
the 'real' world in which we have to live."[82] Vattimo also links art with
anxiety. He refers to the "shock" of art engendering an unsettling but potentially transformative disruption of worldviews: "The analogy of the *Stoss* of
art with this experience of anxiety may be appreciated if one recalls that the
work of art does not allow itself to be drawn back into a pre-established
network of significance."[83] In this way, the pluralization of representational
worlds yields new perspectives, paralleling and enacting the clash between
the semiotic and the symbolic. This transformative dimension is implicitly
indicated in Freud's arguments in *Civilization and Its Discontents* concerning
the role of art and beauty in ongoing, multifaceted cultural modification of
the experience of reality. This aspect of art also complements Freud's analyses of the developmental effects of religious iconoclasm in *Moses and
Monotheism*. In each case, cultural ideals and means of representation
dislodge the subject from an adherence to a closed imaginary identity and
worldview.

Therefore the term iconoclasm is not applicable solely to the *abolition* of
images in the name of a non-representable ideal. Rather, the iconoclastic
process occurs when representational forms subvert the imaginary
congealing of specific modes of seeing and experiencing, indirectly opening
new vision. Mark C. Taylor discusses this iconoclastic, unsettling quality of
both art and religion under the rubric of *disfiguring*. In doing so, he further
elaborates the interconnections between aesthetic and linguistic expression
as modes of meaningful distancing from immediacy. "Disfiguring," he states,
"enacts denegation in the realm of figure, image, form, and representation."
Disfiguring is revolutionary, in Kristeva's sense, because it disrupts static
figuration, representation, and ways of seeing. Simultaneously, in disrupting
(imaginary) formation, disfiguring allows glimpses of complex, overdetermined modes of awareness not susceptible to direct representation. That is,
"disfiguring figures the unfigurable in and through the faults, fissures,
cracks, and tears of figures."[84] The expansion and differentiation of subjectivity, in conjunction with transformations of expressive modes forming and
mediating subjective experience, serve to displace the habitual attitudes of
the imaginary ego mode. Here art's transformative qualities intersect with
the religious project of meaningfully restructuring subjectivity, when the
iconoclastic moment provides a means of opening to a non-reified, cultur-

ally constituted ideal or universal. Iconoclasm maintains a space between, as it were, true and false universals; that is, between those which foster reflection and inclusive other-directedness, and those which are particularistic and exclusive. Here subjective renewal intersects with cultural critique, because it brings new attitudes, perspectives, and representational forms into play within cultural existence.

Kristeva's explorations of the dynamics between semiotic and symbolic provide a model for a critical and reflective process that is more than merely conceptual. Subjective transformation straddles the agencies, insofar as it is at once rational or discursive, emotional or affective, and ethical or relational. It involves the communicative modes of both the semiotic and the symbolic in dynamic interplay. In other words, it is predicated on cultural symbol systems but continually pressures the confines of those systems as they become closed and reified. In these respects, Kristeva augments and extends Freudian and Lacanian inquiries into the exigencies of subjective formation and re-formation within symbolic worlds.

Concluding reflections

My object in the present inquiry has not been to refute or dismiss the critical arguments at the surface of Freud's inquiries into religion. Of course, as with any attempt at a sweeping explanation of vast and complex cultural phenomena, Freud's analyses fall short of the conclusiveness to which they aspire. Nevertheless they contain important insights into regressive psycho-cultural aspects of religion. In addition to these well-known and well-worn arguments, however, I have illustrated alternative lines of inquiry uneasily coexisting with the surface arguments. These latent and marginal insights open other levels of meaning in Freud's analyses of religio-cultural forms and also reflect on psycho-cultural issues central to psychoanalytic theory.

In effect, Freud's discussions of religion point to the problem of accultur-ation, and specifically delineate the difference between human existence with and without the symbolic and ethical resources of culture. In this regard, one can speak of the *constitutive function of symbolic forms*. Because human formation and development always occur within cultural symbol systems, we tend to take these for granted. The point, however, is not to imagine how symbol systems came into being, but rather to understand how such cultural resources function in psychoanalytic terms. What is at issue here already extends beyond a simple adaptation to culture, because it overlaps with an inquiry into how we become, to a greater or lesser extent, thinking, speaking, rational, ethical, and creative beings within culture. These issues open reflection on *modes* of subjective formation, and do so in a way that focuses on the intersections between subjective development and cultural resources.

Freud's writings, failing to establish the origins of religion, shed consider-able light on how faculties associated with religion originate within psycho-cultural dynamics. As we have seen, these faculties, capacities, and modes of being are explored under a variety of interrelated rubrics. Among the most important of these is the issue of rational ethical capacity, discussed in *The Future of an Illusion*. In different ways, both *Totem and Taboo* and *Civilization and Its Discontents* show such reflective, ethical capacity to be intrinsically related to cultural representations, symbols, and structuring forces. The latter text discusses the intertwinings of *Eros*, aesthetic media, and ethical codes in establishing cultural reality. These explorations return to a theme in the margins of *Totem and Taboo*: subjective formation involves symbolically constituted distanciation from immediacy. Modifications of subjectivity ensuing from internalizations of cultural structures foster an ability to become oriented by principles and ideals, rather than immediate gratifications of drives and ego-narcissism. In *Moses and Monotheism* the inner transformations related to these capacities are further developed under the headings of the advance in *Geistigkeit* and the capacity for renunciation. With these interdependent concepts, Freud strives to delineate an acculturated subjectivity incorporating intellectual, ethical, and representational (symbolic and linguistic) capacities.

Freud's analyses do more than illustrate the function of cultural symbol systems and ideals in psychological formation. Given the benefit of a Lacanian reading, they also provide tools for differentiating between closed, reified symbolic frameworks and those which foster autonomous reflective and ethical capacities. This differentiation is not always clearly made, but it appears in many forms. Examples are the distinctions between ethical ideals which are irrational and repressive, and those which enhance personal and communal existence; the distinction between spirituality (*Geistigkeit*), as signifying psycho-cultural transformation, and the literalized spirits discussed in *Totem and Taboo*; and the differentiation between the imaginary gratification symbolized by the golden calf and Mosaic iconoclasm in *Moses and Monotheism*. These and other such critical, functional distinctions can be categorized under the Lacanian headings of the imaginary and the symbolic. Ricoeur's discussions of psychoanalysis as fostering reflective ethical capacity are also relevant in this regard. Here ethics involves a capacity to relate to others, and to respond to life questions and situations, in terms of ideals, principles, and values. Such cultural universals are not fixed and do not exist in themselves, but are reflective tools applicable in multiple contexts. Therefore they must become *subjectified* – that is, freely and consciously incorporated into individual existence. For this to occur, a sometimes painful and traumatizing disconnection from a habitual attachment to a socialized mode of being must occur.

While Freud and Lacan complement each other in elucidating these issues, Kristeva more explicitly takes the analysis to the next level. Her work sketches some of the pathways where individuals struggle with the task of subjectifying cultural ideals. In relation to my inquiry, one might say that her work explores *reconstituting* possibilities within psycho-cultural dynamics. That is, Kristeva addresses issues related to the problem of cultural forms becoming rigid, constricting, or split off from subjective experience. When this occurs, as it inevitably does, cultural vehicles for subjective development are weakened. Subjects are curtailed and disempowered by the inefficacy of existing representational and expressive resources. Although there are elements of more direct social and political thinking in Kristeva's work, she has turned increasingly to a concern with subjectivity. However, the subject is always understood to be acculturated, a speaking subject. Because of this, her analyses actually respond to collective concerns with modes of symbolization by focusing on individual patterns of breakdown and reconstitution. Suffering and trauma, discussed in the context of severe melancholia, can be the unhappy vehicles of personal transformation. Melancholia also serves as a *paradigm* for the representational fissuring and reconfiguring that can occur in art and literature.

Here a gap in Lacanian theory is rectified. Overly concerned with subjective formation *within* the symbolic, Lacan neglects the creative attributes of personal imagination irreducible to the narcissistic mirroring of the imaginary. Kristeva's analyses are in this respect more dynamic. Her notion of the semiotic links up with marginalized, constructive aspects of the Lacanian imaginary that form an essential counterpart to symbolic orders. The semiotic expresses individual creative capacity, manifest in differentiated, affect-laden forms that pressure the more restricted communicative modes of cultural life, surging into the symbolic. This dynamic can effect a rebuilding of inner space, allowing for greater freedom, individuality, and responses to questions of meaning that are *posed as one's own*. In resolving (or at least addressing) personal crises of meaning, one can introduce new experience and expression into the collective communicative space, and this provides a vehicle for cultural critique and renewal.

We are indeed dependent on cultural forms to provide ideational tools and resources to actualize our human potentialities, and this certainly makes us vulnerable to cultural conditioning. However, Kristeva's work emphasizes that the relationship between subject and culture is neither unidirectional nor passive. In the interplay between semiotic and symbolic, there appear new, shared representations in the form of art, literature, religion, and other cultural vehicles. Critical, ameliorative cultural transformations emerge from a capacity to re-engage and rethink our ideals and values within the media that embody them. That is, we can harness the symbolic resources of given cultures to push ideals beyond their more limited and sometimes limiting actual forms. This is not simply a rational procedure, however, since these forms function and take root at deeper, irrational and affective levels. Thus critical distancing and the opening of possibility are connected with the differentiations within meaningful subjectivity articulated by psychoanalysis.

The Lacanian and Kristevan models of subjectivity incorporate and activate the play between the multiple psychical functions and qualities Freud differentiated into id, ego, and super-ego. Their work builds on the insight, implicit in Freud, that human development occurs across a spectrum of capacities within cultural frameworks. Subjective formation includes emotional, aesthetic, and ethical, as well as intellectual or cognitive, dimensions. *Eros*, super-ego, and ego, in communicative interplay, all contribute meaningfully to human subjectivity. Their work may thus be seen as thematizing the umbrella concept of *Geistigkeit* sketched by Freud. This is indicative of a reflective, ethical capacity irreducible to a single agency or function. Both Lacan and Kristeva also extrapolate on Freud's insight that these agencies are formed within interpersonal and cultural interaction, so that the very being of the subject is interrelational.

A consequence of the interactive constitution of human beings is a congruence between modes of subjectivity and modes of being-with-others. Because of the intermeshing of self and other through the involvement of culture, language, and individual others in the formation of subjectivity, the problem of self-development becomes one of relational modes. Personal maturation, as involving heightened awareness and sensitivity to interrelationality, brings with it an increase in empathic capacity. That is, there is a necessarily ethical dimension to the developmental model emerging from Lacan's and Kristeva's extrapolations on Freud. This ethical dimension is, moreover, enabled or actualized by linguistic and aesthetic vehicles. It is a matter not simply of following abstract rules, codes, or ideals, but of a capacity to experience, imagine, and understand beyond the confines of narcissistic orientations. Since we are not transparent to ourselves, symbolic media are intrinsic to the possibility of what is conjointly the development of subjectivity and of meaningful, mutual relations with others. The issue of how one *sees* or envisages the other indicates the confluence of ethical and symbolic concerns.

Thus the formulations of Lacan and Kristeva develop many of the implicit and explicit insights appearing in Freud's analyses of religion. The problem of religion is, of course, tremendously complex. Even within the parameters of the present inquiry, the emerging view of religion is both overdetermined and unfinished. However, as interrogated by Freud and extended by Lacan and Kristeva, one facet of religious forms has been clarified. What appears in the overview is insights into religious dimensions of human existence as having to do with *ethical transformations of subjectivity within cultural symbol systems*. Conversely, this body of work also alerts us to one of the core issues of modern culture: the breakdown and relativization of traditional vehicles for the transmission of ethical ideals and meaningful worldviews. This problem is exacerbated by the enormous influential power of new forms of media, usually disconnected from any concern with qualitative enhancement of subjective existence.

The main contribution of the present inquiry has been to show that symbol systems and ideals are intrinsic to the formation of differentiated and reflective modes of subjectivity. In doing so, my hope is that it will have increased awareness of our locatedness within cultural forms. This serves, on the one hand, to foster appreciation for these forms, including the religious. In making this point, I hope to have pushed psycho-cultural inquiry beyond the simplistic reductionism often associated with psychoanalysis. On the other hand, my goal has equally been to increase awareness of the conditioning forces of acculturation. Again, this takes critical thinking concerning the status and function of religion and ideals beyond empiricism to a qualitative level of analysis. The issue becomes that of the *modality* of cultural representations; that is, do they enhance or inhibit reflective and ethical capacity?

It might be excessive to claim that this project delineates a new psychoanalytic approach to religion and culture superseding prior versions. Nevertheless, the interplay between Freud, Lacan, and Kristeva indicates more complex and seminal relationships among psychoanalytic theory, cultural inquiry, and religious thought than have generally been assumed.

Notes

Introduction: tensions in Freud, extensions in Lacan and Kristeva

1 Anthony Wilden, *The Rules Are No Game: The Strategy of Communication* (London: Routledge & Kegan Paul, 1987), p. 60.
2 Erik Erikson employs the expression *psycho-social* in a manner which partially anticipates the present focus on intersections of psychological and cultural realities. See, in particular, *Childhood and Society* (New York: Norton, 1950), pp. 257ff. In Freud's writings, some of the most direct expressions of this overlapping occur in *Group Psychology and the Analysis of the Ego*, SE XVIII: 69; and *Civilization and Its Discontents*, SE XXI: 142. Unless otherwise noted, all references to Freud are to *The Standard Edition of the Complete Psychological Works of Sigmund Freud*, translated under the general editorship of James Strachey, 24 vols. (London: Hogarth Press, 1953–74), hereafter SE. German references, where given, are to *Gesammelte Werke: chronologisch geordnet*, edited by A. Freud, E. Bibring, W. Hoffer, E. Kris, and O. Isakower, 18 vols. (London: Imago, 1940–50), hereafter GW.
3 Wilden, *The Rules Are No Game*, pp. 168–9.
4 Jean-Luc Nancy, *The Experience of Freedom*, translated by Bridget McDonald (Stanford, CA: Stanford University Press, 1993), p. 30.
5 Luce Irigaray, *Speculum of the Other Woman*, translated by Gillian C. Gill (Ithaca, NY: Cornell University Press, 1985), p. 133.
6 Gilbert Chaitin, *Rhetoric and Culture in Lacan* (Cambridge: Cambridge University Press, 1996), p. 4.
7 Paul Ricoeur, *Freud and Philosophy: An Essay in Interpretation*, translated by Denis Savage (New Haven, CT: Yale University Press, 1970), p. 46.
8 Jean Laplanche, *Life and Death in Psychoanalysis*, translated by Jeffrey Mehlman (Baltimore, MD: Johns Hopkins University Press, 1976), pp. 1–3.
9 Jane Flax, *Thinking Fragments: Psychoanalysis, Feminism, and Postmodernism in the Contemporary West* (Berkeley, CA: University of California Press, 1990), p. 16.
10 *Ibid.*
11 Freud's definition of overdetermination may be found in *The Interpretation of Dreams*, SE IV: 266, 279, 383–4. Overinterpretation is discussed in SE V: 353 and 471. For further definitions of overdetermination and overinterpretation, see J. Laplanche and J.-B. Pontalis, *The Language of Psychoanalysis*, translated by Donald Nicholson-Smith (New York: Norton, 1973), pp. 292–4. See also Paul Ricoeur, *Freud and Philosophy: An Essay in Interpretation*, p. 193.

12 Jacques Derrida, *Positions*, translated by Alan Bass (Chicago, IL: University of Chicago Press, 1981), p. 45.
13 Jacques Derrida, *Aporias*, translated by Thomas Dutoit (Stanford, CA: Stanford University Press, 1993), p. 9.
14 Jacques Derrida, "Freud and the scene of writing," *Writing and Difference*, translated by Alan Bass (Chicago, IL: University of Chicago Press, 1978); *The Post Card: From Socrates to Freud and Beyond*, translated by Alan Bass (Chicago, IL: University of Chicago Press, 1987); and *Archive Fever: A Freudian Impression*, translated by E. Prenowitz (Chicago, IL: University of Chicago Press, 1996).
15 Nicola Abbagnano, "Positivism," in Paul Edwards (ed.), *The Encyclopedia of Philosophy* (New York: Macmillan, 1967), vol. 6, p. 414.
16 Jacques Derrida, *Of Grammatology*, translated by Gayatri Chakravorty Spivak (Baltimore, MD: Johns Hopkins University Press, 1976), p. 60.
17 Jacques Derrida, *Positions*, pp. 64–5.
18 Jacques Derrida, "Freud and the scene of writing," p. 211.
19 Quoted in Susan Handelman, *The Slayers of Moses: The Emergence of Rabbinic Interpretation in Modern Literary Theory* (Albany, NY: SUNY Press, 1982), p. 80.
20 Donald Spence, *Narrative Truth and Historical Truth: Meaning and Interpretation in Psychoanalysis* (New York: Norton, 1982), p. 31.
21 *Ibid.*, p. 28.
22 *Ibid.*, p. 32.
23 See Mircea Eliade, *The Sacred and the Profane*, translated by Willard Trask (New York: Harcourt, Brace, & World, 1959). See also Mircea Eliade, *Cosmos and History: The Myth of the Eternal Return*, translated by Willard Trask (New York: Harper & Row, 1959).
24 For a clear statement on this point, see Freud, *An Outline of Psychoanalysis*, SE XXIII: 183–4. See also Michel Foucault, *Madness and Civilization*, translated by Richard Howard (New York: Random House, 1965), p. 198, for related advances in psychoanalytic theory and practice over those of asylums. However, Foucault also criticizes Freud for transferring excessive authority to the analyst (*ibid.*, p. 278).
25 Freud, *Moses and Monotheism*, SE XXIII: 123.
26 Elisabeth Roudinesco, *Jacques Lacan*, translated by Barbara Bray (New York: Columbia University Press, 1997).
27 Jacques Lacan, *The Four Fundamental Concepts of Psychoanalysis*, translated by Alan Sheridan (London: Penguin Books, 1977), p. 265.

1 Trauma, Oedipus complex, and the exigencies of subjective formation

1 Sigmund Freud, *Introductory Lectures on Psychoanalysis*, SE XVI: 275; GW XI: 284.
2 Ian Hacking, *Rewriting the Soul: Multiple Personality and the Sciences of Memory* (Princeton, NJ: Princeton University Press, 1995), p. 192.
3 William J. McGrath, *Freud's Discovery of Psychoanalysis* (Ithaca, NY: Cornell University Press, 1986), p. 194.
4 *Ibid.* Also important in tracing changes in Freud's thinking on the issues of trauma and fantasy are *The Complete Letters of Sigmund Freud to Wilhelm Fliess 1887–1904*, translated and edited by J. M. Masson (Cambridge, MA: Harvard University Press, 1985). For Freud's earlier theories, see pp. 239–40. For his abandonment of the theory of seduction, see pp. 264–6.

5 SE XVI: 370; and cf. SE XXIII: 187.
6 SE XVI: 276.
7 Sigmund Freud, *New Introductory Lectures on Psychoanalysis*, SE XXII: 120. An excellent discussion of these issues can be found in Ned Lukacher, *Primal Scenes* (Ithaca, NY: Cornell University Press, 1986), pp. 52–8.
8 See, e.g., Alice Miller, *The Drama of the Gifted Child*, translated by Ruth Ward (New York: Basic Books, 1990), p. vii.
9 McGrath, *Freud's Discovery of Psychoanalysis*, p. 307.
10 SE V: 620; GW II/III: 625.
11 SE XVI: 368; GW XI: 383.
12 SE XIII: 159; GW IX: 192. A good discussion of this issue is found in Gananath Obeyesekere, *The Work of Culture* (Chicago, IL: University of Chicago Press, 1990), p. 66.
13 Sigmund Freud, *Beyond the Pleasure Principle*, SE XVIII: 13.
14 Freud notes that the game can be understood as providing the means of moving from a *passive* situation, in which his grandson was "overpowered by the experience" of his mother's departure, to taking an *active* part in this experience (SE XVIII: 16). As Maud Mannoni states, "what was apparent from the 'gone–here' game was that the Symbolic dimension had entered into the mother–child relationship" (*The Child, his "Illness", and the Others* (Harmondsworth: Penguin, 1970), p. 17). Two of many other places where this transition is explicitly linked to language and symbolizing are: Jacques Lacan, *Écrits: A Selection*, translated by Alan Sheridan (London: Routledge, 1977), pp. 103–4; and Samuel Weber, *The Legend of Freud* (Minneapolis, MN: University of Minnesota Press, 1982), pp. 140ff.
15 Cathy Caruth, *Unclaimed Experience: Trauma, Narrative, and History* (Baltimore, MD: Johns Hopkins University Press, 1996), p. 59.
16 McGrath, *Freud's Discovery of Psychoanalysis*. p. 197.
17 Maud Mannoni, *The Child, his "Illness", and the Others*, p. 23.
18 SE XXII: 120.
19 Jean-Joseph Goux has formulated an extended, illuminating interpretation of the Oedipal mythos of Sophocles that differs significantly from Freud's readings. Specifically, Goux focuses on Oedipus as a narrative of "failed initiation." In light of this, it may well be that the Oedipus complex is a misnomer. See Jean-Joseph Goux, *Oedipus, Philosopher*, translated by Catherine Porter (Stanford, CA: Stanford University Press, 1993). Nevertheless, for my present concerns the issue remains the psycho-cultural phenomena Freud sought to understand in terms of what he *called* the Oedipus complex, rather than the accuracy and comprehensiveness of Freud's analyses of Greek drama.
20 See, for example, Sigmund Freud, "The dissolution of the Oedipus complex," SE XIX: 173–9; "Some psychical consequences of the anatomical distinction between the sexes," SE XIX: 256–7; and *An Outline of Psychoanalysis*, SE XXIII: 188ff.
21 Sigmund Freud, *Introductory Lectures on Psychoanalysis*, SE XV: 207–8.
22 See Jane Flax, *Thinking Fragments: Psychoanalysis, Feminism, and Postmodernism in the Contemporary West* (Berkeley, CA: University of California Press, 1990), p. 106; see also Madelon Sprengnether, *The Spectral Mother: Freud, Feminism, and Psychoanalysis* (Ithaca, NY: Cornell University Press, 1990).
23 For a thorough critique, see Luce Irigaray, *Speculum of the Other Woman*, translated by Gillian C. Gill (Ithaca, NY: Cornell University Press, 1985). A partial defense of Freud and correction of some of Irigaray's sweeping arguments is

provided by Sarah Kofman, *The Enigma of Woman*, translated by Catherine Porter (Ithaca, NY: Cornell University Press, 1985), pp. 114–21.

24 Sigmund Freud, *Totem and Taboo*, SE XIII: 57, note 1; GW IX: 189, note 1.

25 Sigmund Freud, *The Ego and the Id*, SE XIX: 31.

26 *Ibid.*, p. 33.

27 Robert Samuels, *Between Philosophy and Psychoanalysis: Lacan's Reconstruction of Freud* (New York: Routledge, 1993), p. 28.

28 Gananath Obeyesekere, *The Work of Culture*, p. 94.

29 Sigmund Freud, *Introductory Lectures on Psychoanalysis*, SE XV: 205–6. Paul Ricoeur also emphasizes that "the Oedipus complex involves the family and in general the social phenomenon of authority." *Freud and Philosophy: An Essay in Interpretation*, translated by Denis Savage (New Haven, CT: Yale University Press, 1970), p. 188.

30 SE XXIII: 146.

31 One of many places where Freud relates libido to "love in the wider sense" is *Group Psychology and the Analysis of the Ego*, SE XVIII: 90–1.

32 Jane Flax, *Thinking Fragments*, p. 49.

33 A similar awareness of the need to conjoin cognitive and libidinal developmental models underpins the project of Hans G. Furth in *Knowledge As Desire: An Essay On Freud and Piaget* (New York: Columbia University Press, 1987).

34 Freud, "A short account of psycho-analysis," SE XIX: 208.

35 Jacques Lacan, *Speech and Language in Psychoanalysis*, translated by Anthony Wilden (Baltimore, MD: Johns Hopkins University Press, 1981), p. 126.

36 Jacques Lacan, *The Seminar of Jacques Lacan, Book VII: The Ethics of Psychoanalysis*, translated by Dennis Porter (New York: Norton, 1992), p. 142.

37 Jacques Lacan, *Écrits: A Selection*, p. 67.

38 Anthony Wilden, *The Rules Are No Game: The Strategy of Communication* (London: Routledge & Kegan Paul, 1987), p. 77.

39 As Elizabeth Grosz argues, "in his formulation of this [Oedipal/symbolic] structure as an inevitable law, patriarchal dominance is not so much challenged as displaced, from biology to the equally unchangeable, socio-linguistic law of the father" (*Jacques Lacan: A Feminist Introduction* (New York: Routledge, 1990), pp. 144–5). The question is, to what extent does Lacan view social laws and norms as unchangeable? Moreover, to what extent are extant social forms homologous with the symbolic as a mode of being? While there is some ambiguity on this matter, the interdependent nature of the three registers resists closure of the symbolic order. In addition, it is noteworthy that, following the above comments, Grosz argues that Lacan "proposes a theory of the socio-linguistic genesis of subjectivity which enables male and female subjects to be seen as social and historical effects, rather than pre-ordained biological givens" (*ibid.*, p. 148).

40 Sigmund Freud, *New Introductory Lectures on Psychoanalysis*, SE XXII: 73.

41 SE XXII: 61–2.

42 Hans W. Loewald, *Sublimation* (New Haven, CT: Yale University Press, 1988), p. 7. Lacan similarly discusses Freud's awareness that "the operations of sublimation are always ethically, culturally, and socially valorized." He further notes that the extra-psychological character of these cultural criteria "creates a difficulty" for Freud. See Lacan, *The Seminar of Jacques Lacan, Book VII: The Ethics of Psychoanalysis*, p. 144.

2 Religion, ethics, and acculturation

1 Paul Ricoeur, "Psychoanalysis and the movement of contemporary culture," translated by Willis Domingo, *The Conflict of Interpretations*, ed. Don Ihde (Evanston, IL: Northwestern University Press, 1974), p.145. Similar assumptions, unqualified by the alternative insights supplied by Ricoeur, continue to govern the reception of Freud's writings on religion. This limited view appears, for example, in James W. Jones's assertion that "Freud's biological determinism and Newtonian atomism set the terms in which he analyzed religion" (*Contemporary Psychoanalysis and Religion* (New Haven, CT: Yale University Press, 1991), p. 33).

2 Sigmund Freud, *The Future of an Illusion*, SE XXI: 16.

3 *The Future of An Illusion*, SE XXI: 7; GW XIV: 328.

4 SE XXI: 10; GW XIV: 331. The polysemy of the term *seelisch*, which might also be translated as *spiritual*, becomes increasingly significant when juxtaposed with other such terminological overdeterminations. Of particular interest will be Freud's extensive use of the term *Geistigkeit* in *Moses and Monotheism*.

5 SE XXI: 12–13.

6 *Ibid.*, p. 39.

7 *Ibid.*, p. 14.

8 *Ibid.*, p. 31; GW XIV: 353.

9 Sigmund Freud, *The Interpretation of Dreams*, SE V: 550ff.; *The Psychopathology of Everyday Life*, SE VI: 164; *Introductory Lectures on Psychoanalysis*, SE XV: 77–8.

10 SE XXI: 43.

11 *Ibid.*, p. 19.

12 Sigmund Freud, *Beyond the Pleasure Principle*, SE XVIII: 36ff.

13 An excellent critical analysis of the death drive is developed by Richard Boothby in *Death and Desire: Psychoanalytic Theory in Lacan's Return to Freud* (London: Routledge, 1991).

14 Sigmund Freud, *Civilization and Its Discontents*, SE XXI: 129.

15 Sigmund Freud, *The Ego and the Id*, SE XIX: 44.

16 *The Future of an Illusion*, SE XXI: 31.

17 *Ibid.*, p. 30.

18 SE XXI: 31; GW XIV: 354.

19 *Ibid.*, p. 43.

20 SE XXI: 44; GW XIV: 368.

21 SE XXI: 47; GW XIV: 370.

22 SE XXI: 48; GW XIV: 371.

23 *Ibid.*, p. 49 (italics in original).

24 *Ibid.*, p. 53.

25 Sigmund Freud, *Civilization and Its Discontents* SE XXI: 109. See also Ernest Wallwork, *Psychoanalysis and Ethics* (New Haven, CT: Yale University Press, 1991), pp. 193ff.

26 Wallwork, *Psychoanalysis and Ethics*, p. 205.

27 SE XXI: 39.

28 *Ibid.*, p. 44.

29 SE XXI: 53; GW XIV: 317.

30 Further elaborations of a constructive ethic also appear in the discussions of *Eros* throughout *Civilization and Its Discontents*. A related argument, illustrating the limits of reason as a basis for ethics and stressing the importance of Freud's invocations of *Eros* in this regard, is formulated by Eli Sagan, *Freud, Women, and*

Morality: The Psychology of Good and Evil (New York: Basic Books, 1988), pp. 153ff.

31 See D. W. Winnicott, *Playing and Reality* (New York: Routledge, 1971). See also William Meissner, *Psychoanalysis and Religious Experience* (New Haven, CT: Yale University Press, 1984), p. 181. The convoluted nature of this *constructive* use of the term illusion has been noted by James W. Jones, *Contemporary Psychoanalysis and Religion*, p. 41.

32 *Civilization and Its Discontents*, SE XXI: 81.

33 *Ibid.*, p. 75.

34 *Ibid.*, p. 76.

35 Freud thus speculates that "it is not only the pressure of civilization but something in the nature of the [sexual] function itself which denies us full satisfaction and urges us along other paths" (SE XXI: 105).

36 SE XXI: 82; GW XIV: 441.

37 SE XXI: 88; GW XIV: 446.

38 SE XXI: 89; GW XIV: 448.

39 SE XXI: 64.

40 *Ibid.*, p. 66; and cf. *The Ego and the Id*, SE XIX: 23.

41 *Civilization and its Discontents*, SE XXI: 66–7.

42 *Ibid.*, p. 67.

43 *The Ego and the Id*, SE XIX: 25.

44 Paul Ricoeur, *Freud and Philosophy: An Essay in Interpretation*, translated by Denis Savage (New Haven, CT: Yale University Press, 1970), p. 458.

45 Paul Ricoeur, *The Conflict of Interpretations*, p. 164.

46 Freud, *Civilization and Its Discontents*, SE XXI: 101.

47 Ricoeur, *Freud and Philosophy*, p. 320.

48 SE XXI: 80; GW XIV: 439 (emphasis added).

49 SE XXI: 80; GW XIV: 439 (emphasis added).

50 Julia Kristeva, *Black Sun: Depression and Melancholia*, translated by Leon S. Roudiez (New York: Columbia University Press, 1989), pp. 13–14.

51 Dylan Evans, *An Introductory Dictionary of Lacanian Psychoanalysis* (New York, Routledge, 1996), p. 98. Evans also notes that "this legal-linguistic structure is in fact no more and no less than the symbolic order itself" (*ibid.*, p. 99).

52 Jacques Lacan, *The Seminar of Jacques Lacan, Book I: Freud's Papers on Technique 1953–1954*, translated by John Forrester (Cambridge: Cambridge University Press, 1988) (hereafter *Seminar I*), p. 66.

53 *Seminar I*, p. 262. Lacan is, of course, deeply influenced by Sauserrian linguistics, for which "no signification can be sustained other than by reference to another signification" (Jacques Lacan, *Écrits: A Selection*, translated by Alan Sheridan (London: Routledge, 1977), p. 150; *Écrits* (Paris: Éditions du Seuil, 1966), p. 498). That is, the terms within a particular language take on meaning in their differentiation from each other and in relation to the system of rules of that language (*la langue*). Reference to specific objects will be shaped and informed by the wider, open-ended system.

54 *Seminar I*, p. 263, and cf. *ibid.*, p. 228:

> Before speech nothing either is or isn't [*rien n'est, ni n'est pas*]. Everything is already there, no doubt, but it is only with speech that there are things which are – which are true or false, that is to say which are – and things which are

not. Truth hollows out its way into the real thanks to the dimension of speech.

Lacan also refers to "the symbolic relation" as being the "power of naming objects [which] structures the perception itself. The *percipi* of man can only be sustained within a zone of nomination" (Jacques Lacan, *The Seminar of Jacques Lacan, Book II*, translated by Sylvana Tomaselli (Cambridge: Cambridge University Press, 1988), p. 169; hereafter *Seminar II*).

55 See Kaja Silverman, *The Subject of Semiotics* (New York: Oxford University Press, 1983), p. 162.
56 Emmanuel Levinas, *Totality and Infinity*, translated by Alphonso Lingis (Pittsburgh, PA: Duquesne University Press, 1969), p. 62. For comparable Lacanian views, see Jacques Lacan, *Écrits: A Selection*, p. 286. See also Elizabeth Grosz, *Jacques Lacan: A Feminist Introduction* (London: Routledge, 1990), pp. 59ff.
57 Pathologies of the super-ego, particularly in terms of culturally fostered authoritarianism, are discussed in Sagan, *Freud, Women, and Morality*; see pp. 3–15.
58 See Stuart Schneiderman, *Jacques Lacan: The Death of an Intellectual Hero* (Cambridge, MA: Harvard University Press, 1983), pp. 33–5. As Schneiderman notes, the Borromean knot also illustrates the interdependence of inner and outer.
59 Jacques Lacan, *Écrits: A Selection*, pp. 18–19. John P. Muller and William Richardson note that the image of the mirror need not be taken literally. It signifies a captation by an external image that allows for the formation of the ego in identification (*Lacan and Language: A Reader's Guide to Écrits* (New York: International Universities Press, 1982), p. 30).
60 *Seminar I*, p. 188. This pejorative account of identification is contextualized by John P. Muller, who introduces a qualitative distinction between imaginary and symbolic modes into the discussion. As he states, "imaginary identification reinforces likeness and constrains the field of desire in a mirroring relation; symbolic identification structures difference and opens desire onto the field of substitution and displacement" (*Beyond the Psychoanalytic Dyad: Developmental Semiotics in Freud, Pierce, and Lacan* (New York: Routledge, 1996), p. 146). This notion of symbolic identification will resurface in a significant way in my discussion of Freud's discourse on the figure of Moses.
61 Jacques Lacan, *Écrits: A Selection*, p. 4.
62 *Seminar II*, p. 50.
63 Samuel Weber, *Return to Freud: Jacques Lacan's Dislocation of Psychoanalysis*, translated by Michael Levine (New York: Cambridge University Press, 1991), p. 14.
64 *Seminar II*, p. 155. For the connection between imaginary orientations and identification, see *Seminar I*, p. 116. In *The Ego and the Id* (SE XIX: 48) Freud discusses identification in the formation of the super-ego. In these passages Freud stresses that the ego is *dependent* on the super-ego (and hence identification is formulated in terms close to those emphasized by Lacan, i.e. as related to compulsions that qualify the ego's autonomy). On the other hand, identification is also indicated as the basis for further ethical development, an issue that Lacan discusses in terms of symbolic identification.
65 Muller and Richardson emphasize that "when Lacan speaks of the 'reality principle' he means the ego's distorting, negating, and oppositional manner of adjusting things to suit its own rigid style – especially its resistance to the growth of the subject" (*Lacan and Language*, p. 63).

66 *Seminar I*, p. 116 (emphasis added).
67 Sigmund Freud, *The Future of an Illusion*, SE XXI: 41; GW XIV: 365.
68 *Seminar I*, p. 267. Similarly, Lacan emphasizes that "it is in this negativity in so far as it is a pure negativity – that is, detached from any particular motive – that lies the junction between the symbolic and the real" (*Écrits: A Selection*, p. 95).
69 See Ferdinand de Saussure, *Course in General Linguistics*, translated by Roy Harris (LaSalle, IL: Open Court, 1986), p. 120.
70 *Ibid.*, p. 128.
71 Jacques Lacan, *Écrits: A Selection*, p. 126; *Écrits*, p. 414.

3 Displacement, supplementarity, and symbolic meaning in *Totem and Taboo*

1 Sigmund Freud, *Totem and Taboo*, SE XIII: 100.
2 Sigmund Freud, *Totem and Taboo*, SE XIII: 156; GW IX: 188.
3 Edwin R. Wallace, *Freud and Anthropology* (New York: International Universities Press, 1983), pp. 113–69.
4 Some of the relevant sources are: Herbert Marcuse, *Eros and Civilization* (Boston, MA: Beacon Press, 1955), p. 60; Patrick Mahoney, "The budding International Association of Psychoanalysis and its discontents: a feature of Freud's discourse," *Psychoanalysis and Discourse* (London: Tavistock, 1987), pp. 175ff; Tomoko Masuzawa, *In Search of Dreamtime: The Quest for the Origin of Religion* (Chicago, IL: University of Chicago Press, 1993), pp. 76–161. The antithesis of approaches discerning layers of symbolic meaning in Freud's text would be represented by René Girard, *Violence and the Sacred*, translated by Patrick Gregory (Baltimore, MD: Johns Hopkins University Press, 1977), pp. 193–222. As Peter Rudnytsky summarizes, "Girard promotes what is at best speculation to the status of a 'fact'" (*Freud and Oedipus* (New York: Columbia University Press, 1987), p. 347).
5 Sigmund Freud, *Moses and Monotheism* SE XXIII: 81; GW XVI: 186. Freud also refers to *Totem and Taboo* as a "construction of primaeval history" composed of "large portions of the past which have been linked together here into a whole" (SE XXIII: 84).
6 Paul Ricoeur, *Freud and Philosophy: An Essay in Interpretation*, translated by Denis Savage (New Haven, CT: Yale University Press, 1970), p. 208. Similarly, Jacques Lacan refers to *Totem and Taboo* as "le mythe freudien" (*Le Séminaire, Livre XVII: L'Envers de la psychanalyse* (Paris: Éditions du Seuil, 1991), p. 143).
7 SE XIII: 32.
8 SE XIII: 3–4.
9 *Ibid.*, p. 6.
10 *Ibid.*
11 *Ibid.*, p. 7.
12 *Ibid.*, pp. 16–17.
13 *Ibid.*, p. 27.
14 SE XVI: 264ff.
15 SE XIII: 27.
16 *Ibid.*, pp. 28–9.
17 *Ibid.*, p. 53.
18 *Ibid.*, p. 29.
19 *Ibid.*
20 *Ibid.*, p. 30.
21 *Ibid.*, p. 30.

22 *Ibid.*, pp. 50–1 (emphasis in original).
23 *Ibid.*, p. 34.
24 *Ibid.*, pp. 65; see also p. 95.
25 Paul Ricoeur, *Freud and Philosophy*, p. 93.
26 Lacan, *Écrits: A Selection*, translated by Alan Sheridan (London: Routledge, 1977), pp. 160–1. See also Sigmund Freud, *The Interpretation of Dreams* SE IV: 277ff.; GW II/III: 283ff., for the dream work involving condensation, displacement, and representation; and SE V: 488ff.; GW II/III: 492ff., for secondary revision. These constitute the four categories by which Freud discerns the construction of dreams, and they reveal numerous indications of language-like processes. J. Muller and W. Richardson, *Lacan and Language: A Reader's Guide to Écrits* (New York: International Universities Press, 1982), pp. 11–17, provide a lucid account of the Lacanian view of the broadly linguistic nature of these processes (predicated on the work of Jakobson and Halle). See also Julia Kristeva, *Revolution in Poetic Language*, translated by Margaret Waller (New York: Columbia University Press, 1984), p. 59.
27 SE IV: 266. The point is elaborated by Barnaby B. Barratt, *Psychoanalysis and the Postmodern Impulse* (Baltimore, MD: Johns Hopkins University Press, 1993), p. 41: "the generation of extrinsic manifest meanings – the translation, elaboration and annunciation of what the patient thought or spoke into another code – is not what makes psychoanalysis psychoanalytic."
28 Sigmund Freud, *The Ego and the Id*, SE XIX: 45.
29 SE XIII: 67–8; GW IX: 85.
30 See Jacques Derrida, *Of Grammatology*, translated by Gayatri Chakravorty Spivak (Baltimore, MD: Johns Hopkins University Press, 1976), p. 36:

> There is no longer a simple origin. For what is reflected is split *in itself* and not only as an addition to itself of its image. The reflection, the image, the double, splits what it doubles. The origin of speculation becomes a difference.

Similarly, Freud's constructed origin seems to be founded on differences that are both intra-psychic and interrelational.
31 SE XIII: 71; GW IX: 88.
32 SE XIII: 73; GW IX: 91.
33 SE XIII: 74.
34 SE IX: 127.
35 Jacques Derrida, "Freud and the scene of writing," *Writing and Difference*, translated by Alan Bass (Chicago, IL: University of Chicago Press, 1978), p. 212. Elsewhere, Derrida further reflects on the co-constitution of supplement and origin: "One wishes to go back *from the supplement to the source*: one must recognize that there is a *supplement at the source*" (*Of Grammatology*, p. 304).
36 Derrida, *Of Grammatology*, p. 244.
37 Freud, *New Introductory Lectures on Psychoanalysis*, SE XX: 97.
38 Laplanche and Pontalis define working-through as "a sort of psychical work which allows the subject to accept certain repressed elements and to free himself from the grip of mechanisms of repetition" (J. Laplanche and J.-B. Pontalis, *The Language of Psycho-Analysis*, translated by Donald Nicholson-Smith (New York: Norton, 1973), p. 488).
39 Julia Kristeva, *Powers of Horror: An Essay on Abjection*, translated by Leon S. Roudiez (New York: Columbia University Press, 1982), p. 89.
40 See, for example, SE XIII: 1.
41 *Ibid.*, p. 77.
42 SE XIII: 22; GW IX: 32.

43 Yosef Hayim Yerushalmi, *Freud's Moses: Judaism Terminable and Interminable* (New Haven, CT: Yale University Press, 1991), p. 51.

44 SE XIII: 61; GW IX: 77.

45 SE XIII: 64; GW IX: 81.

46 SE XIII: 64–5; GW IX: 81.

47 SE XIII: 85; GW IX: 106.

48 Stuart Schneiderman, *Rat Man* (New York: New York University Press, 1986), p. 96.

49 *Ibid.*, p. 106.

50 SE XIII: 79.

51 *Ibid.*, p. 82.

52 *Ibid.*, p. 83.

53 *Ibid.*, p. 91.

54 *Ibid.*, p. 91.

55 *Ibid.*, p. 88.

56 Freud, *New Introductory Lectures On Psychoanalysis*, SE XXII: 170.

57 SE XIII: 35.

58 The status of any given form of traditional religion with respect to this critical, ethical task is, of course, ambiguous. As Max Weber established, religions can function to critique social injustice, but they can also serve as legitimations for entrenched power structures (Max Weber, *The Sociology of Religion*, translated by Ephraim Fischoff (Boston, MA: Beacon Press, 1963), p. 107).

59 SE XIII: 90; GW IX: 111.

60 A relevant analysis of the theme of incest as representing self-enclosure or "autism" is formulated by Jean-Joseph Goux. See *Oedipus, Philosopher*, translated by Catherine Porter (Stanford, CA: Stanford University Press, 1993), p. 136.

61 SE XIII: 93; GW IX: 114.

62 SE XIII: 93; GW IX: 114.

63 SE XIII: 97–8; GW IX: 119–20.

64 SE XIII: 95–6.

65 SE XXI: 124; and cf. SE XIII: 123–4.

66 SE XIII: 125; GW IX: 152.

67 See Sigmund Freud, *New Introductory Lectures on Psychoanalysis*, SE XXII: 95; and "Why war?," SE XXII: 211. For a discussion of the constructive function of myth in Freud's theorizing, see Anthony Wilden, *System and Structure* (London: Tavistock, 1980), p. 198.

68 Lévi-Strauss refers to "the mythopoetical power of *bricolage*" as constituting an "abandonment of all reference to a *center*, to a *subject*, to a privileged *reference*, to an origin or to an absolute *archia*" (*Le Cru et le cuit*, p. 419, quoted in Anthony Wilden, *System and Structure*, p. 259).

69 SE XIII: 125.

70 *Ibid.*, p. 126.

71 Robert Samuels, *Between Philosophy and Psychoanalysis: Lacan's Reconstruction of Freud* (New York: Routledge, 1993) p. 76.

72 See Freud, "Analysis of a phobia in a five-year-old boy," SE X: 5–149.

73 SE XIII: 127–8; GW IX: 155.

74 SE XIII: 129; GW IX: 157.

75 Julia Kristeva, *Powers of Horror: An Essay in Abjection*, p. 35.

76 *Ibid.*, pp. 4–6.

77 *Ibid.*, p. 37.

78 SE XIII: 132; GW IX: 160.

79 SE XIII: 139.
80 SE XIII: 133; GW IX: 161.
81 SE XIII: 150; GW IX: 181.
82 It is instructive to compare Georges Bataille's reading of sacrifice as instituting and/or representing "separation from the world of things" and "negation of the real order" (see *Theory of Religion*, translated by Robert Hurley (New York: Zone Books, 1992), pp. 43–5).
83 SE XIII: 133; GW IX: 162.
84 SE XIII: 136; GW IX: 165 (original emphasis removed).
85 SE XIII: 141–2; GW IX: 171–2.
86 SE XIII: 143; GW IX: 173.
87 See Tomoko Masuzawa, *In Search of Dreamtime*, pp. 101, 127.
88 Julia Kristeva, *Revolution in Poetic Language*, p. 25. Specific reference to the *chora* as having *maternal* associations is given in *ibid.*, p. 65.
89 *Ibid.*, p. 26.
90 Julia Kristeva, *Powers of Horror: An Essay on Abjection*, p. 94.
91 Julia Kristeva, *Revolution in Poetic Language*, p. 70. See also Kristeva, *Powers of Horror: An Essay on Abjection*, p. 61, where the representational status of these formulations "on the level of the subjective history of each individual" is further developed, specifically in terms of "the *advent of language*, which breaks with the perviousness if not with the chaos that precedes it and sets up denomination as an exchange of linguistic signs" (emphasis original).
92 SE XIII: 143; GW IX: 173.
93 Julia Kristeva, *Revolution in Poetic Language*, p. 75.
94 Robert Samuels, *Between Philosophy and Psychoanalysis*, p. 81. Compare Jacques Lacan, *Speech and Language in Psychoanalysis*, translated by Anthony Wilden (Baltimore, MD: Johns Hopkins University Press, 1981), p. 271.
95 Jean-Joseph Goux, *Symbolic Economies: After Marx and Freud*, translated by Jennifer Curtiss Gage (Ithaca, NY: Cornell University Press, 1990), pp. 17–18.
96 *Ibid.*, p. 23. Goux continues: "This role is played by gold in the world of commodities; by the father in the world of others; and by the sexual organ, becoming a phallus, in the world of part objects."
97 Freud, *Totem and Taboo*, SE XIII: 148; GW IX: 179.
98 Goux, *Symbolic Economies*, p. 155.
99 Luc Ferry and Alain Renaut, *Heidegger and Modernity*, translated by Franklin Philip (Chicago, IL: University of Chicago Press, 1990), pp. 4–5.
100 *Ibid.*, p. 5.
101 Freud, *Totem and Taboo*, SE XIII: 146; GW IX: 176. Further "doublings" of ideals, indicating the link with Freud's subsequent analyses of religion, are found in the statement that "while the totem may be the *first* form of father-surrogate, the god will be a later one" (*ibid.*, p. 148). A relevant discussion of the relation of Freud's account to socialization is offered by Wallace, *Freud and Anthropology*, p. 203:

> Only with the covenant of the brothers did the private inhibition become the public institution – the taboo. It is this implicit attempt to take account of both the intrapsychic and the interpersonal factors in institutionalization that seems to me the laudable core of an otherwise preposterous hypothesis.

102 See Wallace, *Freud and Anthropology*, p. 216, and pp. 247–9. This model of socialization is based on Freud, "A short account of psychoanalysis," SE XIX: 208.
103 SE XIII: 145; GW IX: 175.

104 SE XIII: 157–8; GW IX: 189–90. Lacan points out that Darwin would have "demolished" this aspect of *Totem and Taboo* (*Le Séminaire, Livre XVII: L'Envers de la psychanalyse* (Paris: Éditions du Seuil, 1991), p. 132).
105 SE XIII: 159–61; GW IX: 192–4.

4 Moses and Monotheism: the trauma of symbolization

1 Sigmund Freud, *Moses and Monotheism*, SE XXIII: 104.
2 *Moses and Monotheism*, SE XXIII: 16.
3 Yosef Hayim Yerushalmi has stressed a point of difference between the subject matter of the two texts:

> In *Totem and Taboo* Freud did not have to be a historian, for the pivotal event it presupposes does not really take place in historical time....Not so with *Moses and Monotheism*. The man and the religion he established are situated within history and are therefore legitimately subject to the historian's insistent demand for specific historical proofs.

(Yerushalmi, *Freud's Moses: Judaism Terminable and Interminable* (New Haven, CT: Yale University Press, 1991), p. 21.) While this point is certainly valid, Yerushalmi makes it after acknowledging that *Moses and Monotheism fails* as history and needs to be understood in other terms (*ibid.*, p. 2). Later on Yerushalmi quotes Freud's unpublished original introduction to *Moses and Monotheism*, which stresses that the work is a "mixture of historical writing and fiction" (*ibid.*, p. 17). It is on this other level of psychoanalytic narrative that the parallelisms I emphasize occur.
4 Martin Buber, *Moses: The Revelation and the Covenant* (New York: Harper & Row, 1958), p. 7, note 1.
5 W. W. Meissner, *Psychoanalysis and Religious Experience* (New Haven, CT: Yale University Press, 1984), p. 128. See also Paul Ricoeur, *Freud and Philosophy*, translated by Denis Savage (New Haven, CT: Yale University Press, 1970), pp. 245 and 545.
6 Yerushalmi, *Freud's Moses*, p. 2.
7 Yerushalmi, *Freud's Moses*, p. 2. Marthe Robert, *From Oedipus to Moses: Freud's Jewish Identity*, translated by R. Manheim (Garden City, NJ: Anchor Books, 1976), has also focused on the relation of *Moses and Monotheism* to Freud's life and personality.
8 Jan Assmann, *Moses the Egyptian* (Cambridge, MA: Harvard University Press, 1997), pp. 10–11.
9 *Ibid.*, pp. 5–6. It is noteworthy that a similar point, with an opposite emphasis, had been made by Leo Strauss. He argued that Freud was "too concerned with" and "remained vulnerable to" anti-Semitism. That is, a preoccupation with such hostile attitudes was related to Freud's (putative) disavowal of the uniqueness of Judaism. See Leo Strauss, "Freud on Moses and Monotheism," *Jewish Philosophy and the Crisis of Modernity: Essays and Lectures in Modern Jewish Thought*, edited by Kenneth Hart Green (Albany, NY: State University of New York Press, 1997), pp. 286–7.
10 Julia Kristeva, "The true-real," *The Kristeva Reader*, edited by Toril Moi (New York: Columbia University Press, 1986), p. 223. Another discussion of *Moses and Monotheism* as "situated at the intersection of history and fiction" is offered by Michel de Certeau's "The fiction of history: the writing of *Moses and Monotheism*" in his *The Writing of History*, translated by Tom Conley (New York: Columbia University Press, 1988).

11 Jacques Lacan, *The Seminar of Jacques Lacan, Book VII: The Ethics of Psychoanalysis*, translated by Dennis Porter (New York: Norton, 1992), pp. 142–3.
12 *Ibid.*, p. 181.
13 *Moses and Monotheism*, SE XXIII: 16.
14 *Ibid.*, p. 20.
15 *Ibid.*, p. 21 (emphasis added).
16 *Ibid.*, p. 24.
17 *Ibid.*, p. 65; and cf. *ibid.*, p. 85.
18 *Ibid.*, p. 23.
19 *Ibid.*, p. 28.
20 *Ibid.*, p. 23; and cf. *ibid.*, pp. 59–60.
21 *Ibid.*, p. 60.
22 *Ibid.*, pp. 32–3.
23 *Ibid.*, p. 41.
24 *Ibid.*, p. 43.
25 *Ibid.*, p. 77.
26 *Ibid.*, p. 43.
27 *Ibid.*, pp. 44–5.
28 *Ibid.*, p. 47.
29 *Ibid.*, p. 48.
30 This principle is discussed in Freud's essay "Negation," SE XIX: 235–9. Interpreting denial and negation as key points of resistance within the context of the analytic session allows repressed materials to come to consciousness (because questions eliciting further associations can be directed towards the point of resistance). This procedure does not, however, transpose easily into a hermeneutic of texts, because it can lead to *arbitrary* inversions of meaning on the part of the interpreter.
31 Jean-Joseph Goux, *Symbolic Economies: After Marx and Freud*, translated by Jennifer Curtiss Gage (Ithaca, NY: Cornell University Press, 1990), p. 136.
32 *Ibid.*, p. 137.
33 Sigmund Freud, "The Moses of Michelangelo," SE XIII: 233.
34 SE XXIII: 50; GW XVI: 151.
35 SE XXIII: 50–1.
36 *Ibid.*, p. 129.
37 See SE XXI: 91–2.
38 Gianni Vattimo, *The Transparent Society*, translated by David Webb (Baltimore, MD: Johns Hopkins University Press, 1992), p. 93.
39 SE XXIII: 52.
40 *Ibid.*, pp. 65–6.
41 *Ibid.*, p. 66. See *ibid.*, p. 72, for the blurring between analogy and identity.
42 SE XXIII: 73; GW XVI: 178. See also *Introductory Lectures on Psychoanalysis*, SE XVI: 347 and 362–4; *New Introductory Lectures on Psychoanalysis*, SE XXII: 94–5, for discussions of "traumatic moments."
43 SE XXIII: 72–3; GW XVI: 177.
44 SE XXIII: 74; GW XVI: 179 (emphasis added).
45 SE XXIII: 77.
46 Bruce Fink, *The Lacanian Subject: Between Language and Jouissance* (Princeton, NJ: Princeton University Press, 1995), p. 26. See also Cathy Caruth, *Unclaimed Experience: Trauma, Narrative, and History* (Baltimore, MD: Johns Hopkins University Press, 1996), pp. 59–61.
47 SE XXIII: 88–9; GW XVI: 195.

48 SE XXIII: 75.
49 *Ibid.*, p. 76.
50 *Ibid.*, pp. 77–8.
51 *Ibid.*, p. 80.
52 *Ibid.*
53 Paul Ricoeur, *Freud and Philosophy*, p. 230.
54 Julia Kristeva, "The true-real," *The Kristeva Reader*, pp. 223–4.
55 SE XXIII: 50; and compare: "the most powerful effects of the people's experience were to come to light only later and to force their way into reality in the course of many centuries" (*ibid.*, p. 62).
56 Jean Laplanche, *Life and Death in Psychoanalysis*, translated by Jeffrey Mehlman (Baltimore, MD: Johns Hopkins University Press, 1976), p. 33.
57 *Ibid.*.
58 Tomoko Masuzawa has explored the status of originary events in psychoanalytic theory with specific reference to Freud's "From the history of an infantile neurosis," the case history of the Wolf Man. She argues that this text provides an instance of a theory of origins, built around Freud's postulation of the "primal scene," paralleling the originary thinking of *Totem and Taboo* (and, I might add, *Moses and Monotheism*). One of Masuzawa's points of focus is the issue of the complex, constituted nature of temporality. The point of origin turns out to be a construction requiring several retrospectively operative experiences, including dreams and fantasies as well as memories and observations. Indeed, at one point in the case history Freud suddenly overturns his own literalistic postulation of the primal scene as observed event with a far more complex, and persuasive, account that involves fantasy and symbolism as much as recollected observation (Freud, "From the history of an infantile neurosis," SE XVII: 49–51). What emerges in the course of Freud's presentation of the case is that "it takes at least two moments, not one, to constitute an experience" (Masuzawa, *In Search of Dreamtime: The Quest for the Origins of Religion* (Chicago, IL: University of Chicago Press, 1993), p. 101). Temporality is experienced through a mechanism of deferred action and effect, *Nachträglichkeit*, that displaces a strictly linear formulation. This displacing also serves to "disable the question of priority" in the literal sense (*ibid.*, p. 113). It opens another level of insight, related to how we structure our understanding of experience narratively and symbolically.
59 SE XVI: 371.
60 It is tempting to refer to Freud's postulation of inherited memory as "Lamarckian." However, as Jean Laplanche points out, in Freud's account "the inherited element does not really relate to adaptation," and this differentiates it from Lamarckian theory in the strict sense (*New Foundations for Psychoanalysis*, translated by David Macey (London: Blackwell, 1989), p. 34).
61 SE XXIII: 99.
62 *Ibid.*, p. 101.
63 *Ibid.*
64 SE XXI: 47.

5   *Moses and Monotheism*: the psychodynamics of *Geistigkeit*

1 Sigmund Freud, *Moses and Monotheism*, SE XXIII: 107; GW XVI: 214.

2 SE XXIII: 107; "vielmehr scheint jedes Ereignis überdeterminiert zu sein " (GW XVI: 214).
3 Paul Ricoeur, *The Symbolism of Evil*, translated by Emerson Buchanan (Boston, MA: Beacon Press, 1969), p. 134.
4 SE XXIII: 108; "den überragenden Einfluß einer einzelnen Persönlichkeit" (GW XVI: 215). "Transcendent," given by Strachey, is but one of several translations of *überragend*, which might also be rendered as "towering."
5 SE XXIII: 108; GW XVI: 215.
6 "Let us, therefore, take it for granted that a great man influences his fellow-men in two ways: by his personality and by the idea which he puts forward" (SE XXIII: 109; GW XVI: 216).
7 Jacques Derrida, "The laws of reflection: Nelson Mandela, in admiration," in *For Nelson Mandela*, ed. J. Derrida and M. Tilli (New York: Seaver Books, 1987), pp. 26, 15, and 34. Quoted in Rodolphe Gasché, *Inventions of Difference: On Jacques Derrida* (Cambridge, MA: Harvard University Press, 1994), pp. 17–18.
8 SE XXIII: 111.
9 SE XXIII: 109–10.
10 These arguments are my own, rather than Freud's, although they extrapolate on aspects of his thinking. One place where a related issue is addressed is in the final chapter of *The Ego and the Id*. Freud is discussing the formation of the super-ego "from an identification with the father taken as a model. Every such identification is in the nature of a desexualization or even of a sublimation." Freud goes on to characterize sublimation as "an instinctual defusion," such that the *erotic* components of the relation to embodied carriers of cultural ideals and values are diminished. Freud continues: "This defusion would be the source of the general character of harshness and cruelty exhibited by the ideal – its dictatorial 'Thou shalt'" (SE XIX: 54–5). Here Freud is indirectly touching upon the problem of the dehumanization and reification of ideals.
11 SE XXIII: 112; GW XVI: 219.
12 SE XXIII: 112–13.
13 SE XXIII: 113; GW XVI: 220.
14 SE XXIII: 113 (emphasis has been added to indicate Freud's differentiation between two modes of subjective orientation).
15 SE XXIII: 113; GW XVI: 221.
16 "But this turning from the mother to the father points in addition to a victory of intellectuality over sensuality [*ein Sieg der Geistigkeit über die Sinnlichkeit*] – that is, an advance in civilization, since maternity is proved by evidence of the senses while paternity is a hypothesis, based on an inference and a premise. Taking sides in this way with a thought-process in preference to a sense perception has proved to be a momentous step" (SE XXIII: 114; GW XVI: 221–2).
17 SE XXIII: 114.
18 SE XXIII: 114; GW XVI: 222. Strachey adds a note to this passage emphasizing that it is essentially untranslatable because of the multiple meanings of the terms *Geist* and *Seele*. See also Bruno Bettelheim, *Freud and Man's Soul* (New York: Knopf, 1983), pp. 71ff., on the frequency and significance of the term *Seele* in Freud's work. The very mixture of spirit, soul, mind, and intellect indicates dimensions of human psychology irreducible to isolated faculties, narrow rationalism, and utilitarian models of adjustment.
19 SE XXIII: 114; GW XVI: 222.
20 SE XXIII: 118; GW XVI: 226.
21 Part of my argument here parallels that of Gananath Obeyesekere, who likewise notes varying admixtures of regressive and progressive tendencies in cultural

symbol systems. He provides numerous case studies to support the argument that a key feature differentiating regression from progression is "that they operate at different degrees of remove or closeness to archaic motivations of childhood" (*The Work of Culture* (Chicago, IL: University of Chicago Press, 1990), p. 19).

22 SE XXIII: 114; GW XVI: 222.
23 SE XXIII: 114–15; GW XVI: 222.
24 SE XXIII: 115; GW XVI: 223.
25 Judith Van Herik, *Freud on Femininity and Faith* (Berkeley, CA: University of California Press, 1982), p. 18.
26 SE XXIII: 116; GW XVI: 223.
27 SE XXIII: 116; GW XVI: 223.
28 Sigmund Freud, "On narcissism: an introduction," SE XIV: 76–7.
29 Sigmund Freud, *Civilization and Its Discontents*, SE XXI: 118.
30 SE XXIII: 116.
31 SE XXIII: 116; GW XVI: 224.
32 Steven Marcus, *Freud and the Culture of Psychoanalysis* (New York: Norton, 1984), p. 171. Marcus also notes that, as the "heir to the Oedipus complex," the super-ego conjoins higher faculties with more infantile elements.
33 SE XXIII: 116–17.
34 *Ibid.*, p. 117.
35 SE XXIII: 117; GW XVI: 225. Compare the following passage from *The Future of an Illusion*:

> It is only through the influence of individuals who can set an example and whom masses recognize as their leaders that they can be induced to perform the work and undergo the renunciations on which the existence of civilization depends.
>
> (SE XXI: 8)

While this statement contains an element of elitism, it is one based on quality and ability, rather than, for example, heredity.
36 SE XXIII: 118; GW XVI: 226.
37 This way of expressing things should not be construed as indicating a chronological priority, on any level of analysis, of distinct inner and outer realms. The mediating realm is co-constitutive of both inner and outer experience; this is, of course, one of the main points of my argument.
38 SE XXIII: 118.
39 SE XXIII: 118–19.
40 *Ibid.*, p. 119.
41 *Ibid.*
42 See my discussion in Chapter 3 and also Paul Ricoeur, *Freud and Philosophy*, translated by Denis Savage (New Haven, CT: Yale University Press, 1970), p. 487.
43 *Civilization and Its Discontents*, SE XXI: 95; GW XIV: 450.
44 SE XXI: 96.
45 SE XXIII: 122–3; GW XVI: 230.
46 Freud, *Inhibitions, Symptoms and Anxiety*, SE XX: 128.
47 Richard Boothby, *Death and Desire: Psychoanalytic Theory in Lacan's Return to Freud* (New York: Routledge, 1991), p. 149.
48 Jacques Lacan, *Écrits: A Selection*, translated by Alan Sheridan (London: Routledge, 1977), p. 324.
49 Boothby, *Death and Desire*, p. 151. See also Kaja Silverman, *The Subject of Semiotics* (New York: Oxford University Press, 1983), p. 183. In addition, Silverman addresses the issue of *gender* in relation to the Freudian and Lacanian

language of Oedipal dynamics and castration. She notes that "Lacan has extended the notion of lack to include the male subject as well as the female through his insistence on the distinction between the penis and the phallus" (*ibid.*, p. 139). While still a patriarchal symbol, the phallus designates the power of the symbolic order that is the "property" of neither male nor female subjects *per se.* "Castration," then, is experienced by the subject insofar as inherent incompleteness or lack requires that it be "subordinated to a symbolic order which will henceforth entirely determine its identity and desires. It will from this point forward participate in the discourse of the Other, and regard itself from the space of the Other" (*ibid.*, p. 172).
50 SE XXIII: 128; GW XVI: 236.
51 SE XXIII: 129; GW XVI: 237.
52 SE XXIII: 129; "es habe irgendwelche dauernden Spuren, einer Tradition vergleichbar, in der menschlichen Seele hinterlassen" (GW XVI: 238).
53 Jean Laplanche, *Life and Death in Psychoanalysis*, translated by Jeffrey Mehlman (Baltimore, MD: Johns Hopkins University Press, 1976), p. 33.

6 Psycho-cultural inquiry from Freud to Kristeva

1 Mark C. Taylor, *NOTS* (Chicago, IL: University of Chicago Press, 1993), p. 174.
2 See Kaja Silverman, *The Subject of Semiotics* (New York: Oxford University Press, 1983), pp. 215ff; Jean-Joseph Goux, *Symbolic Economies: After Marx and Freud*, translated by Jennifer Curtiss Gage (Ithaca, NY: Cornell University Press, 1990), pp. 155–7; and Slavoj Zizek, *The Sublime Object of Ideology* (London: Verso, 1989), pp. 87ff.
3 Paul Ricoeur, *Lectures on Ideology and Utopia* (New York: Columbia University Press, 1986), p. 136.
4 *Ibid.*, p. 173.
5 Kaja Silverman, *The Subject of Semiotics*, p. 199.
6 Sigmund Freud, " 'Civilized' sexual morality and modern nervous illness," SE IX: 181–204.
7 See Ernest Wallwork, *Psychoanalysis and Ethics* (New Haven, CT: Yale University Press, 1991), pp. 108ff., for a thorough discussion of psychological hedonism and its qualification and counterbalancing by alternative emphases in Freud's work.
8 Sigmund Freud, *Civilization and Its Discontents*, SE XXI: 142.
9 This view appears throughout the discussions of Lacan in, for example, Joel Whitebook, *Perversion and Utopia* (Cambridge, MA: MIT Press, 1995).
10 Jean Laplanche, *Life and Death in Psychoanalysis*, translated by Jeffrey Mehlman (Baltimore, MD: Johns Hopkins University Press, 1976), p. 50.
11 *Ibid.*, p. 51.
12 The ego's narcissistic tendencies, and the ongoing task of overcoming these tendencies, is discussed by Freud in "On narcissism: an introduction," SE XIV: 73–107. One of many comments concerning the defensive nature of the secondary process occurs in Freud, *The Interpretation of Dreams*, SE IV: 146. For an overview and explication of the positive and negative dimensions of the ego in Freud's work, see Elizabeth Grosz, *Jacques Lacan: A Feminist Introduction* (London: Routledge, 1990), pp. 24ff.
13 Jacques Lacan, "Some reflections on the ego," *International Journal of Psychoanalysis*, vol. 34, p. 11.

14 Sigmund Freud, "On the history of the psychoanalytic movement," SE XIV: 50; quoted in Samuel Weber, *The Legend of Freud* (Minneapolis, MN: University of Minnesota Press, 1982), pp. 8–9.
15 Weber, *The Legend of Freud*, p. 13.
16 *Ibid.*, p. 94.
17 Sigmund Freud, "Instincts and their vicissitudes," SE XIV: 136; quoted in Leo Bersani, *The Freudian Body* (New York: Columbia University Press, 1986), p. 86. Also compare Freud, "Mourning and melancholia," SE XIV: 252, where he refers to "the hostility which relates to an object and which represents the ego's original reaction to objects in the external world."
18 Bersani, *The Freudian Body*, p. 87.
19 Jacques Lacan, *Écrits: A Selection*, translated by Alan Sheridan (London: Routledge, 1977), p. 27; *Écrits* (Paris: Éditions du Seuil, 1966), p. 122.
20 Jacques Lacan, *The Seminar of Jacques Lacan, Book I: Freud's Papers on Technique 1953–1954*, translated by John Forrester (Cambridge: Cambridge University Press, 1988), p. 193 (hereafter *Seminar I*).
21 Lacan, *Écrits: A Selection*, p. 15; *Écrits*, p. 109.
22 See, for example, *Seminar I*, p. 267. Many of Jung's formulations, emphasizing images of circles, quaternities, and wholes, certainly lend themselves to this critique. Whether his model is *necessarily* totalized is a different issue.
23 Jacques Lacan, *The Four Fundamental Concepts of Psychoanalysis*, translated by Alan Sheridan (London: Penguin Books, 1977), p. 22.
24 Mark C. Taylor, *Erring: A Postmodern A/Theology* (Chicago, IL: University of Chicago Press, 1984), p. 147.
25 *Ibid.*, p. 146.
26 Lacan, *Écrits: A Selection*, p. 172; *Écrits*, p. 524: "l'inconscient est le discours de l'Autre avec un grand A." Lacan also states:

> If the subject is what I say it is, namely the subject determined by language and speech, it follows that the subject, *in initio*, begins in the locus of the Other, in so far as it is there that the first signifier emerges.
> (Lacan, *The Four Fundamental Concepts of Psychoanalysis*, p. 198)

27 Lacan, *Écrits: A Selection*, p. 284; *Écrits*, pp. 688–9.
28 Jacques Lacan, *Television*, translated by D. Hollier, R. Kraus, and A. Michelson (New York: Norton, 1990), p. 10.
29 Lacan, *Écrits: A Selection*, p. 90; *Écrits*, p. 304.
30 Lacan, *Écrits: A Selection*, p. 81; *Écrits*, p. 293.
31 Richard Boothby, *Death and Desire* (London: Routledge, 1991), p. 163.
32 Lacan, *Écrits: A Selection*, p. 194; *Écrits*, p. 549. Here we reconnect with Lacan's definition of religion, as cited in my Introduction.
33 Boothby, *Death and Desire*, p. 213; and cf. Lacan, *Seminar I*, p. 108.
34 Gilbert Chaitin, *Rhetoric and Culture in Lacan* (Cambridge: Cambridge University Press, 1996), p. 136.
35 Weber, *The Legend of Freud*, p. 33.
36 Lacan, *Seminar I*, p. 102.
37 Discussions of the problem of personality dissociation can be found in Ian Hacking, *Rewriting the Soul: Multiple Personality and the Sciences of Memory* (Princeton, NJ: Princeton University Press, 1995).
38 Lacan, *Écrits: A Selection*, p. 287.
39 Lacan argues that his work extrapolates on Freud's insight that

at the level of the unconscious there is something at all points homologous
with what occurs at the level of the subject—this thing speaks and functions
in a way quite as elaborate as at the level of the conscious, which thus loses
what seemed to be its privilege.

(Lacan, *The Four Fundamental Concepts of Psychoanalysis*, p. 24)

The point is also made by Julia Kristeva, who supports Lacan's view that "the
drives are signifying" (*Tales of Love*, translated by Leon S. Roudiez (New York:
Columbia University Press, 1987), p. 183).

40 Kaja Silverman, *The Subject of Semiotics*, p. 73.
41 *Ibid.*, pp. 73–4.
42 *Ibid.*, p. 81.
43 *Ibid.*, p. 133.
44 *Ibid.*, p. 134.
45 In a more poetic moment, Freud declares that

civilization is a process in the service of *Eros*, whose purpose it is to combine
single human individuals, and after that families, then races, peoples and
nations, into one great unity, the unity of mankind. Why this has to happen,
we do not know; the work of *Eros* is precisely this.

(Freud, *Civilization and Its Discontents*, SE XXI: 122)

46 I establish this connection while remaining aware that Silverman has been rather
critical of Kristeva. See Kaja Silverman, *The Acoustic Mirror: The Female Voice
in Psychoanalysis and Cinema* (Bloomington, IN: Indiana University Press,
1988), pp. 101ff.
47 Julia Kristeva, *Revolution in Poetic Language*, translated by Margaret Waller
(New York: Columbia University Press, 1984), p. 25.
48 See Kristeva, *Revolution in Poetic Language*, p. 68:

Although originally a precondition of the symbolic, the semiotic functions
within signifying practices as a result of a transgression of the symbolic....It
exists in practice only within the symbolic and requires the symbolic break to
obtain the complex articulation we associate with it in musical and poetic
practices.

49 Kristeva, *Revolution in Poetic Language*, p. 17.
50 *Ibid.*, p. 79.
51 *Ibid.*, p. 80.
52 *Ibid.*, p. 27.
53 Julia Kristeva, *Black Sun: Depression and Melancholia*, translated by Leon S.
Roudiez (New York: Columbia University Press, 1989), p. 24; *Soleil noir: dépres-
sion et mélancolie* (Paris: Éditions Gallimard, 1987), p. 35. Here Kristeva seems
to be using the term "imaginary" in a standard, non-Lacanian sense.
54 Julia Kristeva, *In the Beginning Was Love: Psychoanalysis and Faith*, translated
by Arthur Goldhammer (New York: Columbia University Press, 1987), p. 18. In
a similar vein, William Meissner, informed by object-relations theory, particularly the work of Winnicott, resists the classification of religion as delusion and
indicates the value of illusion:

Psychotic delusion is wholly made up of the subject's disordered imagination
and his fragmented relationship to reality. Illusion, on the other hand, retains

not only its ties to reality but also the capacity to transform reality into something permeated with inner significance.

(Meissner, *Psychoanalysis and Religious Experience* (New Haven, CT: Yale University Press, 1984), p. 17)

55 Julia Kristeva, "Georgia O'Keefe: la forme inévitable," in *Georgia O'Keefe* (Paris: Éditions Adam Biro, 1989), p. 8.
56 Kristeva, *Black Sun*, p. 5; *Soleil noir*, p. 15.
57 Kristeva, *Black Sun*, p. 14; *Soleil noir*, p. 24.
58 Kristeva, *Black Sun*, p. 9; *Soleil noir*, p. 18. Compare the similar definition given by Freud in "Mourning and melancholia," SE XIV: 244.
59 Kristeva, *Black Sun*, p. 10; *Soleil noir*, p. 19.
60 Kristeva, *Tales of Love*, p. 15. "Le psychisme est un système ouvert connecté à un autre, et dans ces conditions seulement, il est renouvelable" (*Histoires d'amour* (Paris: Éditions Denoël, 1983), p. 21).
61 Kristeva, *Black Sun*, pp. 13–14.
62 Kristeva, *Black Sun*, p. 33; *Soleil noir*, p. 45.
63 Kristeva, *Black Sun*, p. 91; *Soleil noir*, p. 103.
64 Julia Kristeva, *New Maladies of the Soul*, translated by Ross Guberman (New York: Columbia University Press, 1995), p. 9.
65 Kristeva, *Black Sun*, p. 13; *Soleil noir*, p. 22. Note the appearance of similar imagery in the experience of one of R. D. Laing's patients, discussed in *The Divided Self* (Harmondsworth: Penguin, 1965), pp. 112, 201, 204.
66 Lacan, *Seminar I*, p. 66.
67 Lacan, *The Seminar of Jacques Lacan, Book VII: The Ethics of Psychoanalysis*, translated by Dennis Porter (New York: Norton, 1992), p. 54.
68 Kristeva, *Black Sun*, p. 72; *Soleil noir*, p. 83.
69 Kristeva, *Black Sun*, p. 87; *Soleil noir*, p. 99.
70 Kristeva, *Black Sun*, p. 43; *Soleil noir*, p. 54. This is also called the denial of the signifier (*le déni du signifiant*) (*Black Sun*, p. 37; *Soleil noir*, p. 49). Mark C. Taylor points out that Freud's *Verneinung* is more adequately translated by the French *dénégation*. As he states: "*Verneinung* is at once an affirmation that is a negation and a negation that is an affirmation. To de-negate is to un-negate, but un-negation is itself a form of negation" (*Disfiguring: Art, Architecture, Religion* (Chicago, IL: University of Chicago Press, 1992), p. 7).
71 Kristeva, *Black Sun*, pp. 43–4; *Soleil noir*, p. 55; and cf. Monique David-Ménard, *Hysteria from Freud to Lacan*, translated by Catherine Porter (Ithaca, NY: Cornell University Press, 1989), p. 114.
72 Kristeva, *Black Sun*, p. 42.
73 Kristeva, *Black Sun*, p. 41; *Soleil noir*, p. 53. Here Kristeva draws upon, and extends, Freud's analyses in "Mourning and melancholia," SE XIV: 243–58.
74 Julia Kristeva, *Powers of Horror: An Essay on Abjection*, translated by Leon S. Roudiez (New York: Columbia University Press, 1982), p. 11,
75 Kristeva, *Black Sun*, p. 14; *Soleil noir*, p. 24; and cf. *Powers of Horror*, p. 11.
76 Kristeva, *Black Sun*, p. 99; *Soleil noir*, p. 111.
77 Kristeva, *Black Sun*, p. 159; *Soleil noir*, p. 170.
78 Kristeva, *Black Sun*, p. 128.
79 Kristeva, *Revolution in Poetic Language*, p. 70.
80 Kristeva, *Powers of Horror*, p. 17. Kristeva also refers to literature as becoming "a substitute for the role formerly played by the sacred, at the limits of social and subjective identity" (*ibid.*, p. 26).

81 Karsten Harries, *The Meaning of Modern Art* (Evanston, IL: Northwestern University Press, 1968), p. 116.
82 Gianni Vattimo, *The Transparent Society*, translated by David Webb (Baltimore, MD: Johns Hopkins University Press, 1992), p. 10.
83 *Ibid.*, p. 50. Also compare Goux, *Symbolic Economies*, p. 192: "abstract painting puts an end to the metaphysics manifested in perspectival representation, of the transcendental subject reflecting the object without changing it."
84 Mark C. Taylor, *Disfiguring*, pp. 7–8.

Index